Java Persistence for Relational Databases

RICHARD SPERKO

Java Persistence for Relational Databases
Copyright ©2003 by Richard Sperko

ISBN (pbk): 1-59059-071-6

Printed and bound in the United States of America 12345678910

Trademarked names may appear in this book. Rather than use a trademark symbol with every occurrence of a trademarked name, we use the names only in an editorial fashion and to the benefit of the trademark owner, with no intention of infringement of the trademark.

Technical Reviewer: Robert Castaneda

Editorial Board: Dan Appleman, Craig Berry, Gary Cornell, Tony Davis, Steven Rycroft, Julian Skinner, Martin Streicher, Jim Sumser, Karen Watterson, Gavin Wright, John Zukowski

Assistant Publisher: Grace Wong

Project Manager: Tracy Brown Collins

Copy Editor: Ami Knox

Compositor: Argosy Publishing

Indexer: Kevin Broccoli

Proofreader: Lori Bring

Cover Designer: Kurt Krames

Production Manager: Kari Brooks

Manufacturing Manager: Tom Debolski

Distributed to the book trade in the United States by Springer-Verlag New York, Inc., 175 Fifth Avenue, New York, NY, 10010 and outside the United States by Springer-Verlag GmbH & Co. KG, Tiergartenstr. 17, 69112 Heidelberg, Germany.

In the United States, phone 1-800-SPRINGER, email orders@springer-ny.com, or visit http://www.springer-ny.com. Outside the United States, fax +49 6221 345229, email orders@springer.de, or visit http://www.springer.de.

For information on translations, please contact Apress directly at 2560 Ninth Street, Suite 219, Berkeley, CA 94710. Phone 510-549-5930, fax 510-549-5939, email info@apress.com, or visit http://www.apress.com.

The information in this book is distributed on an "as is" basis, without warranty. Although every precaution has been taken in the preparation of this work, neither the author(s) nor Apress shall have any liability to any person or entity with respect to any loss or damage caused or alleged to be caused directly or indirectly by the information contained in this work.

The source code for this book is available to readers at http://www.apress.com in the Downloads section.

For Tracey and Josh

Contents at a Glance

v

Contents

Chapter 3　Using JDBC 1 for Relational Database Work 35

Chapter 4　What Is New in JDBC 2 and 3 63

Chapter 12   Commercial Java Persistence Libraries and Frameworks 267

Chapter 13   Summary 307

Foreword

IN THE INFORMATION TECHNOLOGY (IT) ECOSYSTEM, one true constant is that applications need to retrieve and manipulate data. Think about it for a moment: Business needs, processes, and rules change on a regular basis. Oftentimes the applications that support the rules and processes must be rewritten or replaced. New systems and technologies are brought in and old ones get phased out.

The data that is contained in these applications rarely goes away. Instead the data is massaged and loaded into the new application. Developers will then write code to retrieve, manipulate, and integrate this data. One of the more mundane aspects of a developer's career is that a large chunk of time and effort is spent writing data access code. (And you thought librarians had exciting jobs.)

The data will live in the new application until that application is replaced. The cycle then starts over. It is unfortunate that when it comes to having a clear, consistent data access architecture for building applications, most developers do not look beyond their immediate project needs for the data access technology and design strategy they are going to use.

Developers often write data access code with little thought of the reusability opportunities or the long-term maintenance costs their decisions might afford or incur. Instead, the data access code they write oftentimes "evolves" into a mixed tangle of technologies and point-to-point system integrations. While the written code might solve the immediate business need, over time it can become a serious liability to an organization's ability to adapt its IT systems to changing business needs.

Building an enterprise-level data access tier involves two distinct decision points: *tactical* and *strategic*. Tactical decision points are those in which developers have to decide what data access technology is going to best meet their application needs. This is often not a straightforward decision, because there are a lot of choices available. The Java development environment alone offers a number of different choices for writing data access code. These choices include

- Java APIs (JDBC, Entity Enterprise JavaBeans, Java Data Objects)

- Commercial products (TopLink, CocoBase)

- Open source projects (ObJectRelationalBridge, Hibernate, Castor JDO)

Each of these technologies has its own advantages and disadvantages. To leverage these technologies successfully, developers must understand how their applications are going to use data. Is the application going to be based on online transactional processing (OLTP) or online analytical processing (OLAP)? How much data is the application going to be working with for a given call?

The answer to these types of questions will force developers to make tactical decisions on which technology will work best for their specific needs. Tactical decisions are made in the context of a specific point and time. If situations change, a once good tactical decision can very quickly turn bad.

The second type of decision point for building a data access tier is the strategic decision point. The strategic decision point involves making design decisions that are going to increase the overall maintainability and extensibility of your applications. These decisions are going to revolve around such tasks as the following:

- Minimizing the impact of structural changes in an organization's database(s). Does changing a column type in a database table force the organization's developer to make changes in multiple spots in applications?

- Facilitating the easy migration of applications to different data access technologies and data stores. How does an organization build an abstraction layer that hides the particular details of what technology is being used to access the data and what type of data stores (Oracle, Sybase, XML) the data is residing in? Hiding these types of implementation-specific details can make migrating applications to a new technology a smooth and manageable process rather than an absolute nightmare.

In this book, Richard Sperko has provided a balanced view of both the tactical and strategic decision points involved in using Java-based data access technology. He starts with the essentials of persistence management and then systematically explores the different data access technologies available to a Java programmer.

This book is a roadmap and should be used as such. As a reader, you will not be given the minutest, and often useless, technical details associated with each Java data access technology. Instead you will be given working code examples and an excellent narrative that examines the strengths and trade-offs involved with using each particular technology.

Richard's words resonate with the hard-earned experience of a veteran Java developer.

After reading this book, you will gain an appreciation for the amount of time and effort involved in building an enterprise data access tier that can meet the ever-changing needs of your organization.

John Carnell
Principal Architect
NetChange, LLC

About the Author

How is that for a thinker's pose?

Richard Sperko is an architect-level consultant for Centare Group, Ltd. Richard has 11 years of software development experience and has been working with emerging technologies that entire time. He has extensive knowledge in Java/J2EE and other object-oriented technologies. He is currently certified as a Sun Microsystems Java Developer and working on his Sun Microsystems Java Architect and Microsoft Certified Application Developer certifications. He spends as much time as he can with his lovely wife and beautiful son.

About the
Technical Reviewer

Robert Castaneda is principal architect at CustomWare Asia Pacific, where he
provides architecture consulting and training in EJB/J2EE/XML-based
applications and integration servers to clients throughout Asia and America.
Rob's multinational background, combined with his strong real-world business
experience, enables him to see through the specifications to create realistic
solutions to major business problems. He has also contributed to and technically
edited various leading EJB and J2EE books.

Acknowledgments

NO BOOK IS WRITTEN by any one person. This book is not an exception. I need to acknowledge some of the many people who made this opportunity possible for me. First and foremost, my wife, Tracey, literally took over all other parts of our life to allow me to work on this project. I thank my son, Joshauh, for his tolerance and patience for all of those times I could not play "choo-choo" with him.

Next I need to thank all of the mentors I have had in technology: Randy Parr for his tutorage, Ed Chaltry for being a great example and teacher and helping me move into consulting, all of the "old" Smalltalkers at Compuware Milwaukee, and my project team members from all my projects.

Lastly I want to thank the Centare Group. The respect and help they have given me while working on this project is absolutely amazing. Within that organization I need to specifically thank Dave Glyzewksi for his help and Andrew Patzer for leading me to Apress.

Introduction

WELCOME TO *Java Persistence for Relational Databases*. This book is wholly concerned with the problem and solution of storing Java objects in relational databases. There are many different solutions to this problem. I want to give an overview that will help developers maximize their time solving interesting application-related challenges and minimize the time spent with the same old problem of converting objects to and from SQL.

The idea for this book came a long time ago when I was part of a team that wrote a semitransparent persistence layer. What that means is that we were able to store our objects in a generic way without having to write much new code for a new object. After the wonder of not losing 30 percent of my development time to persistence, I ended up on several projects where there was no such emphasis. I watched developers, myself included, on these projects repeat the same solution to the same problem over and over again. We also needed to debug and test those same solutions over and over again.

Since that time, I have had the opportunity to use and learn about many different ways to do that same work with less effort. I want to convey that information in a way that may help those who does not feel they have the time to learn a new product or framework, even if it will save them time in the long run.

The intended audience of this book is any Java developer or manager who does not want to waste time, energy, and money solving the same old problem in the same old expensive way. This book is for people who do not have the time to go out and research different persistence mechanisms, but want to use best practices anyway. This book is written for people who already know the Java programming language. It does not assume knowledge of JDBC, SQL, or relational databases; those topics will be covered.

One note concerning the opening sentence of each chapter: Each chapter begins with the first sentence of a piece of classic literature. It all started with me trying to get my brain working by typing "It was the best of times, it was the worst of times." I continued it because I enjoy the irony of starting technical chapters with literary references. I tried to use books that I had either read or knew about.

This book consists of twelve chapters. Each is intended to build on the earlier chapters. The breakdown goes like this:

Chapter 1 is a basic introduction to object persistence. I cover the definition of persistence and give some nonrelational database persistence examples. I then talk briefly about object-to-relational persistence.

Chapter 2 focuses on relational databases. This chapter covers the definition of relational databases, as well as relational database design and practices. The chapter finishes with an introduction to SQL.

Chapter 3 is concerned with JDBC 1. This is the first version of the Java API that is used to talk to relational databases. I cover all of the major classes in the framework. This chapter also discusses transactions and performance tips for using JDBC.

Chapter 4 discusses JDBC 2 and 3. I cover all the new features that were added after JDBC and introduce you to such topics as scrollable result sets, batching SQL, data sources, distributed transactions, row sets, and more.

Chapter 5 is about creating a persistence layer by hand. You learn several options for querying in this chapter. I show you various types of unique identifiers in this chapter including ways to generate UUIDs. This chapter also covers inserting, updating, and deleting objects through a hand-built persistence layer.

Chapter 6 shows design patterns that help when writing persistence-related code. The chapter talks briefly about what a design pattern is, then delves into some code examples that illustrate the usefulness of design patterns.

Chapter 7 is one of the most important chapters in this book because it covers unit testing persistence layers. This chapter looks at JUnit as well as discussing in-container testing and Mock Objects. I introduce you to several best practices in this chapter.

Chapter 8 talks about EJBs and Container Managed Persistence. This chapter covers persistent fields, primary keys, and relationships. It also details the life cycle of a CMP EJB and querying through EJB QL. The chapter ends with examples using Sun's J2EE Reference Implementation.

Chapter 9 is about ODMG 3.0. This is a specification meant for persistence of objects to any type of data store. In this chapter I talk about the specifications in general including Object Query Language, then show you examples of using ODMG from Java.

Chapter 10 covers Sun's JDO specification. This is Sun's intended standard for using the same Java code to persist objects to any data store. The chapter covers the specification including JDOQL. It also uses the same example from Chapter 9 modified to use JDO.

Chapter 11 is about open source object-relational persistence frameworks. Specifically, I introduce you to Hibernate, OJB, and Castor JDO. After I discuss each framework, I show how to apply them to the same application used in Chapters 9 and 10.

Chapter 12 focuses on commercial object-relational persistence frameworks. This chapter covers TopLink and CocoBase. I discuss both frameworks in depth, explore their graphical mapping tools, and then demonstrate their differences and similarities using the same application from the previous chapters.

So a lot of material is covered. I hope this book helps you to better plan, design, and implement your next application. Of all the applications I have worked on, I have yet to build one that does not need some sort of persistence. This book is intended to help you focus on the fun part and not sweat the mundane.

If you want to discuss any topics covered in this book I am easily reached via e-mail at javapersistence@sperko.com. I am also happy to discuss any object-oriented or design topic.

Thank you,

Richard Sperko

CHAPTER 1

All Kinds of Methods for Persisting Objects

IT WAS THE BEST OF TIMES, it was the worst of times. For months, the development team I was working on had been writing a large Java system to support utility companies. The best part was working on a great project with an innovative team. We had built our own storage mechanism for the system, and that is what sometimes made it the worst of times. The storage mechanism included hundreds of classes, all with one purpose: to make our objects persistent (which means that the objects exist even after the application is done running). We could always re-create or use any object we wanted kept around.

As with most projects with home-built persistence, much of our development time was spent storing objects to the database and getting them back, locking the data of those objects before modifying them, and again searching for objects that we had previously stored. No matter how clean and elegant the various applications in the system were, there was always a nasty, hard-to-maintain layer of Java classes underneath the application that kept our objects safe. These persistence objects were a tough-to-read mixture of Structured Query Language (SQL) and Java. For every significant business object, there were groups of objects to support it.

Most software aims to take an object that has been created, possibly modified, and store it for later use. Often much of our work as developers is spent focusing on persistence—turning off the power, stopping and restarting the application, having objects garbage collected, and still being able to get the original data back. It can be a daunting task to keep it all straight.

For example, if I have a human resources application in which I want to keep track of employees, I would take an employee object that contains the employee's first name, last name, and ID and store the employee object to persistent storage, usually on a hard disk.

This is different from storing the object in a system's memory. Memory is transient, meaning that if you take away the power, the contents are lost. Transient memory is faster, but not durable; therefore it is inappropriate for long-term storage. By using durable storage, if I turn off the computer and turn it back on, I will still be able to see what employees work for the company. Then I could gather statistics on the employees and find out just how many Bobs work at the company.

Once I have stored the employee objects, I have to tackle another problem, and that is retrieving the stored objects. When I've placed a few objects into storage, the question becomes how to get a single employee record back, particularly after the system has been shut down and restarted. What if I want to search for a particular employee? I cannot simply ask the hard disk for this information, as it is concerned with files, not with providing search capabilities to my application.

These problems are not new; they're the same ones faced by almost all non-trivial pieces of software. It also is not unique to object-oriented software. Back in the 1950s, IBM was storing this type of data on tape drives, long before objects were even a thought. Before tape drives, data was stored in paper with holes punched in it.

Persistence in this book's context means saving an object in a durable way. You can save your data to a disk file using XML or Java serialization, or your own data format. You could also store your data to a relational database or object database. Work is even being done to save data to organic material. Once the data has been stored, it can then be retrieved from whatever medium it was stored to.

Figure 1-1 shows a system where power is lost, and with it all the employee data in the HR application on that system is lost as well. You can see that without persistence, you can lose your data due to power outage, error, or simply because you think you are done with it, when you are not.

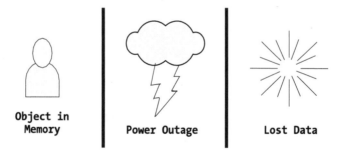

Figure 1-1. Employee information lost due to power outage

In Figure 1-2, you can see the value of making your data persistent and durable. This image shows an employee's information that has been saved to disk and can be recovered at any time in the future. This is persistence in action. The data is durable because it is stored to the file system.

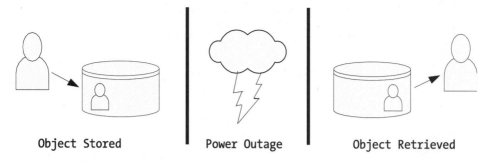

Figure 1-2. Employee data is saved to disk, and recovered after a power outage.

Persistence means making it possible to access an object even after the object has been removed from memory. This can also be referred to as making the object *durable*. Throughout the rest of this chapter, I will introduce various methods of persisting objects, briefly touching on storing objects to files. I will discuss object databases and introduce relational databases. Finally, I will discuss the primary focus of this book, which is writing and using object-to-relational-database frameworks.

Storing Objects to Simple Data Files

One option for storing objects is to put them directly into simple flat files on the hard disk. This can make for a clean and simple solution, provided simplicity is all you need. If your data is complex or your needs extend beyond what a simple system can provide, then flat files probably won't fit the bill due to poor performance. Another reason to shy away from basic data files is lack of organized data support. Unlike writing data to the end of a file, which is easy, adding or removing objects in the middle of a file requires moving all the data that follows.

When storing objects to data files, you simply create a data file on a disk and put your objects into it, one after another. The format they are stored in is not important, so long as you can read that format in order to retrieve the objects later. The disk doesn't care what format you use because it is acting as a dumb medium. You care because you need to reconstitute the data.

In the situation of using data files, no process is provided to manage data files as it is in a relational database. The files can usually be written to by one program at a time. Oftentimes because of the writing limitation I mentioned previously, the objects come out in the same order they went in, meaning they follow a first in, first out (FIFO) method for data storage and retrieval.

In Figure 1-3, you can see a Java object that exists in memory and is then stored directly to disk. In this situation, an application opens a disk file and simply writes out its data. This is great for quickly and easily storing the object, but provides little help in recovering the object later.

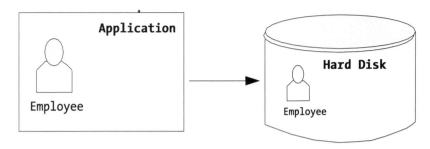

Figure 1-3. Storing an object to a data file

Briefly I want to discuss two common methods of persisting objects to simple data files. The first is through serialization, which has been a part of the Java language since version 1.0. The second way to store objects to data files is using XML, which is becoming more and more prevalent.

Using Java Serialization

Though the focus of this book is on relational databases, one of the easiest ways to make your Java objects persistent in a data file is through Java serialization. Just to make sure you understand serialization so that we can compare it to other mechanisms, let's take a minute to look over what it entails. Java serialization is a built-in mechanism that comes with Sun's Java implementation. Essentially, you can use serialization to turn an object into a serial stream of data. *Serial* means one byte after the other, all in a row. Java also knows how to reconstitute the object from that same stream of data.

Java serialization makes a wonderfully simple persistence mechanism. I can turn my Java object into a stream of data, and then write that stream of data out to a file. Later when I need that object, I can read the stream of data from that file and let Java turn it back into an object. There are built-in mechanisms to handle skipping attributes I don't want saved. If I want data stored in a different format, I can override a couple of methods for reading and writing and manage the serialization myself.

Listing 1-1 shows a very simple Employee Java class. It consists of a constructor that ensures all required attributes and the associated accessor methods are set. This class also implements the interface java.io.Serializable. The Serializable interface is a tagging interface, and does not require any persistence-specific methods to be implemented. Serializable tells the system that this object can be serialized.

Listing 1-1. Employee Object

```
package com.apress.javapersist.chapter1.serialization;

import java.io.Serializable;

public class Employee implements Serializable {
    private String firstName;
    private String lastName;
    private long employeeId;

    public Employee( String firstName, String lastName, long employeeId ) {
        this.firstName = firstName;
        this.lastName = lastName;
        this.employeeId = employeeId;
    }

    public String getFirstName() {
        return firstName;
    }

    public String getLastName() {
        return lastName;
    }

    public long getEmployeeId() {
        return employeeId;
    }
}
```

Now Listing 1-2 shows some code that takes an employee object and persists it to disk. First, I open a FileOutputStream to a file on the hard disk named employees.ser. Next I open an ObjectOutputStream that will wrap my FileOutputStream. This is the stream that will take the employee object and hand it off to the Java serialization mechanism. The stream then delegates the writing to the FileOutputStream. I store my object by calling the writeObject method, which serializes the object. After I store the employee object, I close the file.

Listing 1-2. Writing Objects with Serialization

```
FileOutputStream fout = null;
ObjectOutputStream oout = null;

try {
  fout = new FileOutputStream( "employees.ser" );
  oout = new ObjectOutputStream( fout );

  Employee employee = new Employee( "Bob", "Smith", 2230045 );
  oout.writeObject( employee );
}
catch( Exception e ) {
  e.printStackTrace();
}
finally {
  try { if( oout != null ) oout.close(); }
  catch( IOException e ) {}
  try { if( fout != null ) fout.close(); }
  catch( IOException e ) {}
}
```

Next, Listing 1-3 presents the code for reading the stored object from the file. First, I create a FileInputStream that opens the same file that I have just written to. I then create an ObjectInputStream that wraps that FileInputStream. On the ObjectInputStream, I call the readObject method. This method draws its data from the wrapped file stream and uses the Java serialization mechanism to reconstruct the original object.

Listing 1-3. Reading Objects with Serialization

```
FileInputStream fin = null;
ObjectInputStream oin = null;
try {
  fin = new FileInputStream( "employees.ser" );
  oin = new ObjectInputStream( fin );

  Employee savedEmployee = (Employee) oin.readObject();
  System.out.println( savedEmployee.getFirstName() );
}
catch( Exception e ) {
  e.printStackTrace();
}
finally {
```

```
      try { if( oin != null ) oin.close(); }
      catch( IOException e ) {}
      try { if( fin != null ) fin.close(); }
      catch( IOException e ) {}
   }
```

There are some issues with the built-in Java serialization, however. Primarily it is fragile. Java serialization breaks down when you are working with different versions of a class. For example, you create an `Employee` class with a first name, last name, and employee ID, and then serialize a copy of an employee to a file. If you add a "number of dependants" attribute to the class, you will not be able to read the saved file back into the new `Employee` class, even though all saved attributes are still part of the new class.

```
public class Employee implements Serializable {
  private int numDependants;
...
  public void setNumDependants( int numDependants ) {
    this.numDependants = numDependants;
  }

  public int getNumDependants() {
    return numDependants;
  }
}
```

If you try to read a previously stored employee object into the preceding modified `Employee` class, you will receive a `java.io.InvalidClassException` and be told that the classes are incompatible. The reason for this is that all classes have serial numbers, and the serial number for the Employee class is stored with a serialized object. When you read the object in, the JVM detects you are trying to populate a class with a different serial number, and it throws the exception.

Another problem with serialization is the same for all simple data file storage: There is no inherent way to search those stored employee objects. In order to find an employee named Frank, you will need to reconstitute all employee objects and run through them until you find the object representing Frank. This can be hugely inefficient, particularly if you have thousands of employees.

The final issue with serialization is that it is an inexact form of persistence. This is partially due to the inability to search through the stored objects. The larger problem is the fact that you cannot access part of the data. Serialization is an all-or-nothing situation, as you can either retrieve a whole object or nothing at all. One final missing piece in serialization is the lack of transactions. I will discuss transactions throughout this book, but for now suffice it to say that there is now a way to make the writing of several objects "all or none," meaning that storage could have partial data before an error stops the persistence.

Because this book is about persistence to relational databases, I will not go into all of the specifics of serializing Java objects. All I want to convey is that there is a simple process for making your objects durable. For more information on Java serialization, JavaSoft has a wonderful tutorial that explains it very well at http://java.sun.com/docs/books/tutorial/essential/io/serialization.html.

Storage Using XML

eXtensible Markup Language (XML) is a simple, clean language that can be used to describe data. One nice feature about XML is that it is easy for people to read, and because so many supporting libraries are available, it can be straightforward for developers to make computers read the same data. In order to support this read-ability, it needs to be very flexible.

It is this flexibility that helps XML overcome some of the obstacles that you see in Java serialization. With XML, the data description can change and grow; and so long as the software that is reading the data is reading the same data description, it can reconstitute an object even if the data format has changed.

Using an off-the-shelf tool like Castor from Exolab (available at http://castor.exolab.org), you can convert your Java objects to XML in a fashion that is almost simpler than serialization. You don't need to open or close an ObjectOutputStream. To use Castor, you simply open a FileWriter, then call the marshall method on the Marshaller class as shown in Listing 1-4.

Listing 1-4. Writing Data as XML

```
import java.io.*;
import java.util.*;
import org.exolab.castor.xml.*;
...
    FileWriter writer = null;
    try {
      writer = new FileWriter("employees.xml");

      Employee employee = new Employee();
      employee.setFirstName( "Bob" );
      employee.setLastName( "Smith" );
      employee.setEmployeeId( 2230045 );
      Marshaller.marshal(employee, writer);
    }
    catch( Exception e ) {
```

```
      e.printStackTrace();
    }
    finally {
      if( writer != null ) {
        try { writer.close(); }
        catch( IOException e ){}
      }
    }
```

This code will create an XML file that contains the following representation of the employee object:

```
<employee employee-id="2230045">
         <last-name>Smith</last-name>
         <first-name>Bob</first-name>
</employee>
```

Reading an object from XML is just as easy as writing the object. Just use the unmarshall method on the Unmarshaller to do the reading, as shown in the following code. Once again, this is simpler than serialization.

```
import java.io.*;
import java.util.*;
import org.exolab.castor.xml.*;
...
    FileReader reader = null;
    try {
      reader = new FileReader("employees.xml");

      Employee savedEmployee
        = (Employee) Unmarshaller.unmarshal(Employee.class, reader);
      System.out.println( savedEmployee.getFirstName() );
    }
    catch( Exception e ) {
      e.printStackTrace();
    }
    finally {
      if( reader != null ) {
        try { reader.close(); }
        catch( IOException e ){}
      }
    }
```

Slightly simpler reading and writing is a product of Castor, not XML. The gain that you get from using XML is seen in the flexibility mentioned earlier. With XML, you can read an old class's data into a new version of your class. If you add the numDependants attribute to your class, you do not lose access to your previously stored employee objects. All future stored employee objects would generate XML that looks like the following:

```
<employee employee-id="938005" num-dependants="2">
    <last-name>Smith</last-name>
    <first-name>Bob</first-name>
</employee>
```

It is also possible to use the old version of the class to read this new XML because attributes that are not supported by the class will be ignored. This is much more robust than serialization.

Castor is only one of many libraries and tools available for free and for fee. You can take your pick, as most will help you do the job of reading and writing your objects. In many cases, you will still need to write Java code to turn your Java objects into XML. As for Castor specifically, the tool also provides a mechanism for persisting objects to relational databases, which I will cover more in depth in Chapter 11.

Though XML helps overcome some of the issues raised in serialization, it still has some of the same issues that will plague any storage method that uses flat files—namely, the lack of search capability, the need to read all objects into memory until you find the one you need, and the lack of transactions.

As with serialization, in depth discussion of storing objects with XML is outside of this book's scope. For more information, check out the great work being done on XML at http://www.w3c.org; you can also read up on storing data to files using Java in JavaSoft's tutorial at http://java.sun.com/docs/books/tutorial/essential/io/index.html.

Object Databases for Transparent Persistence

Another method of persisting objects is with an Object Database Management System (ODBMS). An ODBMS, or object database for short, provides a transparent method of persistence. It allows you to query for and work with objects directly. By *transparent*, I mean you usually do not need to add a lot of code to store and retrieve your objects. Those hundreds of classes I mentioned in my opening paragraphs can be reduced to a few lines.

There are a wide variety of ODBMS implementations available. How they work can vary widely. Some implementations provide an environment where your Java objects run. They essentially replace the Java Virtual Machine (JVM) that runs Java code with their own environment. Most others simply interact with running Java objects in whatever JVM they exist in.

Object databases store data together with the methods for the data. This fits in well with the object-oriented paradigm, where data and the methods that work on that data are kept together. In this way, complex objects and their related methods can be stored simply. Because entire objects are stored, there is no need to reconstitute objects when they are retrieved. In other words, you do not need to read a name value and assign it the name attribute of the employee object. You simply read the whole employee object from the object database.

In Figure 1-4, you can see that storage of objects in an object database is similar to storing those objects to a data file through serialization. In this case, however, you hand the object off to a running object database system. There is usually a running process that the application connects to in order to store the object. As well as providing help in storing the object, the object database system provides help in recovering the stored object.

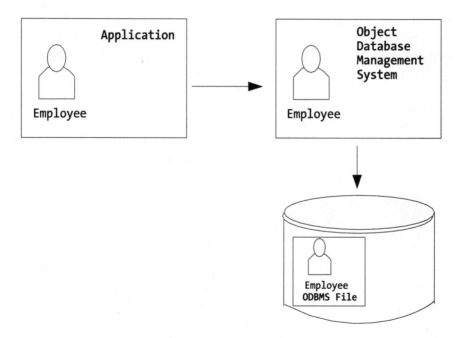

Figure 1-4. Storing an object to an object database

With a little thought, you might develop a concern about what objects are loaded and when. For instance, if I am making a list of employees' first names, I don't want to instantiate an entire object's graph in order to find the first names. I don't want to load the employee, her address object, her employer object, all of the employer's other employee objects, and so on. In order to overcome this problem, a lot of object databases rely on lazy initialization for instantiating objects. You will be provided with a reference to an object, but not until you try to use it does the database initialize the object.

In the past, there were performance concerns with object databases. They were considered much slower than relational databases, although object database providers have now largely rectified these issues. Many of the current crop of object databases provide object caches that help the performance immensely. Instead of an object being read from disk, it is read directly out of memory.

Reducing or eliminating code to store objects is a huge savings in time and effort as well. Using an object database can shorten development time considerably, as it spares you from writing persistence layers. With an object database, you simply say "store this employee," and you don't need to specify how or where.

There are concerns with using an ODBMS, however. While many ODBMSs have been around for years, there are none with the maturity and user base of some of the larger relational databases. In addition, a host of tools are available that can provide functionality if they have direct access to the data without the objects. An example could be reporting tools. You don't have to load all the employees when you just need to know the number of people who started over 10 years ago. However, the reporting tool may not be suited to Java, in which case its associated object database would not be suited at all.

Another concern is the way in which object databases mark objects as persistable. Some object databases add additional code to either the source of an object or the compiled byte code. Although this code may not affect the ability to run these objects in other JVMs, there is a concern that this is violating Java's write once, run everywhere ideal.

The Value of Relational Databases

Relational Database Management Systems (RDBMSs) represent a more mature technology than ODBMSs. Relational databases have been around since the 1970s. The software companies behind many of them are some of the largest and most powerful in the world. There is a level of confidence that comes with using a product from IBM, Oracle, or even Microsoft. There can also be a level of confidence in using products like PostgreSQL or MySQL, since they are well known and documented in the open source community.

Another positive for relational databases is that most companies already have some sort of relational database in place. This goes back to the maturity and amount of time these products have been available.

One consideration too often overlooked by excited new designers and developers is what a company can best support. If there are five Oracle database administrators (DBAs) on site, Oracle is probably a good choice. It is very rare today to find a company with object database administrators on staff.

This is, unfortunately, the same type of argument you can hear for not using an open source relational database. PostgreSQL DBAs may be less expensive than Oracle DBAs, but the former is virtually impossible to find in many places. They are around, but not many companies have a PostgreSQL practice.

For simple queries and accessing data, you will find few things that can match the performance and stability of a relational database. Do keep in mind accessing data is only part of the problem I am talking about in this book though. Once you have the data, you still need to turn it into objects.

One key to a relational database is how easily the data is made available to other applications. I can have a human resources application written entirely in Java that uses Oracle databases as its back end. That data is not limited to my HR application, nor is it restricted to Java. I can purchase and use a third-party reporting tool like Crystal Reports or Actuate with that data very easily.

Figure 1-5 shows an object that is being stored to a relational database system. In concept it is very similar to storing an object database. This is not entirely the case, however. There is an impedance mismatch between the object to be stored and the medium it will be stored to. You application needs to do a lot more work in order to store the objects in the relational database. It needs to speak the relational database's language. The specifics of this work are what this book will address.

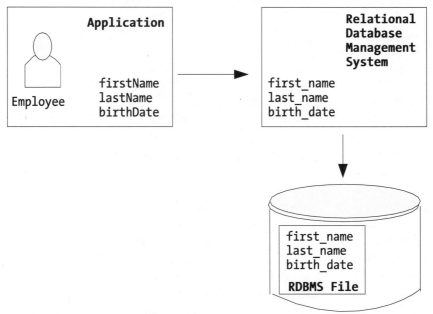

Figure 1-5. Storing an object to a relational database

Using an Object-Relational Persistence Layer

Most business applications developed today need to support both object databases and relational databases. By supporting both, a company can leverage the strengths of both. This can be accomplished by implementing an object-relational (OR) persistence layer between your application and the relational database. This layer can be home built or off the shelf. The ways these layers are implemented vary widely, and it is this method of persistence I will most directly address.

Whether the OR layer is off the shelf or home built, it must provide the following functionality: a way to tie an object's attribute to a relational database field, a way to query for objects, and a way to lock an object for updating.

All OR layers also need to have some sort of mapping layer. In a mapping layer, an object is connected to database tables and columns through mapping. The firstName field of an employee object is related to the first_name column of an Employees table. The mapping layer determines the way objects are connected to tables.

An OR layer that does not allow you to retrieve stored objects is of no value (like write-only memory), so it must employ some form of query language, even if that language is hard coded in objects through method calls. Sometimes the layer will require you to use a query language to look for objects, and sometimes you will make calls. For instance, you could use either a request like the following object query statement:

```
SELECT e FROM Employee e WHERE e.firstName = 'wilbur'
```

or a request like this one:

```
employeeDM.findForFirstName( "wilbur" ).
```

Another requirement for OR layers is the capability to lock an object in order to update it. You don't want to have people overwriting the same object. I will talk more about methods of locking objects in Chapter 5.

In a home-built system, you can decide for yourself the best way to implement this functionality. You can implement your mapping layer in XML or in serialized objects, or you can use reflection to get an object's metadata. You can create a language that you parse in order to do your querying. Also, you can implement whatever locking mechanism makes the most sense in your application.

In off-the-shelf products, these days a lot of work is going on to make these layers act and perform similar to an object database. These off-the-shelf products can use the same query language as many object databases and can include a caching mechanism to help with performance. Locking can be implemented in various ways to best suit the users. This applies to both commercial products and open source products.

Figure 1-6 illustrates storing an object to a relational database through an OR layer. This is very similar to storing objects to a relational database, but I have added one piece, the OR layer. This layer gives you many of the benefits of object databases, while allowing you to keep the benefits of the relational database. So in this diagram, the object is handed off to the OR layer from the application. The OR layer may or may not cache the object, but it does remove the impedance mismatch using OR mapping. The object is then stored in the relational database using the relational database's language.

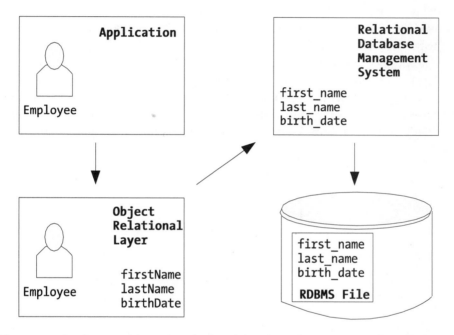

Figure 1-6. Storing an object to a relational database through an object-relational layer

Summary

In this chapter, I have introduced the concept of persistence. I have talked about various ways you can store your objects to data files on a file system, including using Java serialization. I also briefly went over using XML to store objects in a way that can be updated without breaking previously stored objects. This is a simple form of persistence. It is easy to implement, but lacking in features that are often needed for nontrivial applications.

Object databases were introduced as another way of persisting objects. Remember that an object database can provide some of the cleanest methods of persisting objects, because little overhead and little extra work need to go into storing objects to this type of storage. However, some issues with using object databases can make them less than ideal, including the need to make data available to non–object-oriented systems.

Relational databases constitute a more mature technology than object databases. Often they are already available in a company's information technology suite. The data is easily accessible to both object and nonobject systems. You can find a lot of tools and products off the shelf that can help you work with your data when it is in a relational database.

An object-relational persistence layer can provide you with many of the positives of both an object database and a relational database. A lot more work can be involved if you write it yourself, but you can specialize your layer to your needs that way. Many off-the-shelf products are also available that provide OR persistence for both commercial and open source databases.

The last method of persistence, object-relational, is what this book is about. In the next chapter, I will discuss relational databases in more detail. The relational database is your repository. Not understanding relational databases can result in a poor performing and short-lived application. So with no further ado, on to the next chapter.

CHAPTER 2

Understanding Relational Database Management Systems

CALL ME ISHMAEL. We are about to learn about the White Whale: the Relational Database Management System (RDBMS). RDBMS is the most common type of data storage in business today, because it is a proven and well-supported technology. In this chapter, I will discuss what a relational database is and how you can use one. I will try to touch on most aspects of the relational database, but a relational database is too large of a whale to cover in one chapter.

The best part about a relational database is that it has something in it for everyone. RDBMS origins are based on mathematics. The database's query language, which I will cover in this chapter, is based on spoken English. A nicely designed database is to some a form of art, created from carefully drawn diagrams. You can focus on the big picture by looking at overall design. An opportunity to delve down and get your hands dirty presents itself when you're figuring out the best field type to store data as; or, for those who are a little obsessive-compulsive, RDBMS has a lot of redundancy. Plus, speed freaks will appreciate the in-memory caching. So hold on to your hat and let's take a whale of a ride.

What Does a Relational Database Do?

The purpose of a relational database is to store data in a way that allows high performance and is very safe. The relational database is often high performance because of all the work that has gone into making it the central data repository of business since the late 1970s. It is usually considered stable for the same reason. Companies like IBM, Oracle, Microsoft, and many more have poured untold billions into development of these systems.

The *table* is the central unit of the relational database, and it is where data is stored. Tables represent a collection of like data. For example, all employee records would be stored in an Employees table. All GM car models would be stored in an Automobiles table.

Inside of a table, the data is broken down into columns and rows. A *column* describes the data. It tells what name the data goes by; for example, num_dependants is the name for a column of data. It also describes what type of data the column holds. The column num_dependants is a whole number, and probably doesn't need to be that large of a number (if anyone has over 255 children, we can refactor the database later).

A *row* is a record in the table. The row intersects every column in the table. Our employee Bob Smith from the last chapter would have his very own row. That row would contain an employee_id value, a last_name value, a first_name value, and a num_dependants value. Not all of these entries in the row need to be filled in. A relational database will allow you to make the values empty or undefined.

If, for example, you were connecting to the HR database created in Chapter 1, you could see a table similar to Table 2-1 that has four columns: employee_id, last_name, first_name, and num_dependants. Every row in the table would have a value or field that is assigned to each column, even if that field is undefined, because you are still making a statement about its value.

Table 2-1. Example of a Database Table

EMPLOYEE_ID	LAST_NAME	FIRST_NAME	NUM_DEPENDANTS
0716456	Patzer	Andrew	2
005657	Busse	Dale	1
2230045	Smith	Bob	2

Most rows of data require some unique identifier. This is called the table's *primary key*. A primary key could be a Social Security number or it could be database or application specific. In the preceding example, the employee_id column is the primary key, as it is unique for each employee.

A *view* in a relational database is a way of grouping the data of one or more tables as a new virtual table. The data is kept in its original tables rather than actually stored in the view. The view simply brings the data together as defined. Views can also contain other views. So views are actually groupings of multiple table or view data put together in a specific way. Views make it easy to write complex queries. The database has already grouped the data in the view, and queries are run by simply asking for data from that view.

A History of Relational Databases

Relational databases are a technology that was first introduced in the 1970s by IBM researcher E. F. Codd. At the time there were two popular types of databases: the network model and the hierarchical model.

Users of network and hierarchical databases were finding limitations in them. Specifically, it was difficult to change an existing database without breaking the applications that used them. This was because both designs required the application to have a good knowledge of the internal structure of the database.

Codd suggested a database design based on mathematical relations, which is how this type of database derived its name. The "relational" in relational database comes from the assumption that database tables relate to each other.

Codd proposed making the data independent of the applications that used it. He described how the data could exist and how it could be referenced. He also suggested designing this type of database in such a way as to reduce duplication of data.

While it was Codd at IBM who came up with the idea of relational databases, it was Relational Software's Oracle product that was the first commercially available relational database. IBM did eventually release their relational database, System/R, followed by DB2.

How Relational Databases Work

There are two types of relational databases: those with a server process and those without one. Within Java, there is little difference in interacting with either type. Usually a relational database that does have a server will have much higher performance. For this chapter, I am going to talk exclusively about relational databases with a server process. Specifically, all the examples in this chapter were written for and tested with the MySQL relational database, which is open source and can be obtained from http://www.mysql.com.

In a relational database with a server process, the server process answers client requests for data. The server is a program that is running, waiting for requests. When the server receives requests from client software, it answers those requests, returning whatever data it finds in its repository.

Usually relational databases will have a cache mechanism that keeps data in system memory in order to improve response performance. By implementing such a cache, there is less need to go to the hard disk for commonly accessed data. With the price of memory falling, some businesses are loading their entire databases into the cache.

In order to retrieve data from the database, the client needs to use a language that the database understands. The language most commonly used today is Structured Query Language (SQL). It is in SQL that requests are made to the server. Although most implementations of SQL are similar, usually some differences exist, such as how to create a join, or what data types are available. Make sure you are familiar with the exact syntax of the database you are using.

Figure 2-1 shows a query coming into the relational database. The cache is checked. If the results are not found there, then the server checks the disk files. After finding the results, the data is cached and returned to the client. Subsequent requests for the same data will not need to go to the disk. The data will be found in the cache.

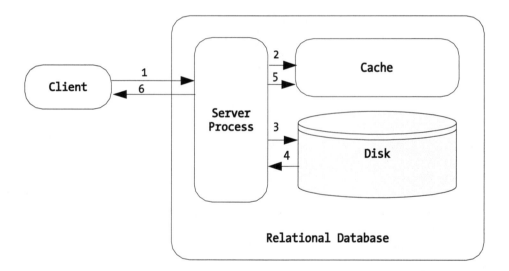

Figure 2-1. Interaction with a relational database

Ensuring Good Data Through Transactions

When a lot of clients are interacting with a database, the database needs to be able to handle all the data interaction. Specifically, there is a concern when reading and writing to any data storage that two processes will try to work on the same chunk of data at the same time. If this were to happen, the validity of that chunk of data would be in question.

For example, if one process is updating the address of an employee and another process tries to read that employee's address at the same time, there is a chance that the data could be only half updated at the time of the read. If there was nothing to manage these reads and writes, the best you could hope for is bad data. Probably you would end up with a crashed server, client, or both.

Figure 2-2 shows data as it exists initially in the repository. At the same time, two processes go for the same employee's address. One tries to write a new street address while the other is reading it. The requests get there at almost the same time, and the process that is reading the data gets half a correction, which means it is entirely wrong.

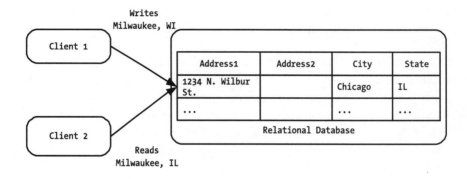

Figure 2-2. Multiple processes trying to work on the same data at the same time

It was because of this concern that the concept of transactions was created. A *transaction* is a unit of work on the data. By separating work performed on data into units, one process could read an employee's address while another process writes to it. Neither knows the other is working. In a transaction, there is no possibility that the two processes are working on the same piece of data at the same time.

In order for transactions to be safe, they need to follow certain requirements. The transactions must be Atomic, Consistent, Isolated, and Durable (ACID). These ACID properties keep the database in a stable state. The following list details these ACID properties:

- *Atomicity:* All changes are committed or all changes are rolled back. No single part of the transaction is saved without all parts of the transaction. No single part of the transaction is skipped without all being skipped.

- *Consistency:* The database is left in a consistent state. The transaction must obey integrity constraints. If you have set a constraint that no employee shall be added to the Employees table without an entry in the Payroll table, then the database is not consistent if there is an employee in the Employees table and none in the Payroll table.

- *Isolation:* Transactions shall operate independently of each other. Never can one transaction see a half-finished second transaction. One transaction cannot be affected by a second transaction until the first is completed.

- *Durable:* Once the transaction is committed, it is saved. Even if there is a system failure, that transaction is saved. It will not be lost.

It is through the ACID properties that relational databases keep data safe. If a transaction does not have success in ensuring all of these properties work, the transaction is rolled back, meaning that all work is undone. All major relational databases handle ACID transactions. Note that at the time of this writing MySQL by default does not support these ACID properties. However, MySQL-Max, a version of the MySQL database program that does support transactions, is available from the MySQL site.

Database Design

Before any database is created, you need a design for that database. By spending some time up front designing your database, you will save a lot of time and headaches later on. When designing a database, you need to take into account the data that needs to be stored, the types of queries that will be run, the load that you expect, and the type of database you are deploying on. Database design is performed in three parts: gathering requirements, data modeling, and normalization.

Gathering Requirements

The first part of database design is the same as that of any other type of design: You need to gather your requirements. There will be many sources for these requirements, but for the most part they will come from your users and the project sponsors. What you want to find in these requirements are entities that you will be storing, such as customers, employees, invoices, and parts; any object that you want to store data for is an entity.

Data Modeling

The second phase of database design is data modeling. When you design a database, you want to draw a diagram using the entities you discover in the requirements phase. You also want to determine the relationships between the entities. For example, an employee has any number of addresses. Another example is that an invoice should never exist without an item associated with it. You can also set the requirement that a customer exists only if there is one or more invoices. These relationships are captured in the same diagram.

By capturing those entities and relationships in a diagram, you create an entity relationship (ER) diagram. This is the language used to communicate database design. These diagrams consist of entities, relationships, and constraints.

Figure 2-3 shows an ER diagram. In this diagram, one invoice is related to many items. Each box is an entity, and the line and diamond represent the relationship between the entities.

Figure 2-3. Example of a basic entity relation diagram

Normalization in Database Design

The third phase of database design is normalization. Normalization was another idea pioneered by E. F. Codd. After working with relational databases for some time, he discovered some best practices in laying out a database. Going back to mathematics, he coined the term *normalization* for these practices. In fact, Codd initially proposed three forms of normalization:

- First Normal Form (1NF) occurs when you connect two tables through a foreign key.

- Second Normal Form (2NF) involves taking any dependencies between two tables and moving them into a third table.

- Third Normal Form (3NF) is used to keep related data together and move unrelated data to another table.

Using First Normal Form

In First Normal Form, you use the primary key from one table as a foreign key in another table. Say for example that you want to store information on invoices and items within the invoice. A table based on First Normal Form would have a lot of duplicate information, as shown in Table 2-2.

Table 2-2. Invoices Table with Item Data

INVOICE_DATE	TOTAL_SALES_TAX	FREIGHT	CUSTOMER_NAME	QTY	ITEM_DESC	PRICE
10/13/2002	2.03	5.95	Dave Glyzewski	3	Picture frame	6.95
10/13/2002	2.03	5.95	Dave Glyzewski	1	American flag	15.95
10/14/2002	.76	3.95	Ed Chaltry	2	Picture frame	6.95

Here you have data from distinctly different entities combined into one table. You will also end up with duplicate data for every second item in an invoice. You have two options: to only allow people to order one item or to normalize your data.

In First Normal Form, you take the data that would be duplicated and create an Items table (Table 2-3). You then give each item and invoice its own unique ID, which is its primary key. You associate the item with the invoice by adding one field to your Invoices table that contains the primary key from the Items table (see

Table 2-4). That is the foreign key. The same data that is a primary key in one table is a foreign key in another.

Table 2-3. Items Table

ITEM_ID	ITEM_DESC	PRICE
567	Picture frame	6.95
456	American flag	15.95

Table 2-4. Invoices Table with Items Table Foreign Key

INVOICE_ID	INVOICE_DATE	TOTAL_SALES_TAX	FREIGHT	CUSTOMER_NAME	ITEM1	ITEM1_QTY	ITEM2	ITEM2_QTY	ITEM3	ITEM3_QTY
3456	10/13/2002	2.03	5.95	Dave Glyzewski	567	3	456	1		
3457	10/14/2002	.76	3.95	Ed Chaltry			567	2		

In Figure 2-4, you can see that the Invoices table is related to the Items table. This relationship is through the foreign key. The Invoices table contains three foreign keys to the Items table—specifically, the fields item1, item2, and item3.

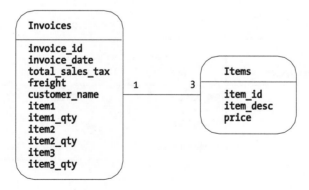

Figure 2-4. First Normal Form normalization

First Normal Form can define dependencies between tables. A designer could say that an item should not exist without an invoice. When the last invoice containing an item is removed, the item itself should be removed.

Using Second Normal Form

One issue with 1FN in the preceding example is you can only have three items per invoice. You also have storage allocated for items that you are not filling. What you need is a way to organize your tables that removes this restriction, such as a dependent table to allow you flexibility in your relationships (see Tables 2-5 through 2-7).

Table 2-5. Invoices Table with Items Table Foreign Key

INVOICE_ID	INVOICE_DATE	TOTAL_SALES_TAX	FREIGHT	CUSTOMER_NAME
3456	10/13/2002	2.03	5.95	Dave Glyzewski
3457	10/14/2002	.76	3.95	Ed Chaltry

Table 2-6. Invoice_Line Table

INVOICE_ID	ITEM_ID	QTY
3456	567	3
3456	456	1
3457	567	2

Table 2-7. Items Table

ITEM_ID	ITEM_DESC	PRICE
567	Picture frame	6.95
456	American flag	15.95

Figure 2-5 shows how these tables are connected. It is the Invoice_Line table that connects an item with an invoice. In this way, you are able to add as many items to an invoice as needed.

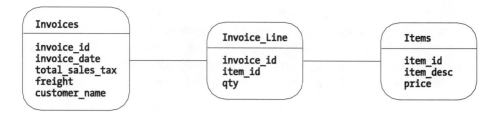

Figure 2-5. Second Normal Form normalization

Using Third Normal Form

Third Normal Form deals with removing redundant data from tables by moving it into a separate table. This is especially true where the redundant data is part of a complete entity that is not a part of that table.

The Invoices table in this example includes each customer's name. A customer is an entity unto itself. In a true Invoices table that is unnormalized, there would be customer address information, contact information, and much more. Third Normal Form suggests taking all of the customer information and putting it into a Customers table. Then when Dave Glyzewski places another order, you do not have to repeat his information. You simply refer to the foreign key that represents him.

In 3NF the information being extracted from the table is nondependent. A customer does not depend on an invoice. Removing an invoice will not remove the customer.

The Other Normal Forms

Codd later produced three other normal forms: Boyce-Codd Normal Form (BCNF), Fourth Normal Form (4NF), and Fifth Normal Form (5NF). These other normal forms helped to address problems in the First Normal Form and added rules as to how data should be stored in the tables themselves.

Reviewing Structured Query Language

Structured Query Language (SQL) is the language that was designed to work with Codd's relational database. It was originally developed at IBM for the System/R database. Although IBM invented SQL, it was first commercially available in the Oracle database.

SQL is a huge topic that already has many good books devoted to it. For our purposes, I want to give some quick reference material that should help with most of the examples presented in this book. I highly suggest spending some time mastering this powerful query language if you haven't already done so.

There are some properties that pertain to all SQL statements that we can address:

- SQL is case insensitive. `INSERT INTO` is the same as `insert into` is the same as `InSeRt InTo`.

- Strings in quotes are case sensitive. "Bob Smith" does not equal "bob smith." This can be overridden, but doing so can be very costly in terms of performance.

- SQL is not white space sensitive. `INSERT`   `INTO` is the same as `INSERT INTO`.

The main functionality you will need from SQL is to do basic database management. You will need to create a database in order to have somewhere to store your tables. You will need to create a table to store your data and add data to the table. Once the data is there, you often have to update it. And when the data is no longer applicable, you should be able to delete it. And data has no value without the ability to query for it in order to use it. These are the SQL commands we will go over next.

All of these commands need to be executed from some type of database SQL client. In MySQL, the command is `mysql`. For Oracle, the environment is `SQL*Plus`. There are similar tools for Microsoft SQL Server and IBM's DB2. You can also use a tool like WinSQL through an ODBC driver if you wish; or, if you are ahead of the game, you can write your own application using JDBC, which I will cover in Chapter 3. One last point before we dive into the commands themselves is to remember that most databases provide extensions to standard SQL—some even provide quirks.

Creating a New Database

First you need somewhere to work on and store all the wonderful tables you have designed, and that is the database. In order to use SQL or interact with a relational database, you need to create a database. The database itself is simply the grouping of your tables, views, and other objects.

The command for creating a database is very easy:

```
CREATE DATABASE database_name
```

For example, to create a database named HRApp, you would issue this command:

```
CREATE DATABASE HRApp
```

Creating New Tables

Once you have a database created, you need to create the tables you designed. In the CREATE TABLE command, you need to tell the database not only the table name, but the names and types of all of the columns. You can additionally specify some column constraints here, like whether the column can contain a null value or not.

The format of the create table command is

```
CREATE TABLE table_name (
  column1_name data_type[(length)] [NULL|NOT NULL],
  column2_name data_type[(length)] [NULL|NOT NULL],
  …)
```

Before you can create the tables, though, you need to be in the database's context. You do this through the USE database_name command like this:

```
USE HRApp
```

Now you can create your Employees table with the simple CREATE TABLE command as follows:

```
CREATE TABLE employees (
  employee_id      INTEGER       NOT NULL,
  last_name        VARCHAR(128)  NOT NULL,
  first_name       VARCHAR(128)  NOT NULL,
  num_dependants   SMALLINT      NULL )
```

Note that in the preceding command, I made any field that I felt should be filled in have the constraint of NOT NULL, particularly the employee_id field, which is the primary key field for this table. Look at your business requirements to decide if you can enforce data constraints in this way. My application, for instance, could not handle the musician Sting unless he was willing to use his given name. But even Sting would have a primary key, so make sure that is enforced.

Adding these constraints gives your database some protection. Remember, not all the developers who use your database are going to be as smart as you are. By ensuring that a primary key is set, your application is protected from future applications not following conventions.

Inserting Data into Tables

You have created your database and your tables. Now you need to insert some data into the tables. This command will require the table name, the list of columns you are setting values for, and the values themselves.

```
INSERT [INTO] {table_name|view_name} (
  column1_name, column2_name, …
    ) VALUES (
  column1_value, column2_value, …
    )
```

An example of the INSERT statement for our employees table would look like this:

```
INSERT INTO employees (
   employee_id, last_name, first_name
   ) VALUES (
   123456, 'Glyzewski', 'Dave'
   )
```

In the preceding statement I add an employee named Dave Glyzewski, by filling in all of the fields that have the constraint NOT NULL, but I leave out the field that is allowed to be null. You should only enforce the minimum required fields. If the entity makes sense without a field filled in, allow nulls for that field.

Updating Data with SQL

Now that you have some data in the table, you need to make a change to it. If you need to change some values in an existing row, use the UPDATE statement. An UPDATE statement is similar to an INSERT statement. It contains the name of the table you are writing to, as well as a list of columns you are providing values for, and the values themselves. The exact format of this statement is

```
UPDATE {table_name|view_name}
    SET column1_name = column1_value, column2_name = column2_value,…
    WHERE conditions
```

This is useful for when you find out that Dave's real name is David, and when you find out that he has three dependants, and you are ready to capture that information. An example for updating the Dave Glyzewski record to David Glyzewski would look like this:

```
UPDATE employees
SET first_name = 'David', num_dependants = 3
WHERE employee_id = 123456
```

In the preceding statement, I have changed Dave's first name, and set a new value to the row for his number of dependants.

Deleting Data with SQL

In most business situations, you do not delete many business records from the database. For the most part, you want to put a record into an inactive state so that it can be skipped in queries. This is because data is hard to come by, and you never know when you might need it again.

In some situations though, you will need to delete data. The need to delete data usually presents itself in temporary tables or when an employee is sure never to come back. The syntax for the DELETE statement contains the name of the table you are deleting the row from followed by a criteria to ensure you delete the correct row.

```
DELETE FROM {table_name|view_name}
    WHERE conditions
```

Say the you want to get rid of all traces of the employee Dave Glyzewski. To do so, you would execute a DELETE statement that looks like this:

```
DELETE FROM employees
    WHERE employee_id = 123456
```

You ensure that you are removing the correct record by using the unique primary key, rather than some other attribute that could be duplicated.

Selecting Data from Tables

The SELECT statement is how you perform queries on the database. It is by the SELECT statement that all data is found. Because of this, SELECT statements can be very complex. There is a good chance that most of the SQL code you write for your applications will be SELECT statements.

The syntax of a SQL SELECT statement consists of the SELECT command followed by what columns you want returned, what table the columns can be found in, then an optional series of conditions that the rows need to meet in order to have their columns returned.

```
SELECT {*|column1_name, column2_name,…}
FROM {table_name|view_name}
WHERE conditions
```

If you wanted to get the first and last name of an employee whose ID is 123456, you would list the first_name and last_name columns. You would then tell the database it could find the data in the Employees table. Finally, you would give the query the condition of the employee's ID being 123456.

```
SELECT first_name, last_name
    FROM employees
    WHERE employee_id = 123456
```

Sometimes everything you need is not found in just one table. For example, if you were creating mailing labels for your employees, you might want to return the address as well as the first and last name. *Joins*, such as the one demonstrated in the following code, are a way of putting together multiple table queries:

```
SELECT e.first_name, e.last_name, a.address1, a.city, a.state, a.zip
    FROM employees e
    LEFT JOIN addresses a ON e.employee_id = a.employee_id
    WHERE a.employee_id = 123456
```

Summary

This chapter has covered a lot of material, but only in brief. As I said at the beginning, relational databases and SQL are topics that have been covered very well in numerous books. For our purposes, I have taken a high-level view, and provided a quick summary of SQL.

A relational database is a stable, high-performance system for storing and retrieving data. The data that a relational database works with is stored in tables in the form of columns and rows. Every primary row for an entity that is stored should have a unique primary key.

Transactions are the way in which a database maintains data consistency. Transactions ensure that the reads and writes to the data are atomic. The data will always be consistent. The various processes trying to work in the data will work in isolation, and when any work is done, it is durable and will survive a system shutdown.

Database design follows standard development design procedures. First requirements are gathered. All entities and relationships in the system are modeled in an ER diagram or other modeling system. The second step in the design of a database is to apply the rules of normalization to the design. Related tables are connected through foreign keys.

You create dependent tables of foreign keys to allow flexibility in the number of rows from one table that are related to a row in another table. You want to remove redundant data out of one table and put it into another.

Finally, in a quick review of Structured Query Language (SQL), we specifically, examined how to create databases and tables. I discussed how to insert data, change it after it exists, and how to delete the data. I covered the syntax of querying for data from a table as well.

There are many great sources for information on SQL. Oracle provides references for their databases and SQL at `http://technet.oracle.com/documentation/ content.html`. The MySQL manual is also available online at `http://www.mysql.com/ doc/en/index.html`. This provides much information when writing SQL to use with MySQL. If you are really ambitious, you can contact the American National Standards Institute and purchase a copy of the ISO standard, ISO/IEC 9075: 1992.

CHAPTER 3

Using JDBC 1 for Relational Database Work

THE UNGENTLE LAWS AND customs touched upon in this tale are historical, and the episodes which are used to illustrate them are also historical. The customs and laws I am going to introduce in this chapter are concerned specifically with database interaction from Java. I am going to talk about JDBC, which was introduced by Sun back in the days of Java 1.0 as an add-on package to the Java Software Development Kit (SDK). JDBC promised to make database access easy, consistent across databases, and high performance for the Java platform.

Those promises sounded so good, I wanted to take JDBC for a spin. The first time I used JDBC, I rewrote a referential integrity application for a DOS-based Paradox database. I had written the original referential integrity tool in C++ using Open Database Connectivity and Microsoft's Data Access Objects (no direct relation to the Java Data Access Objects pattern). The tool's job was to run through a specific database and ensure that all child records had parents and the general data format was good.

I was able to rewrite the application in Java with JDBC in less than two days. This was not really surprising because I had written the original tool and knew the problem and solution. The speed did give me a nice sense of accomplishment and really set the stage for me to see Java as a real programming language.

I was surprised to find that the Java/JDBC version of the referential integrity tool ran faster than the C++/ODBC version. To this day I cannot explain why this was true. Most likely the problem was in my C++ code. The increased speed in performance and development did give me good reason to take a better look at Java for future solutions. While I cannot explain the performance benefit, the development time and expense were reduced by the simplicity of Java code.

Now it is important to note, I am not saying that Java 1.0 with JDBC 1 was faster than C++/ODBC. What I am saying is that the technologies were interesting. Fortunately, at that time, there were no real JDBC books available, which means I got to go directly to the specification.

Sun has done a very good job of explaining JDBC to both the users of the libraries and to vendors who want to supply drivers for the library. They put both of these explanations into the JDBC specification. This is one of the major advantages Sun provides you with: well-documented specifications.

I am going to give you an overview of JDBC in this chapter. I will focus on the minimum number of parts you will need to start development with JDBC. In the next chapter, I will expand on new features that were added in versions 2 and 3 of the specification. I will also spend some time discussing ways to improve JDBC performance. To fully understand the ins and outs of JDBC, I highly recommend reviewing Sun's specification and API documents.

One thing you will get out of these JDBC chapters that you will not get out of the specifications is some best practices when using JDBC. In Chapter 6, I go even further by showing you some utility classes that make using JDBC much easier and less error prone.

What Is JDBC?

JDBC is to a database what a Java interface is to a Java class. It gives a simple, consistent way to work with relational databases. Regardless of the brand of database, JDBC allows the developer to interact with it in basically the same way. As an interface promises certain functionality from the classes that implement it, so the JDBC specification promises certain functionality from the databases and drivers that meet the standard.

When Sun Microsystems introduced JDBC, it was in the form of a specification document and a basic library. The specification described what JDBC was and how JDBC should be used; it also described what interfaces driver vendors needed to implement in order to release drivers that could be used as part of JDBC.

Vendors who want to produce a JDBC driver can read through the specification to know what functionality they need to provide. This gives users confidence in the providers that their drivers have a chance of being successful. Adhering to the specification also give consumers confidence in what functionality will be available.

I mentioned at the beginning of this chapter that JDBC started out as an add-on library to be used with Sun's Software Development Kit. Today JDBC is built into the standard Java SDK. Sun does, however, release the specification as a separate document.

When Sun releases a new version of the JDBC, they often release optional extension libraries that can be added to older SDKs that do not have the new functionality. For example, to use JDBC 1 features with the Java SDK 1.3.x, you do not need to add anything, you simply use the classes that are part of the SDK. If you want to use JDBC 2 or 3 features with the Java SDK 1.3.x, you needed to include additional library files. The Java SDK 1.4 includes all of the necessary libraries for JDBC 2 as well as JDBC 3. So with the Java SDK 1.4, you do not need any additional libraries.

Besides the libraries and documentation that Sun releases, JDBC also needs drivers for any database that it will support. Sun includes one JDBC driver with JDBC itself, and that driver is a bridge to any other installed ODBC driver on the system. What this means is that you can use one JDBC driver to communicate with various ODBC drivers.

Different Types of Drivers

One strong feature of JDBC is the ability to change drivers that you can use. Sun has included in their specification all the information a company needs to create a driver and distribute it. Specifically, you can choose the driver that best suits your needs.

For example if you go to Sun's JDBC driver page (`http://industry.java.sun.com/products/jdbc/drivers`), you can search on drivers for different databases. A search for all drivers for Microsoft SQL Server returns 36 different drivers. Some have built-in connection pooling, some support transactions, some are free, and others are not. Choose the driver that best fits your needs.

One downside of being able to use multiple drivers with the JDBC library is that not all drivers support all JDBC features. That puts you in the situation where the classes look like they have certain features, but because of the driver you are using, you might not be able to use those features.

Sun specifically describes four different types of drivers. Unfortunately, Sun did not take the time to clearly name the types of drivers, so you are now stuck with calling these drivers type 1 through type 4, which means you need to memorize or look up exactly how each driver works. Table 3-1 explains how each type of driver differs and what you can expect from each driver type.

Table 3-1. JDBC Driver Types

TYPE	NAME	DESCRIPTION
1	JDBC-ODBC bridge	Wraps an installed ODBC driver in the JDBC API. Requires a native ODBC driver to be installed on the computer that is trying to communicate with the database.
2	Native API partly Java driver	Wraps an installed database client in the JDBC API. Once again, this requires a native database client to be installed on any computer that wants to communicate with the database.

Table 3-1. JDBC Driver Types (Continued)

TYPE	NAME	DESCRIPTION
3	Net protocol full Java driver	Converts JDBC calls to a database-independent net protocol, which is then translated into the database protocol by the server. Fits best in a middleware product that the client needs to communicate with anyway. The middleware can then natively talk to the database.
4	Native protocol Java driver	A pure Java driver that knows how to talk directly to the database. This type of driver needs a running database server process and is not possible with a strictly file-based database such as Microsoft Access.

I mentioned before that there could be various trade-offs between drivers. Here you see more flexibility in your options depending on which type of driver fits your needs best. If, for instance, you need to access a Microsoft Access Database from an application server that is running on a mainframe or UNIX box, you would probably go with a type 3 driver. If you want high performance and are working with a full-fledged database server, you could choose a type 4 driver. If you are doing some simple prototyping, Sun's provided type 1 driver may suit your needs.

How to Use JDBC

Using JDBC is simple. Just a few classes and interfaces give you all the database functionality you need. This is particularly true if you focus just on the basic functionality provided by JDBC 1. For the most part, all database work in JDBC 1 can be done using the `java.sql.DataManager` class and the `java.sql.Connection`, `java.sql.Statement`, and `java.sql.ResultSet` interfaces. Because this one class and these three interfaces can do so much work, this is where we will focus first.

Figure 3-1 illustrates the relationship between these parts. Notice in particular that the driver manager provides connections but knows nothing about statements or result sets. Connections know about statements, but not about result sets or even the driver manager. Finally, the result set knows about nothing besides itself. This is a clean object model—it has few interdependencies and does a good job of distributing responsibility between objects.

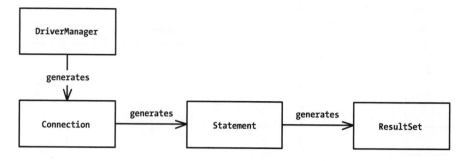

Figure 3-1. Primary class and interfaces of JDBC

In Figure 3-2, you can see how some of these objects interact. Note that a system first must register a driver with the driver manager by loading the driver's class. On loading the class, the driver registers itself with the driver manager.

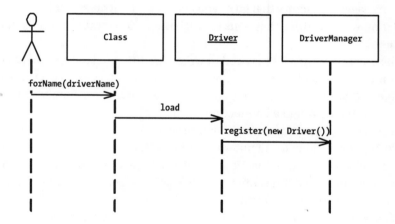

Figure 3-2. Loading a JDBC driver

After the driver is registered, the system can obtain a connection from the driver manager. Once a connection is obtained, the system can obtain a statement for doing the actual work with the database. If the work being done is intended to return data through a SELECT query, then a ResultSet object is returned (see Figure 3-3).

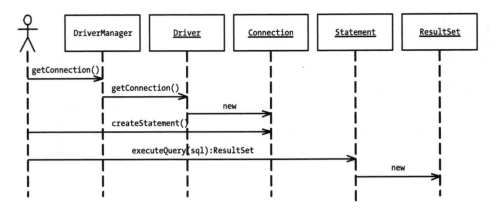

Figure 3-3. Working with the primary class and interfaces of JDBC

The DriverManager class gives you access to connections to the database. The driver manager is a factory that gives you access to and wraps your JDBC driver. All interaction with the driver happens through the various static methods that are provided.

The Connection interface is used to wrap a traditional database client connection. This is your lifeline to your data. Every time you need to get some data from the database, add a new row to the database, or make a change in your database, you go through a connection.

Because java.sql.Connection is an interface, your driver vendor provides the class to support it. So you will not (or should not have to) have any idea of what the underlying class actually is. However, you will be able to interact with it because the interface defines the available methods. For example, it is from the connection that you obtain instances of Statement.

Statement is the interface you use for doing actual work with your database. Statements are meant to wrap units of SQL work. You use SQL through a statement by calling methods that take SQL strings as arguments.

A statement is also used to select or query data from the database. The data that matches your query is returned in the form of a result set. A *result set* is a type of cursor to the database. You can essentially iterate through the values that were returned by the query.

Installing MySQL and Drivers

The MySQL database is a high-performance open source database. One opportunity gained by the database being open source is you can install it and use it to follow the examples in this book without cost. Besides being free, it is also very easy to install. Another advantage is it has many graphical tools that can help you administer the database.

Installation of the database varies depending on the platform you are installing to. The MySQL Web site at http://www.mysql.org contains precompiled versions for most platforms. Simply go to their site, click the Downloads link, then follow the links and instructions to install the database. On a Windows platform, it is a simple install file. For Linux, RPMs and tar files are available. Other OSs have their own installation files.

Once you have installed the database, I suggest installing a graphical tool to help with some of the administration tasks. The MySQL Control Center is available from the MySQL Web site and works on both Windows and Linux. There are many others, including a PHP front end that is always listed as being extremely active on SourceForge at http://www.sourceforge.net.

Creating the Database

Now that you know the basic parts of JDBC, it is time to see it work. First you will create a database. The examples in this chapter use MySQL. Every database will be a little different. With MySQL, there are a few ways to create a new database: You can use a graphical tool such as the MySQL Control Center, you can use the command line tool mysqladmin, which comes as part of MySQL, or, as I am going to demonstrate in these examples, you can use JDBC. Since this is a book about interacting with relational databases through Java, why wouldn't you want to use Java? If you choose to use a database other than MySQL, you will need to modify the sample code to match that database's requirements.

There are several steps to creating a database using JDBC. First you need to load the driver for the database you will be using. This is a simple process of using ClassLoader to load the driver class. Then you need to connect to the database, which you will achieve using the driver manager. Finally, you need to execute the CREATE DATABASE SQL statement, which I described in the last chapter. Once you have created the database, you will follow very similar steps to populate it, and then interact with it.

Loading the Database Driver

In order to do any work in JDBC, you need to work through a JDBC driver that is meant specifically for the database or database API you want to use. For these examples, I choose to use the Connector/J driver, which I obtained from http://www/mysql.com/. Once I downloaded and followed the instructions for installing the driver, I added it to my classpath. The code for this book, available from the Downloads section on the Apress Web site (http://www.apress.com), includes an Ant build script that loads all .jar files in the lib/ and lib/ext directories, so I simply copied the driver there. Ant is a build tool that is freely available from http://ant.apache.org; this tool can be used to manage an application's build process.

Before you can use a driver in your Java code, you need to load it. Referencing the driver class does this. The first time any Java code references a class, the class loader loads that class from the classpath into the virtual machine. When a class is loaded, any static initialization that needs to be done will be done. One task that all JDBC drivers perform in their static initializers is to register themselves with the driver manager. In this way you can simply reference a driver class and make it available through JDBC.

The way to load a driver class is to use the forName static method on the Class class. When calling the forName method, you give it a string containing the name of the class to load. The forName method tells the class loader to search the classpath and find any classes that match the name the method is given. The code for loading the MySQL driver looks like this:

```
Class.forName( "com.mysql.jdbc.Driver" );
```

This line will cause the class loader to find and load the com.mysql.jdbc.Driver class. When the class is loaded, its static initiator is called. The static initializer registers the driver with the driver manager. Once the driver is registered, this driver will handle any requests for connections that this driver can handle.

Obtaining a Connection to the Database Server

In order to create a database, you first need to establish a connection to your database server. With the Connector/J JDBC driver, you actually need to connect to an existing database on that database server. In order to connect to any existing database, you need to have some name to refer to it.

With JDBC, the name of a database takes the form of a Uniform Resource Locater (URL); this is the same type of naming you would use to access a Web page or an FTP server. Where the URL for a Web page consists of http://web.address, the form of the URL for JDBC consists of jdbc:subprotocol:subname.

So to access a MySQL database, you need to create a URL that contains "jdbc", a subprotocol of "mysql" that tells the driver manager which driver to use, and a subname that tells the driver where to look for the database for instance. Usually the subname consists of the server's name, an optional port, and the name of the database to connect to. Since you are trying to create a database, you will use the system database name. In MySQL, the system database name is "mysql". Your URL would be //localhost/mysql, provided you are running MySQL on the default port of 3306.

So a string referencing the complete URL for accessing the MySQL database you created before would look like this:

```
String url = "jdbc:mysql://localhost/mysql";
```

Now that you have loaded your driver and know your URL, you can create a connection to your database server. In order to make a connection, you use the driver manager. DriverManager is a class that has static methods for managing drivers and getting connections. The DriverManager class can only be interacted with through its static methods. It is impossible to create an instance of the driver manager because it has a private constructor. The method you are most interested in is getConnection(String url, String user, String password). You will give the getConnection method your URL and a user name and password that are applicable to your specific database. This will then return a JDBC connection that you can use.

```
connection = DriverManager.getConnection( url, username, password );
```

It is important to note that there are actually two other getConnection methods. The first method takes a single string containing the URL to connect to. You can use this method if the database does not need authentication or if the driver supports having the user name and password as part of the URL. The third version of the method takes a URL and java.util.Properties object. In this method, you can specify the user name and password in the Properties object, as well as any driver-specific parameters that are available.

Using a Statement to Create the Database

Now that you have successfully connected to your database server, you need a way to give the server the SQL that will create your database. The object that handles the communication of SQL is a Statement object. The object itself is a part of the JDBC driver that implements the java.sql.Statement interface.

In order to obtain a `Statement`, you ask for it from the connection you retrieve from the driver manager. The simplest method on the connection that returns a statement is the `createStatement()` method. This is the method you are going to call:

```
statement = connection.createStatement();
```

Now that you have your `Statement` object, you need to define the SQL statement that it will execute. The SQL for creating a database is very simple. As I explained in the last chapter, the statement consists of `CREATE DATABASE database_name`. For this example, you will create a database named hrapp. Your SQL and string referencing it looks like this:

```
String hrappSQL = "CREATE DATABASE hrapp";
```

Once you have your SQL defined, you next need to execute the SQL through JDBC. Your `Statement` object is where this work will be done. Specifically, you can call the method `executeUpdate` to execute your SQL.

```
statement.executeUpdate( hrappSQL );
```

After this method call your database is created. It is here that JDBC takes your SQL and delivers it to the database server. JDBC then tells the database server to execute the SQL.

It is very important to remember that once you have run your SQL, you *must* close and release the resources you have allocated. This is an area where every significant project I have ever seen has had problems at one time or another.

Closing and releasing JDBC resources is easy to do, but is often forgotten. This error usually doesn't show itself during development and sometimes not even during testing, because the amount of time that the application or database runs is often short enough that the unreleased resources aren't noticed. In a production environment, this is a bug that quickly becomes apparent because the performance of the application is impacted or the system crashes.

Because it is so important that the resources are released, you need to ensure the code that closes the resources is run even if exceptions occur in an earlier part of the method. The only way to ensure a code fragment will be run even if an exception happens is to put it in a finally block.

```
        finally {
          if( statement != null ) {
              try {
                  statement.close();
              }
              catch( SQLException e ){} // nothing we can do
          }
          if( connection != null ) {
              try {
                  connection.close();
              }
              catch( SQLException e ){} // nothing we can do
          }
        }
```

Putting It All Together

Now it is time to recap the work you did in order to create your database. First you loaded the correct JDBC driver for the database server you were working with. Next you created a connection to the database server using a URL that pointed to the server. From the connection you obtained a Statement object. With the statement you executed the SQL that your database server needed in order to create a new database instance. Once you were done, you closed your statement, then you closed your connection. In order to keep the code simple, you did not attempt to catch individual exceptions. Do not try this at home. I don't want you to cloud the example code with error handling, but in almost all cases individual exceptions should be caught and handled or rethrown as appropriate.

The code for the complete class looks like this:

```
package com.apress.javapersistence.chapter03.database;

import java.sql.SQLException;
import java.sql.Connection;
import java.sql.Statement;
import java.sql.DriverManager;

public class CreateDatabase {
    private String username;
    private String password;
```

```java
    public CreateDatabase(String username, String password) {
        this.username = username;
        this.password = password;
    }

    /**
     * @param args contains the user name and password to connect to the database
     */
    public static void main(String[] args) {
        if( args.length < 2 ) {
            System.out.println( "usage: CreateDatabase username password" );
            return;
        }

        CreateDatabase createDatabase
            = new CreateDatabase( args[ 0 ], args[ 1 ] );
        createDatabase.execute();
    }

    public void execute() {
        Connection connection = null;
        Statement statement = null;
        try {
            // Load the JDBC Driver
            Class.forName( "com.mysqlJDBC.Driver" ).newInstance();
            String url = "jdbc:mysql://localhost/mysql";
            // Connect to the database
            connection = DriverManager.getConnection( url, username, password );

            // Obtain a statement object
            statement = connection.createStatement();
            String hrappSQL = "CREATE DATABASE hrapp";

            // Execute the SQL
            statement.executeUpdate( hrappSQL );
        }
        // Don't try this at home, catch SQLException and all others
        catch( Exception e ) {
            e.printStackTrace();
        }
```

```
    finally {
        // Time to close everthing up.
        if( statement != null ) {
            try {
                statement.close();
            }
            catch( SQLException e ){} // nothing we can do
        }
        if( connection != null ) {
            try {
                connection.close();
            }
            catch( SQLException e ){} // nothing we can do
        }
    }
  }
}
```

Creating the Tables

Having a database is great, but a database has little value without some table to hold your data. In order to create a table from Java using JDBC, you need to obtain a connection. You then create a statement from the connection and execute the SQL to create the tables. This process is exactly the same as that which you followed to create the database. For this example, you will create one table in your hrapp database named Employees.

As when you created your database, you need to obtain a connection. That means you must load your driver exactly as before, then you must get your connection from the driver manager. This time you can connect to the database you created before instead of connecting to the system database. The URL and string referencing the URL should look like this:

```
String url = "jdbc:mysql://localhost/hrapp";
```

With this URL, you request a connection from the driver manager exactly the same as before. You make a call to the driver manager with your URL, user name, and password for your database. Also as before, you use the getConnection method and the code should look like this:

```
connection = DriverManager.getConnection( url, username, password );
```

Using a Statement to Create Tables

First you need to define the SQL that you will use to create your table. If you refer back to Chapter 2, you see the SQL for creating a table consists of CREATE TABLE table_name followed by the table definition. For this example, you will create one table to hold your employee data. The table will have four columns. The exact SQL is as follows:

```
CREATE TABLE employees (
employee_id     INTEGER         NOT NULL,
last_name       VARCHAR(128)    NOT NULL,
first_name      VARCHAR(128)    NOT NULL,
num_dependants  SMALLINT        NULL )
```

Now you need to tell the database server to execute this SQL. First you create a Statement object from your connection. You create a string reference to hold your SQL. Finally, you execute the SQL through the JDBC executeUpdate method on your Statement object.

```
statement = connection.createStatement();
String employeesSQL = "CREATE TABLE employees ( "
            + "employee_id     INTEGER         NOT NULL,"
            + "last_name       VARCHAR(128)    NOT NULL,"
            + "first_name      VARCHAR(128)    NOT NULL,"
            + "num_dependants  SMALLINT        NULL )";
statement.executeUpdate( employeesSQL );
```

The preceding lines of code are all you need to change from your CreateDatabase class in order to make a CreateTable class. The complete code listing consists of the following:

```
package com.apress.javapersistence.chapter03.database;

import java.sql.SQLException;
import java.sql.Connection;
import java.sql.Statement;
import java.sql.DriverManager;

public class CreateTable {
    private String username;
    private String password;

    /** Creates a new instance of CreateDatabase */
```

```java
    public CreateTable(String username, String password) {
        this.username = username;
        this.password = password;
    }


    /**
     * @param args consists of the username and password required to authenticated
     * against the database server.
     */
    public static void main(String[] args) {
        if( args.length < 2 ) {
            System.out.println( "usage: CreateTable username password" );
            return;
        }


        CreateTable createTable = new CreateTable( args[ 0 ], args[ 1 ] );
        createTable.execute();
    }

    public void execute() {
        Connection connection = null;
        Statement statement = null;
        try {
            Class.forName( "com.mysql.JDBC.Driver" ).newInstance();
            String url = "jdbc:mysql://localhost/hrapp";
            connection = DriverManager.getConnection( url, username, password );

            statement = connection.createStatement();
            String employeesSQL = "CREATE TABLE employees ( "
                + "employee_id     INTEGER        NOT NULL,"
                + "last_name       VARCHAR(128)   NOT NULL,"
                + "first_name      VARCHAR(128)   NOT NULL,"
                + "num_dependants  SMALLINT       NULL )";
            statement.executeUpdate( employeesSQL );
        }
        catch( Exception e ) {
            e.printStackTrace();
        }
        finally {
            if( statement != null ) {
                try {
                    statement.close();
                }
                catch( SQLException e ){} // nothing we can do
```

```
        }
        if( connection != null ) {
            try {
                connection.close();
            }
            catch( SQLException e ){} // nothing we can do
        }
      }
    }
}
```

Note that once again you must close and release all resources that you allocate to make the table. After this code is run, there should be one table in the hrapps database named employees. The table will have the four columns listed in the SQL.

Using a JDBC Statement to Insert Data

Inserting data in the database through JDBC is very similar to creating a database or creating a table. You use the exact same objects including the DriverManager, Connection, and Statement. The only thing you change is the SQL you hand off to the Statement object. Your execute method would change to include the following code fragment:

```
statement = connection.createStatement();
String employees1SQL = "INSERT INTO employees "
    + "( employee_id, last_name, first_name ) "
    + "VALUES ( 123456, 'Glyzewski', 'Dave' )";
statement.executeUpdate( employees1SQL );
String employees2SQL = "INSERT INTO employees "
    + "( employee_id, last_name, first_name ) "
    + "VALUES ( 123457, 'Chaltry', 'Ed' )";
statement.executeUpdate( employees2SQL );
```

In this code, you create two different SQL statements to execute. The first inserts an employee named Dave Glyzewski; the second statement inserts an employee named Ed Chaltry. After both SQL statements are defined, you hand them off to the same Statement object.

Note that the name "Statement" can seem misleading in that you can actually execute multiple SQL statements reusing the same Statement object. Only do this if it makes sense in the code. At least in the first draft, it is better to write clear code than fast code; you can always optimize later. An even better way to handle the multiple inserts is with PreparedStatements, which I will talk about later in this chapter.

Using JDBC to Update Data

Once again, updating or changing data in the database is very similar to creating tables and inserting data. The difference is the SQL you execute.

```
employees1SQL = "UPDATE employees "
    + "SET first_name = 'David', num_dependants = 3 "
    + "WHERE employee_id = 123456";
statement.executeUpdate( employees1SQL );
```

Obtaining Data and Querying via JDBC

Now that you know how to create tables, insert data, and update that data, you need a way to get the data back out. JDBC does a great job of making tasks similar, therefore easy to learn. There are minimal changes to the code you learned previously in order to read data from a database.

The big change is that you add a new object to the mix. The ResultSet object contains your query results. That means that you need to execute a method on the Statement that will return a result set. You also need to add code to your finally block to close the result set.

```
String selectEmployeesSQL = "SELECT * FROM employees";
resultSet = statement.executeQuery( selectEmployeesSQL );
```

The code used to close your result set gets added to your code to close your statement and connection. It works exactly the same way. The code checks for a result set that is not null; if it finds one, the result set is closed.

```
finally {
    if( resultSet != null ) {
        try {
            resultSet.close();
        }
        catch( SQLException e ){} // nothing we can do
    }
    if( statement != null ) {
        try {
            statement.close();
        }
        catch( SQLException e ){} // nothing we can do
    }
    if( connection != null ) {
```

```
                    try {
                        connection.close();
                    }
                    catch( SQLException e ){} // nothing we can do
                }
            }
```

Keeping the results of your query in a result set provides little value if you don't know how to get the data back out. So let's learn a little about result sets.

A ResultSet, like most JDBC classes, is a vendor-provided class that implements an interface. Because of this, I can only speak to general implementations. Usually the ResultSet is a cursor reflecting the results of the query back on the database. The data that is actually loaded in the local Java Virtual Machine can be as little as the row that the result set is currently on.

You interact with the data through the ResultSet interface. The ResultSet interface gives you methods for accessing the data from the database in a Java-centric way. For instance, in your SQL for creating the table, the num_dependants column is of type smallint. There is no smallint type in Java; the ResultSet gives you methods where you can access that value as an int, string, double, byte, or through one of the other accessor methods.

In order to understand querying the database using JDBC, let's print out the contents of the database you have built and updated. Once again, most of the code remains the same. The changes are in the execute method, and the class name is PrintDatabase.

The two main changes are that you run the executeQuery method instead of the executeUpdate method. This leads to the second change: The executeQuery method returns a ResultSet object. Iterate through the result set to display the results of your query.

```
package com.apress.javapersistence.chapter03.database;

import java.sql.SQLException;
import java.sql.DriverManager;
import java.sql.Connection;
import java.sql.Statement;
import java.sql.ResultSet;

public class PrintDatabase {
    private String username;
    private String password;

    /** Creates a new instance of CreateDatabase */
    public PrintDatabase(String username, String password) {
```

```
        this.username = username;
        this.password = password;
    }


    /**
     * @param args username and password to access the database.
     */
    public static void main(String[] args) {
        if( args.length < 2 ) {
            System.out.println( "usage: PrintDatabase username password" );
            return;
        }

        PrintDatabase printDb
            = new PrintDatabase( args[ 0 ], args[ 1 ] );
        printDb.execute();
    }

    public void execute() {
        Connection connection = null;
        Statement statement = null;
        ResultSet resultSet = null;
        try {
            Class.forName( "com.mysql.jdbc.Driver" ).newInstance();
            String url = "jdbc:mysql://localhost/hrapp";
            connection = DriverManager.getConnection( url, username, password );

            statement = connection.createStatement();
            String selectEmployeesSQL = "SELECT * FROM employees";
            resultSet = statement.executeQuery( selectEmployeesSQL );

            while( resultSet.next() ) {
                System.out.print( resultSet.getInt( "employee_id" ) );
                System.out.print( ", " );
                System.out.print( resultSet.getString( "last_name" ) );
                System.out.print( ", " );
                System.out.print( resultSet.getString( "first_name" ) );
                System.out.print( ", " );
                System.out.println( resultSet.getByte( "num_dependants" ) );
            }
        }
        catch( Exception e ) {
            e.printStackTrace();
        }
```

```
        finally {
            if( resultSet != null ) {
                try {
                    resultSet.close();
                }
                catch( SQLException e ){} // nothing we can do
            }
            if( statement != null ) {
                try {
                    statement.close();
                }
                catch( SQLException e ){} // nothing we can do
            }
            if( connection != null ) {
                try {
                    connection.close();
                }
                catch( SQLException e ){} // nothing we can do
            }
        }
    }
}
```

You must be aware of the type of data you are trying to access using JDBC. The reason is that you may end up with data you are not expecting. For instance, you can access num_dependants as either a byte or string. If you access a field that does not contain any data as a byte, you will get back a 0; if you try to get the same field as a string, you could get a null. Remember, a 0 and null are not necessarily the same thing in your application. 0 means none, whereas null can mean not set yet.

Another important point to note is how you run through the contents of the result set. Notice that the example uses a while loop that has resultSet.next() as its test criteria. This is because the next method on a ResultSet has the job of telling you if there are more results, but it also has the side effect of moving your cursor to the next row. That means that you test for next, then you extract the next values. If next is never called, there is no data for you to extract, and you will get a SQLException thrown. Once again, the code looks like this:

```
...
while( resultSet.next() ) {
    // Work with row we just moved to
    ...
}
...
```

Using Basic JDBC Transactions

By default, when using JDBC, a connection is set to auto-commit. That means that once you execute a change in the database, it is immediately stored in the database. Occasionally, it is desirable to execute several commands, and then store them all at once in the database. In order to do this, you need to use transactions.

A *transaction* allows you to group multiple commands, and then either store them all or roll all the changes back to the database's original state. With auto-commit turned on, this is not possible.

While auto-commit gives the ability to execute multiple transactions at once, it does not specify enough to determine what kinds of reads you would have from the database. For that, you first need to determine what type of database reads are possible (see Table 3-2).

Table 3-2. JDBC Transaction Read Types

READ TYPE	DESCRIPTION
Dirty read	A transaction reads data that was written in another transaction, but has not been committed to the database.
Nonrepeatable read	A transaction reads the data from the database as it is. If rows have been modified or updated, those changes will be reflected. In other words, you cannot count on getting the same data twice if there are multiple transactions working on the database.
Phantom reads	A transaction reads data including rows that may have been inserted since last read.

The second part of transactions is the isolation of work done through a connection. Four different transaction levels are defined in standard SQL and supported by JDBC. Since not all relational databases are SQL compliant, JDBC also adds a transaction level of none (see Table 3-3).

Table 3-3. JDBC Transaction Types

LEVEL	DESCRIPTION
TRANSACTION_NONE	Indicates transactions are not supported.
TRANSACTION_READ_COMMITTED	Prevents reading data that is not committed to the database, but allows reads that could be unrepeatable. Allows dirty, nonrepeatable, and phantom reads.
TRANSACTION_UNCOMMITTED	Allows reading data that has not been committed to the database. Also allows reading data that may not be repeatable and/or phantom reads.
TRANSACTION_REPEATABLE_READ	Does not allow reading data that has not been committed to the database. Also disallows changing of data underneath the connection. Dirty reads and nonrepeatable reads are prevented, but phantom reads can occur.
TRANSACTION_SERIALIZABLE	Prevents dirty reads, nonrepeatable reads, and phantom reads.

Optimizing Performance with JDBC

Oftentimes the data access portion of an application can be one of its slowest performing parts. Some of the issues can be difficult to address, and others are easy. You can do some simple things to help reduce resources used in your JDBC code, as well as things to improve performance when using JDBC.

Before you can improve performance, you first need to know where your problems lie. Often developers optimize parts of applications that are not the real performance bottlenecks. The cost of many optimizations is decreased readability and maintainability of the code. So before you attempt to fix the problem, find out where the problem is.

I suggest using a tool for profiling like JProbe. Since JDK 1.2, Sun has also included a basic profiling tool in Java named hprof. By adding a few command line arguments to the JVM, you can dump a lot of profiling information. This is not the easiest to read, but you can use a GUI tool on Sun's Java Developer site named PerfAnal that makes it a little easier to read.

I was on one project where it became my duty to evaluate the performance of a J2EE application and find areas to speed it up. I found that the development team had developed their own ResultSet class that was returned from the system's database utilities. This result set looped through a real result set and put all of the contents into a collection. The collection-based result set was returned and the calling code looped through the contents again. The functionality was there to allow them to query the total number of results that were returned.

I am sure the initial design sounded great; the problem was almost none of the code was using the additional functionality. In only a couple places was the total return number checked. What these developers had done was introduced a double looping through the contents with almost no benefit. My solution was to add a second method to the database utilities that would return a real result set and change the calls in most of the code. I was able to find this problem and realize the savings I would achieve because of profiling tools.

First Culprit Is Probably the SQL

If you find that much of your application's time is spent in the executeUpdate or executeQuery methods of a statement, then the problem is the SQL. My first suggestion is to take the offending SQL to your local neighborhood database administrator and let that person try to figure it out.

Sometimes you don't have a DBA available. There is still much you can do to help your application perform better. First, simplify your SQL. Many times SQL becomes very complex and difficult to understand and troubleshoot. Take the SQL you are working with, copy it to your favorite text editor (such as emacs), format it, and break it down. Add parenthesis where you can to group code. Make the SQL cover multiple lines. Indent related regions.

Once you have done all of these things, see if the problem with the SQL is obvious. You might have multiple joins where you don't need them because the data is available in a different way. Check to see if there are already views or stored procedures that will generate some of what you need.

In queries, watch out for the LIKE keyword and % wild card searches—both of these are very expensive for a database engine. Ensure that you are asking for exactly what you need from the query. Nothing is gained by requesting data from the database that you are not going to use.

Use stored procedures for complex and often used database queries or updates. A stored procedure runs much faster than pure SQL handed over to the database. I suggest not putting too much business logic or knowledge into the stored procedures. Moving business logic into a stored procedure makes it difficult to share that functionality between Java objects.

Know Your Driver

Rarely are you stuck with one JDBC driver for any database. Look into what drivers are available for the database you are using. Look for benchmarks.

Most drivers are optimized for different needs in the database. One driver can have better querying performance, while another has an emphasis on inserting and updating data. Look into the features of the driver you are using.

Try different drivers out. Look at your application and decide what you need to have the highest performance. If your application is mostly used for reporting, you want to write a test for querying large amounts of data. If your application is for new members joining a Web site, write a test that will insert many entries. Create the appropriate test, and then run it after changing drivers. Most driver vendors provide demo versions you can use for this type of testing.

Use Prepared Statements for Repeated SQL

If you are going to use the same SQL statement multiple times in your code, use a prepared statement instead of a statement. The java.sql.PreparedStatement interface extends the java.sql.Statement interface. It is a specialization of a statement. What a prepared statement provides is improved performance on the same SQL. In Figure 3-4, you can see where PreparedStatement resides in the JDBC hierarchy.

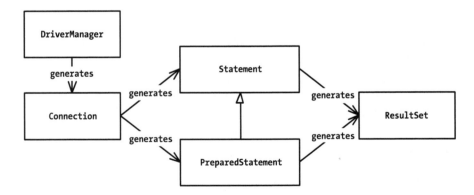

Figure 3-4. Primary classes and interfaces including PreparedStatement

When a statement hands off SQL to the database, the database takes the SQL, compiles, and runs it natively. Each and every call from that statement goes through the same steps. This is because a statement is not created with any one specific piece of SQL, so every execution can be different.

On the other hand, a prepared statement is created with one specific piece of SQL. Because of this, the database does not need to recompile on every request that comes from that prepared statement. This can have a great impact on performance.

If you are updating many instances of the same object, use a prepared statement. If you have many clients running the same query with different arguments, use a prepared statement.

A PreparedStatement object is created from the Connection class just like its parent the Statement object. Instead of calling createStatement, you call the method prepareStatement(String sql). The connection is a factory for your prepared statement.

The way to specify arguments to the prepared statement is to put question marks in the query to represent parameters. For example, if you wanted to write a query that would give all employee IDs that match a specific first and last name, you would write your SQL as

```
SELECT id FROM employees WHERE first_name = ? AND last_name = ?
```

The arguments of a prepared statement are filled by calling setType(index, value), where Type is the data type (e.g., setBoolean, setString), index is the argument number you are providing, and value is what you want the SQL to contain. One important thing to remember about prepared statements is that the arguments are 1 based, not 0 based. That means to set your first_name then last_name argument, you would use the following Java code:

```
preparedStatement.setString( 1, "Dave" );
preparedStatement.setString( 2, "Glyzewski" );
```

The last difference of the prepared statement is that it has methods to execute itself that do not take SQL as arguments. The execute(), executeUpdate(), and executeQuery() methods simply execute the SQL that the prepared statement was created with.

Manage Resources Carefully

Part of the problem with any database-based application is the limited resources. Part of this is because you are often requesting data over a network connection. Issues also arise because you don't account for limited processor power or limited memory.

One solution for limited resources is to always use connection pooling. Connections can be very costly to create. If you use a connection pool, then connections will only be created when they are actually needed. JDBC 2 comes with connection pooling built in, but even with JDBC 1 you can add or implement your own connection pooling. I suggest looking into the DBCP Component from the Jakarta Commons project at `http://jakarta.apache.org/commons/dbcp/index.html`. The DBCP Component is intended to create an efficient and feature-rich connection pooling package.

Another resource-oriented optimization when using connection pooling is to allocate the minimum number of connections you expect to need in the beginning. Don't let the system wait until crunch time to start the expensive process of creating connections.

Finally, as I said before, release your resources. Closing a connection from a connection pool doesn't actually close the connection; it is released back to the pool. Don't leave statements or result sets opened. Databases have very limited resources available, and you are probably holding on to them if you haven't closed your statements and result sets.

Watch Out for Premature Optimization

Premature optimization is the scourge of any development. It is a situation where a developer *knows* there is a performance problem with a section of code, so that developer removes all readability and maintainability in order to make the code go faster.

More often than not, such developers are wrong in what they *know*. Don't assume you know something; use a profiling tool to find out where the problems are. This will allow you to make the most impact on your application in the minimum time.

Summary

JDBC is Sun's answer to providing a consistent SQL interface to Java. The purpose of the libraries is to allow developers to move their code from one database to another with minimal rework. The toolkit also allows the developer to leverage knowledge gained in one application by taking it to another.

JDBC also provides similar interfaces between inserting, updating, and querying data. You can use very similar code, only the meat of it changes. In all cases, the code needs to use the `DriverManager` class. The driver manager is used to obtain a reference to a `Connection` object that is specific to the driver being used. From the connection, a `Statement` object is obtained to actually execute the SQL. If the SQL being executed is intended to return data, then a result set wraps that data.

In optimizing your JDBC code, use a profiling tool. Guessing will often result in wrong optimizations that could hurt the application in the long or even the short term. Find out if the problem is your SQL or just the way the libraries are being used. Check to ensure you have the best driver for your needs.

Have fun. JDBC programming is fun because after you have done it once for one database, you have a leg up for all database work you do going forward.

CHAPTER 4

What Is New in JDBC 2 and 3

IT WAS A FEATURE PECULIAR to the colonial wars of North America, that the toils and dangers of the wilderness were to be encountered before the adverse hosts could meet. So it is with JDBC. After you have fought your way through JDBC 1 and all its basic functionality, you find you have more to learn and overcome. In this chapter, I will discuss what has been added in versions 2 and 3 of JDBC. I will also give examples of how to use the new functionality.

While JDBC 1 is very important and was all we had for a long time, it left quite a few functionality holes to be filled by later versions. As with any product, once it is used in a production environment for any length of time, it becomes easier to see exactly where it can be enhanced and extended. Like so many version 1s of software before it, JDBC has newer versions to extend it.

To date, there are two versions of JDBC since version 1. Both add new functionality that was sorely missed. As you might expect, a lot of the new functionality is not really needed for basic database use that was well covered in JDBC 1. The additions in versions 2 and 3 enhance the library.

In JDBC 2 you see much more functional result sets, you get row sets to hold your data, connection pools are made available, and much more. JDBC 3 brings much of version 2's functionality together in a more integrated way.

What's New in JDBC 2.1

JDBC 2.1 was released to address some omissions of the original JDBC specification. Specifically, people expressed a preference for scrollable result sets, batch updates, and the ability to handle advanced data types such as blobs. There was a need to store user-defined data types and to store data to tabular files rather than having to store data in a relational database.

JDBC 2.1 also includes batch updates and an entire optional package that has even more functionality. In order to obtain JDBC 2.1, you simply need to download a current Java SDK. Versions 1.2.1 and 1.3 both contain JDBC 2.1. The Java SDK 1.4 contains JDBC 3.0, but most of the information in the first part of this chapter is pertinent to that too.

Result Set Running Wild

In JDBC 1, a result set can move in only one direction, from the beginning to the end of the contents. There is no way to jump to the middle or even go back one row after you have passed it. In order to retrieve data again, you needed to requery. And don't even think about trying to change the underlying data through a result set.

To overcome this single direction limitation, a lot of development teams would cache the contents of the result set. This can be very inefficient because you end up looping through the same data multiple times. This solution also does not help if you need the current data, rather than a copy.

A second limitation of the result set in JDBC 1 is that if you come across a record in the result set that you want to modify, you need to run a separate update on the database. Since the data is currently available to the code, this is a less than ideal solution. It would be nice to simply modify the data that your code just read.

These are the two features best addressed in JDBC 2.1. The result set now can scroll backward and forward as well as being able to jump to arbitrary positions within the result set. A result set can also be used to update information in the database. Row sets can even insert new rows into the database or delete an existing row.

How to Use Scrolling Result Sets

Allowing a result set to scroll backwards is optional. If all you need to do with your data is move from beginning to end, you don't need to indicate specific scrolling to JDBC. You can create a result set that moves forward and is read-only by executing the code described in Chapter 3. Alternatively, the code to create a result set would look like this:

```
String url = "jdbc:mysql://localhost/chapter04_jdbc21";
connection = DriverManager.getConnection( url, username, password );
statement = connection.createStatement(
                  ResultSet.TYPE_FORWARD_ONLY,
                  ResultSet. CONCUR_READ_ONLY );
String selectEmployeesSQL = "SELECT * FROM employees";
resultSet = statement.executeQuery( selectEmployeesSQL );
```

In order to create a scrollable result set, you simply pass two parameters to the createStatement method on your connection. The first argument is the result set scroll type. The second argument determines the concurrency of the result set. I will discuss result set concurrency further along; for now let's focus on the different types of scrolling that are available.

The createStatement method on the connection takes two int arguments. The constants that should be used to set the result set type are defined on the ResultSet class, and they are public final static ints. To set the type of scrolling, you can choose from the options in Table 6-1.

Table 6-1. ResultSet Scroll Types

FLAG	DESCRIPTION
TYPE_FORWARD_ONLY	Enables JDBC 1–style scrolling. Can only move forward to the next row.
TYPE_SCROLL_INSENSITIVE	Enables scrolling forward and backward, but the result set will not reflect changes made to the database by others.
TYPE_SCROLL_SENSITIVE	Enables Scrolling forward and backward. The result set will reflect changes made to the database by others.

By setting the result set type to either TYPE_SCROLL_INSENSITIVE or TYPE_SCROLL_SENSITIVE, you can scroll forward and backward. The sensitivity determines if you will see changes that have happened to the underlying database while scrolling. If you do want to see changes others have made to the database, specify the type as TYPE_SCROLL_SENSITIVE; otherwise go with TYPE_SCROLL_INSENSITIVE. Obviously, TYPE_SCROLL_INSENSITIVE will generate less work for the database server.

Once you have created your result set, you want to be able to scroll with it. Scrolling forward is actually exactly the same as it was in JDBC 1. You simply call the next method on the result set. As I noted previously, you can create the statement itself either by using the no-argument createStatement method or by using a scrollable result set to scroll forward.

```
String url = "jdbc:mysql://localhost/chapter04_jdbc21";
connection = DriverManager.getConnection( url, username, password );
statement = connection.createStatement();
String selectEmployeesSQL = "SELECT * FROM employees";
resultSet = statement.executeQuery( selectEmployeesSQL );
resultSet.next(); // Moves to the next record.
```

Once you have moved forward a record, you can move back to that same record. The way to do this is to call a new method, previous, on the result set. The previous method will take you back to the record you just moved off of. This method only works if results are included in the result set and if you are not at the first record. If both of these conditions are not met, you will end up with a SQLException.

```
String url = "jdbc:mysql://localhost/chapter04_jdbc21";
connection = DriverManager.getConnection( url, username, password );
statement = connection.createStatement(
                ResultSet.TYPE_SCROLL_INSENSITIVE,
                ResultSet.CONCUR_READ_ONLY );
String selectEmployeesSQL = "SELECT * FROM employees";
resultSet = statement.executeQuery( selectEmployeesSQL );
resultSet.next(); // Moves forward one record.
resultSet.previous(); // Moves to the previous record
```

You can ensure that you are not on the first record by calling the isFirst method on the result set. If you are on the first record, it will return true so you know not to call the previous method. The reverse can be achieved with isLast, but isLast has a much higher performance penalty because the next record must be obtained.

You can provide hints to the JDBC driver as to which direction you will be going with the setFetchDirection method. This method indicates to the driver which direction you intend to scroll so that it can optionally optimize itself for that direction. Remember, though, that setFetchDirection is only a hint and can very well be ignored by the driver.

Moving backward and forward is great, but if there are a lot of records, it could be time consuming to scroll to the desired record, especially if you know the record number you want to go to. In order to avoid costly looping, you can use absolute positioning with the result set. Absolute positioning works when you call the absolute method with a specific record number to go to. As with much of JDBC, the numbering is from 1 not from 0.

```
String url = "jdbc:mysql://localhost/chapter04_jdbc21";
connection = DriverManager.getConnection( url, username, password );
statement = connection.createStatement(
                ResultSet.TYPE_SCROLL_INSENSITIVE,
                ResultSet. CONCUR_READ_ONLY );
String selectEmployeesSQL = "SELECT * FROM employees";
resultSet = statement.executeQuery( selectEmployeesSQL );
resultSet.absolute( 5 ); // Moves to the fifth record
```

One additional feature of absolute positioning is that you can use a shortcut to move to the last record. By calling absolute with a -1, your result set will move to the last record in the set. In the same vein, a nice shortcut is the ability to use negative numbers to move in from the last record. For example, -2 will take you to the second to last record, -3 to the third from last, and so on.

Additional result set scrolling features include the first, last, and relative methods. The first method will take you to the first record and is the same as calling `absolute` with an argument of 1. The `last` method will take you to the end of the results and is the same as calling `absolute` with a -1. The `relative` method will move the result set the given number of rows in a positive or negative direction. For example, a call to `relative` 4 from the second record would move the result set to the sixth record. From there a relative move of -2 would take the result set back to the fourth record.

Updating Data with Result Sets

The concurrency type of the result set determines if the result set can update the underlying data. A result set is either *updatable* or *read only*. An updatable result set can change the data that is in the current record, add new records, or delete records. All of these changes are then stored to the database. A read-only result set is the same as a JDCB 1 result set and does not have this ability.

The ability to update underlying data can have a huge impact on an application. No longer do you need to read data from the database, decide it needs to be changed, and then make a whole new call to update the data. In JDBC 2, you can read data and change it without any additional database calls.

The way updating data works is that you create a statement with concurrency set to UPDATABLE. Next you query for some data. Once you have found a record you want to update, you simply call the applicable updateString, updateInt, or updateLong method for the fields you want to change. After updating the data, you tell the result set to communicate the changes back by calling the updateRow method.

```
String url = "jdbc:mysql://localhost/chapter04_jdbc21";
connection = DriverManager.getConnection( url, username, password );
statement = connection.createStatement(
                ResultSet.TYPE_SCROLL_INSENSITIVE,
                ResultSet.CONCUR_UPDATABLE );
String selectEmployeesSQL = "SELECT * FROM employees";
resultSet = statement.executeQuery( selectEmployeesSQL );
resultSet.absolute( 5 ); // Moves to the fifth record
resultSet.updateString( "last_name", "NewLastName" );  // Change the value.
resultSet.updateRow(); // Commits the change.
```

As I said earlier, an updatable result set not only gives you the ability to change existing records, but it also allows you to insert new records. The process for this is very similar to updating existing records. You create an updatable statement. Next you query for data. Once you have data, you can call the moveToInsertRow method, which inserts a new row that you can then use to call the various update methods on. Once you have set your new data through the update methods, you call the insertRow method on the result set, which communicates the inserted row back to the database.

```
String url = "jdbc:mysql://localhost/chapter04_jdbc21";
connection = DriverManager.getConnection( url, username, password );
statement = connection.createStatement(
                    ResultSet.TYPE_SCROLL_INSENSITIVE,
                    ResultSet.CONCUR_UPDATABLE );
String selectEmployeesSQL = "SELECT * FROM employees";
resultSet = statement.executeQuery( selectEmployeesSQL );
resultSet.moveToInsertRow();
resultSet.updateString( "employee_id", newId );
resultSet.updateString( "last_name", newLastName );
resultSet.updateString( "first_name", newFirstName );
resultSet.updateString( "email", newEmail );
resultSet.insertRow();
```

Deleting a row is another function that is available through an updatable result set. In this situation, you create the updatable result set. Next you query for some data. On finding a record you no longer want to have in your database, you simply call the deleteRow method on the result set, which communicates the deletion back to the database.

```
String url = "jdbc:mysql://localhost/chapter04_jdbc21";
connection = DriverManager.getConnection( url, username, password );
statement = connection.createStatement(
                    ResultSet.TYPE_SCROLL_INSENSITIVE,
                    ResultSet.CONCUR_UPDATABLE );
String selectEmployeesSQL = "SELECT * FROM employees";
resultSet = statement.executeQuery( selectEmployeesSQL );
resultSet.absolute( 5 ); // Moves to the fifth record
resultSet.deleteRow();
```

Using Batch Updates to Execute Multiple SQL Statements

The second big feature added to JDBC 2 is the ability to execute multiple SQL statements immediately. By grouping SQL statements, you can reduce network traffic and database communication, which will result in better performance.

Three JDBC interfaces are affected by the addition of batch updates. The Statement, PreparedStatement, and CallableStatement interfaces were changed after JDBC 1.

Batch Updates Using Statements

The first interface I am going to talk about that now supports batch updates is the Statement interface. Essentially, you can execute multiple SQL commands all at once. These can even be different types of SQL commands, such as INSERTs and UPDATEs mixed together.

In general, the process for executing batch updates is very similar to executing a single statement. First, you get your connection, create your statement, and execute your updates. The difference is that you should always set auto-commit to off on your connection. Next, you need to add your updates before you execute them. Finally, you execute all of the commands at once through a single method call.

Auto-commit is a feature of a JDBC connection that tells the driver and database to save to the database all commands as they are passed in. This continues to update the database as many pieces of work are executed. Auto-commit is on by default.

Issues arise concerning auto-commit when several updates are related. They should either all be committed or none of them committed to the database. In a situation where you want to insert an employee into an Employees table and insert a record of that employee into a Departments table, you would want to make sure that both commands were successfully executed. You wouldn't want the employee to have a record in the Departments table without existing in the Employees table.

The process then is to turn auto-commit to off, add the updates to the statement, and execute the updates. Once you ensure that all updates are successful, you then commit the changes made.

```
Class.forName( "com.mysql.jdbc.Driver" ).newInstance();
String url = "jdbc:mysql://localhost/chapter04_jdbc21";
connection = DriverManager.getConnection( url, username, password );
connection.setAutoCommit( false );

statement = connection.createStatement();

String update1 = "UPDATE employees "
    + "SET email = 'dglyzewski@centare.com' "
    + "WHERE email = 'dave.glyzewski@centare.com'";
statement.addBatch( update1 );

String update2 = "UPDATE employees "
    + "SET email = 'echaltry@centare.com' "
    + "WHERE email = 'ed.chaltry@centare.com'";
statement.addBatch( update2 );
```

```
String update3 = "UPDATE employees "
    + "SET email = 'dsmith@centare.com' "
    + "WHERE email = 'dustin.smith@centare.com'";
statement.addBatch( update3 );

int updates[] = statement.executeBatch(); // Execute all of the batch
```

In testing for success of the batch update, simply run through the array of integers returned from executeBatch. Any value equal to or greater than 0 indicates the number of rows that were affected. In JDBC 2.1, a value of -2 means that the update executed successfully, but the number of rows affected is unknown. A value of -3 indicates that the updated failed, but the database is configured to keep processing after an error occurs; otherwise a BatchUpdateException is thrown. If one of the statements returns rows from the database, a BatchUpdateException will be thrown also (i.e., a SELECT statement returns rows, whereas an UPDATE, INSERT, or DELETE statement would not). Note that in JDBC 3.0 these hard-coded numbers are changed to constants where -2 is conveyed with SUCCESS_NO_INFO and -3 is referenced as EXECUTE_FAILED.

Using Prepared Statements in Batch Updates

Prepared statements can be used for batch updates as well. If you are using a prepared statement, the SQL commands must be homogeneous. In other words, you cannot mix INSERTs to different tables or even INSERTs and UPDATEs. A batch update through a prepared statement is very much like using a prepared statement any other time.

The first step in using a prepared statement for batch updates is to create the prepared statement. This is exactly the same as creating a regular prepared statement. Build your SQL string using a single "?"to hold a place for each argument and call the prepareStatement method on the connection.

Next, you need to set the arguments for the prepared statement. As always, call the various setter methods (setString, setDouble, setInt, etc.). The first parameter is the SQL argument number beginning with 1, and the second parameter is the value to be set.

Instead of executing the prepared statement for a batch update, you simply call addBatch, which puts the prepared statement into the batch. It also sets the statement up for the next set of arguments. So set the next set of arguments and once again call addBatch, continuing until you have filled your batch update.

Finally, after building up your batch updates, you call the executeBatch method on the prepared statement. The call to this method follows the same conventions as the executeBatch method on the Statement interface.

```
String sql = "UPDATE employees SET email = ? WHERE employee_id = ?";
statement = connection.prepareStatement( sql );

statement.setString( 1, "dglyzewski@centare.com" );
statement.setLong( 2, 1 );
statement.addBatch();

statement.setString( 1, "echaltry@centare.com" );
statement.setLong( 2, 2 );
statement.addBatch();

statement.setString( 1, "dsmith@centare.com" );
statement.setLong( 2, 3 );
statement.addBatch();

statement.executeBatch();
```

JDBC 2.0 Optional Package

The purpose of separating JDBC 2 into two packages was to keep from adding dependencies to the Java Development Kit on optional packages. All functionality that easily stood without any optional packages was included in the Development Kit, and any functionality that relied on products outside of the Development Kit was moved to the JDBC 2.0 Optional Package.

As you might guess, that means several of the more desirable features are found in the optional package—including the ability to retrieve a connection from the Java Naming and Directory Interface (JNDI), thereby removing the need to know about the connections underlying implementation. Connection pooling is available from the optional package. Distributed transactions are available as well as a data-oriented JavaBean called a row set. In this section, I am going to go over these different parts one at a time.

Using JNDI to Obtain a Connection

The original purpose of JDBC was to make it easy for developers to work with different SQL databases without having to know the intricacy of those databases. In other words, the goal was to encapsulate the database and give developers a consistent interface to work with.

JDBC has done a fairly good job of doing this, but one feature that is lacking is the capability to obtain a connection. In order to obtain a connection, you need to do two driver-specific things. First you need to load the driver, and second you need to create a driver-specific URL for connecting to the database.

In order to remove this encapsulation breaking, you need to allow developers to obtain prebuilt connections from an application-independent source. That is where JNDI comes in. JNDI provides an interface for obtaining objects and data from anywhere on the network or within the same JVM.

The purpose of JNDI is to create a directory where applications can ask for services without knowing where the services reside or will come from. JNDI acts much like phone information in that you ask it for a service, and if the service is known, you will be automatically connected.

While JNDI can help you retrieve services, it would be a lot to expect it to be able to create new connections for you. So the service you actually want to obtain is a connection factory. This is an object that can create connections whenever you need one. The DriverManager in JDBC 1 is a type of connection factory. The DriverManager, however, is too tightly coupled to JDBC drivers to be effectively stored in JNDI, so instead you store a data source that can create connections.

Using a Data Source to Create Connections

In order to create connections using a data source, you first need to make that data source available. Unfortunately there is no one single way to do this. An application server such as JBoss, WebLogic, or WebSphere usually makes data sources available. So it is up to those products to determine how to create a new data source.

Once the data source has been created and added to JNDI, it becomes easy to obtain and use. First you create an initial context, which is the usual way of finding resources in JNDI, then you ask for the resource by name. An object implementing the DataSource interface will be returned that you can use to create connections.

```
InitialContext initCtx;
String         jndiName;
DataSource     dataSource;
Connection     connection;

// Application code to access the database
initCtx = new InitialContext();
jndiName = "java:comp/env/jdbc/hr";
dataSource = (DataSource) initCtx.lookup( jndiName );
connection = dataSource.getConnection();
```

Saving System Resources Through Connection Pooling

A serious issue with any large system is the availability of database resources. I have seen many otherwise well-designed and robust systems brought to their knees because of a lack of database connections or slowed while creating new connections. A solution is to reuse these expensive connections whenever possible.

This is where connection pooling comes into play. You can think of a connection pool as a kind of limbo where connections reside until they are needed. When you need a connection, you simply ask for one, and when you are done you give it back to the pool for others to use.

The way connection pooling is defined in JDBC 2 is transparent to the application using it. An application simply obtains a reference to a data source. Whether that data source is pooled or not is irrelevant. A connection is checked out of the pool with a call to DataSource.getConnection and is returned to the pool with a call to Connection.close.

```
InitialContext initCtx;
String          jndiName;
ConnectionPoolDataSource      dataSource;
PooledConnection pooledConnection;
Connection      connection;

// Application code to access the database
initCtx = new InitialContext();
jndiName = "java:comp/env/jdbc/hr";
dataSource = (PooledConnectionDataSource) initCtx.lookup( jndiName );
pooledConnection = dataSource.getPooledConnection();
connection = pooledConnection.getConnection();  // Obtain connection from pool
// Do work with connection
connection.close(); // Release connection back to pool
```

Distributed Transactions

In the last chapter, I discussed basic transactions. These allow reading and writing across transactions going to one database. Occasionally it is necessary to interact with multiple databases at the same time. Transactions are particularly important in this situation. It is a lot harder to find problems when half of your data is stored in one database and the other half does not make it into another database.

These cross-database transactions are possible even across heterogeneous database vendors. You could store all of your personnel data in an Oracle database, while storing all department data in DB2.

The way to interact with these separated databases is through distributed transactions. In this situation, a transaction does not commit changes until all involved databases have successfully committed changes. Fortunately, the JDBC 2.0 Optional Package makes this very easy.

Distributed transactions rely on javax.sql.XAConnection and javax.sql.XADataSource. While there are different interfaces involved, it is not up to the developer to interact with them. To the developer, all interaction is almost exactly the same as interacting with a regular data source and connection. The differences are in what you cannot do to the connection.

Distributed transactions rely on a full transaction system using the Java Transaction API or the related Java Transaction Service. So they are usually used within a full application server. It is therefore the application server's responsibility to handle the committing and rolling back of the transactions.

Because of this, a developer cannot call the methods Connection.commit(), Connection.rollback(), or Connection.setAutoCommit(true). All of these methods try to take over the transaction, which is not allowed.

Row Sets

I have been on multiple projects where I needed data from a database, but did not want to keep a result set open there by maintaining an open connection. This is where the row set comes into play. Essentially a row set is a JavaBean that contains database data. The implementation can store the data offline, or it can simply wrap a connection to make a result set look like a JavaBean. You could even use a row set to access data communicating over HTTP to a servlet, which provides the data for the bean.

A row set is a set of rows that are obtained from a tabular data source. All Sun provides in JDBC 2 is an interface. How the interface is implemented is not specified. The idea is that you can create or obtain any implementation that best fits your needs. Sun does intend to release sample implementations for the RowSet interface.

The three sample implementations that they intend to release include a CachedRowSet, a JDBCRowSet, and a WebRowSet. There could be any number of other implementations in the future as well.

The CachedRowSet is intended to read data from the database, and then make it available without an open database connection. The row set could be created and then sent over the network to devices on which it would be difficult to make actual database connections available, such as handhelds or smart appliances.

The JDBCRowSet simply wraps a result set to give it a JavaBean interface. This allows a visually configurable data source in some integrated development environments (IDEs). Essentially you could add a JDBCRowSet in your visual tool and set the properties for accessing your tabular data source. You can then use that bean within your application.

The last version that Sun is releasing is essentially a proxy object. In the WebRowSet, requests for data from the row set will be turned into HTTP calls, which a servlet will respond to. A call to the next method will invoke a servlet call. The servlet will look up the next row's data and return it.

Sun has made early access implementations of these row sets available on their developer network. You do need an account on that network to obtain these implementations, which can be downloaded from http://developer.java.sun.com/developer/earlyAccess/crs/.

JDBC 3.0

JDBC 3.0 had a few specific goals. One was to consolidate the previous specifications under one specification by pulling the optional packages into the standard JDBC packages. The second goal was to add new functionality. The new functionality they added includes savepoints within transactions, parameter metadata for prepared statements, pooling of prepared statements for performance, auto-generated keys, and many updates to existing classes.

In this section, I will address some of these key features. I will cover the importance of savepoints. I will show how to access and use the parameter metadata. And I will talk about generating and using keys.

Bookmark Your Transaction with Savepoints

Transactions are not always as simple as all or none. Sometimes there are intermediate states that are correct within a transaction and should be retained. Consider a situation where an automated system is populating the example HR database. You could conceivably create a savepoint after each employee was input rather than create a new transaction for each.

A savepoint is like a bookmark. It is a placeholder for a point in the transaction. If a problem occurs, you can roll the transaction back to any specific savepoint. The issue is, of course, that you need to have a savepoint to roll back to, as in the HR database scenario mentioned previously.

It is important to remember that savepoints will only work if auto-commit is turned off. Another point to note is that, as of this writing, neither MySQL or PostgreSQL's JDBC drivers support JDBC 3.0. Hopefully that will not be the case by the time you are reading this text.

```java
connection = DriverManager.getConnection( url, username, password );
connection.setAutoCommit(false);

statement = connection.createStatement();

String update1 = "UPDATE employees "
    + "SET email = 'dglyzewski@centare.com' "
    + "WHERE email = 'dave.glyzewski@centare.com'";
statement.executeUpdate( update1 );
Savepoint savepoint1 = connection.setSavepoint("savepoint1");

String update2 = "UPDATE employees "
    + "SET email = 'echaltry@centare.com' "
    + "WHERE email = 'ed.chaltry@centare.com'";
statement.executeUpdate( update2 );
Savepoint savepoint2 = connection.setSavepoint("savepoint2");

String update3 = "UPDATE employees "
    + "SET email = 'dsmith@centare.com' "
    + "WHERE email = 'dustin.smith@centare.com'";
statement.executeUpdate( update3 );
Savepoint savepoint3 = connection.setSavepoint("savepoint3");

String update4 = "UPDATE employees "
    + "SET email = 'stomczak@centare.com' "
    + "WHERE email = 'susan.tomczak@centare.com'";
statement.executeUpdate( update4 );
Savepoint savepoint4 = connection.setSavepoint("savepoint4");

String update5 = "UPDATE employees "
    + "SET email = 'jcarnell@centare.com' "
    + "WHERE email = 'john.carnell@centare.com'";
statement.executeUpdate( update5 );
Savepoint savepoint5 = connection.setSavepoint("savepoint5");

connection.rollback(savepoint3);
```

Using Database Auto-Generated Keys

Many databases have the ability to auto-generate unique values to use as keys for rows. The reason this is desirable is because many methods of generating unique keys involve two trips to the database: one to find out what the next key should be, and a second to actually store the data.

Allowing the database to generate the keys makes the developer's life that much easier. How exactly the database generates the key or what kind of keys can be generated varies from database to database. In many cases, it will be as simple as auto-incrementing a field in the row. So you can add a row excluding the field that will contain the key. The database will then add 1 to the number held in the previous row's field and insert it along with the data.

While it is great that the database can do this, your Java object will be out of date because it will not automatically know what number was assigned when its data was inserted. What you need to do is read the key from the database after the row is inserted.

The way it works is that instead of calling executeUpdate on the statement with just the SQL involved, you add an additional argument of Statement.RETURN_GENERATED_KEYS. Then after the statement executes, you simply call the statement's getGeneratedKeys method, which returns a result set containing all the values that were auto-generated during the update.

```
Statement stmt = conn.createStatement();
rows = stmt.executeUpdate("INSERT INTO employees "
                + "( last_name, first_name ) "
                + "VALUES ( 'Glyzewski', 'Dave' )",
                Statement.RETURN_GENERATED_KEYS);
// Grab all the generated values
ResultSet rs = stmt.getGeneratedKeys();
boolean b = rs.next();
if (b == true) {
// set generated key value on the business object
...
}
```

Optionally, you can give the executeUpdate method an array of strings containing the names of columns that will contain the generated keys. That way only those values will be returned in the result set. This is particulary useful if you have many values being generated, but only a few are part of the key.

Other JDBC 3.0 Additions

Many other features have been added or enhanced in JDBC 3.0. Two of the more interesting are the inclusion of ParameterMetaData and the pooling of prepared statements.

`ParameterMetaData` tells you about the parameters that are expected for a prepared statement. It can tell you the number of parameters expected, what class a specific parameter should be, the mode of a specific parameter, whether the parameter can be made null, and much more.

Access to this information is most useful to frameworks and automatic persistence tools. You should be aware of it in case you ever need to interact with a prepared statement that was generated outside of your code.

Prepared statement pooling is another nice feature that has been added to help with performance. Instead of just pooling connections, now JDBC can reuse prepared statements. As with `ParameterMetaData`, this will not affect most JDBC developers; it is more a feature that is used by application servers and data source providers.

Summary

I have covered a lot of territory in this chapter, including JDBC 2.1, the JDBC 2.0 Optional Package, and JDBC 3.0. JDBC 2 is a significant enhancement to JDBC 1, which I covered in the last chapter. Many new features were added, including scrollable result sets, the ability to set concurrency on a result set, and batch updates.

Scrollable result sets give you the ability to move backward and forward through your data set. You can peek at data that is coming up and move back to the beginning to ensure you have all the information you need.

Concurrency allows you to edit results in place without making another database call. Combined with scrollable result sets, concurrency is a powerful data management tool. You can scroll through your data and adjust what you find on the fly.

The JDBC 2.0 Optional Package provides a lot of functionality on top of JDBC 2. It gives you a data source, connection pooling, distributed transactions, and row sets. The data source gives you the ability to completely separate your business logic from the database; instead of telling JDBC what driver you need and what server to connect to, you simply ask the JNDI tree for a data source that can generate connections for you.

Connection pooling is a feature that is available to you through application servers. It saves resources and is transparent to the user. The resources saved can be great. Using connection pooling, you can manage how hard you make your database work.

Distributed transactions take the JDBC transaction concept further by allowing you to execute JDBC work accross multiple databases. This is a feature that is tied to your application server. The application server can then manage the transactions and ensure that either all data is persisted or none as needed.

The optional package also provides you with results in the form of JavaBeans in row sets. A row set can have any type of implementation, but it makes data appear as a component unto itself. This is very useful for tools that want to work with the data or dynamically display the data.

Finally, JDBC 3.0 gives you bookmarks within your transactions and the ability to leverage auto-generated keys from databases. These bookmarks are in the form of savepoints, and you can hold on to them and roll back to a saved point at any time. This allows you to do a lot more work in a transaction without worrying about losing it all. The ability to use keys generated by the database saves developers work in creating their own.

CHAPTER 5

Writing a
Persistence Layer

WHEN I REACHED C Company lines, which were at the top of the hill, I paused and looked back at the camp, just coming into full view below me through the grey mist of early morning. Now that you have a thorough understanding of JDBC, we can march on and put it to good use. In this chapter I will show you how to write a clean object persistence layer that will allow you to cleanly separate your domain objects from their storage.

The reason it is important to keep domain or business objects separate from their persistence mechanism is it allows the reuse of those objects in applications that employ different databases.

If the reuse argument isn't enough for you, it also makes your objects much easier to read and therefore maintain. By making your objects clearer, you will have fewer bugs and be better able to extend the software. I also believe firmly that clearer code leads to less code in the long run. It is much easier to refactor a 15-line method than a 100-line method, which means you can create more reuse of code within your objects.

Another value of a persistence layer is the ability to change the repository you store your data to. In a most basic implementation, you can quickly write a layer for a MySQL database, then if your company switched to Oracle for all applications, you only need to replace a few classes. In a situation where you are writing software to sell, you rarely want to force your customers into one database. A persistence layer allows you to provide your customers with the correct storage for their database.

You may be wondering what a persistence layer is. A persistence layer is an imaginary layer of code. Oftentimes in object-oriented systems there is talk about tiers of software, as shown in Figure 5-1. These include the User Interface Tier, Domain Tier, and the Data Management Tier (sometimes there are other tiers, and almost always people have different names for the various tiers). The persistence layer is a Data Management Tier.

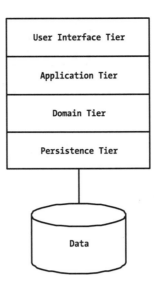

Figure 5-1. Tiers of a object-oriented system

The purpose of the Data Management Tier is to take a Java object and store it in some form of persistent storage, in this case a relational database. From the outside of the tier you should not be able to tell how this is accomplished. The persistence tier should be a clean interface from which you ask for objects and to which you give objects you want added to the database or updated in the database; you should also be able to instruct this interface to remove objects you no longer want stored in the database.

The Data Management Tier has been around since early in the life of object-oriented development, and even without a lot of object-oriented experience, most developers eventually arrive at this solution. This tier is created by taking all of the similar functionality for interacting with a database and encapsulating that functionality in a set of objects that can be replaced if the data storage changes. Because it has been around for so long, this tier goes by many different names including persistence layer, Data Management Tier, Data Access Object, Data Mapper—the list goes on and on. Regardless of what it is called, it performs the same functions.

In this chapter, I am going to show you how to implement a persistence layer for an Employee object.

One point to keep in mind is that you may not want to write a persistence layer. Although most companies still write their persistence layers themselves, it is very costly. It can be cheaper to purchase an off-the-shelf product that takes care of most data storage needs. Even though most companies will end up spending much more to build, test, and debug their own layers, they would rather do this than spend the money for a commercial product, usually because they don't want to take the time and money to explore the options.

Open source products are another option, but they are generally not as developer friendly as commercial offerings. For one project the learning curve for an open source product could easily overshadow any savings received, but subsequent projects should see a huge return on investment for that learning curve.

Writing Your First Data Access Object

Going forward, I will often refer to persistence layers as Data Access Objects (DAOs) because that is what Sun calls such patterns in their Java blueprints. That doesn't mean that the name is any more correct than any other, just that many people working on Java 2 Enterprise Edition applications will have been exposed to this term.

The first part in writing your DAO is to define the interface you want to work with. Usually this interface will include one or more find methods, an insert method, an update method, and a delete method.

Even though I show you how to define an interface for your DAOs, keep in mind that not all domain objects will be persisted in exactly the same way. Nor will all domain objects have the same requirements from the persistence layer. Your interfaces should be about conventions, not compile time checking. To create a simple interface and decide that all your DAOs should implement it is naive and will often cost much more later on when one business object doesn't play nice.

Types of Object Search Criteria

Finding the objects that you have stored is a very important part of any Data Management Tier. For that reason, people have come up with different ways to indicate to the DAO in an object-oriented fashion just what objects they want.

In this section, I will address three search types:

- Search methods

- Search by example

- Search languages

Search Methods

A search method is the easiest way to indicate what you are searching for to a DAO. It does, however, lead to some fragility in the code that uses it. For many applications, this is a simple, straightforward, and relatively complete way to search. For this reason, this is the style of searching that Sun implemented for their Enterprise JavaBean specification.

The process involves creating a method that defines each type of search you need. Any criteria that will change from search to search are handed in as arguments to the method.

In implementing this style of searching, I recommend that you follow Sun's conventions for Enterprise JavaBeans. This will make your search methods obvious to developers who are familiar with that specification.

For every search you create a method; the method name should start with "find," then optionally include the name of what will be returned, and end in "By" or "For" with a series of clearly named arguments. For example, to find an employee by unique object identifier, you would create a method named `Employee findFor(long oid)`.

The type of object returned in the name is particularly important if you are returning more than one object within a collection. For example, to search for all employees with a single last name, you would create a method with a signature like this: `List findFor( String lastName )`. This second way breaks down as soon as you need to search by two different criteria of the same type. For this, you need to make the method clearer by renaming it to `findForLastName`.

By naming your methods in this way, you create a clear, natural search method. Each method is easily translated into English: These examples translate to "Find Employee By employeeId" or "Find Employees For lastName."

How these methods are implemented can vary widely. Since you often are adding these methods directly to a Data Management Tier, you simply put the JDBC code that supports the search right in the method.

A simple `find` method could look like this:

```
public Employee findFor( long oid ) throws FindException {
    Connection connection = null;
    Statement statement = null;
    ResultSet resultSet = null;
    Employee employee = null;
    try {
        connection = getConnection();
        statement = connection.createStatement();

        String sql = "SELECT employee_id, first_name, last_name, email "
            + "FROM employees "
```

```
            + "WHERE employee_id = " + oid;
        resultSet = statement.executeQuery( sql );
        if( resultSet.next() ) {
            employee = newEmployeeFrom( resultSet );
        }
        return employee;
    }
    catch( SQLException e ) {
        e.printStackTrace();
        throw new FindException( e.getMessage() );
    }
    finally {
        closeAll( connection, statement, resultSet );
    }
}
```

A similar method for searching by last name could look like this:

```
public Collection findForLastName( String lastName ) throws FindException {
    Connection connection = null;
    Statement statement = null;
    ResultSet resultSet = null;
    List employees = new ArrayList();
    try {
        connection = getConnection();
        statement = connection.createStatement();

        String sql = "SELECT employee_id, first_name, last_name, email "
            + "FROM employees "
            + "WHERE last_name = '" + lastName + "'";
        resultSet = statement.executeQuery( sql );
        while( resultSet.next() ) {
            employees.add( newEmployeeFrom( resultSet ) );
        }
        return employees;
    }
    catch( SQLException e ) {
        e.printStackTrace();
        throw new FindException( e.getMessage() );
    }
    finally {
        closeAll( connection, statement, resultSet );
    }
}
```

Search by Example

While the implementation of find methods is simple, they become difficult to maintain. If a unique identifier is refactored to include two parts, you need to change all the consumers of the method. This can often stop important refactorings from occurring. The same issue arises if you need to add new search criteria to any existing find method.

One way to prevent this difficulty is to hand in one whole object that defines your query parameters instead of a bunch of separate query parameters.

Once you have decided that you want to pass in a whole object, you need to decide if you will use strongly typed or softly typed example criteria.

Strongly Typed Example

In a strongly typed example, you can use the compiler to indicate if you have incorrectly typed a parameter name; this is because your query objects will either be domain objects or query objects that closely mirror domain objects.

The easiest implementation of this is to simply use existing domain objects to define what you are looking for. Any properties of the objects that are left null are ignored. Any properties that are included are part of the query. For this type of query, you would write two methods for all of your searches. The first method would find either the only instance of a criteria match or return the first instance. A signature for this method would be Employee findFor(Employee exampleCriteria). The signature for the method that returns multiple instances would be Collection findAllFor(Employee exampleCriteria).

```
public Employee findFor( Employee exampleCriteria ) throws FindException {
    Connection connection = null;
    Statement statement = null;
    ResultSet resultSet = null;
    Employee employee = null;
    try {
        connection = getConnection();
        statement = connection.createStatement();

        StringBuffer sql = new StringBuffer( "SELECT employee_id, first_name, "
            +"last_name, email "
            + "FROM employees "
            + "WHERE " );
        if( exampleCriteria.getOid() != 0 ) {
            sql.append( "employee_id = " );
            sql.append( exampleCriteria.getOid() );
```

```
            sql.append( " AND " );
        }
        if( exampleCriteria.getFirstName() != null ) {
            sql.append( "first_name = '" );
            sql.append( exampleCriteria.getFirstName() );
            sql.append( "' AND " );
        }
        if( exampleCriteria.getLastName() != null ) {
            sql.append( "last_name = '" );
            sql.append( exampleCriteria.getLastName() );
            sql.append( "' AND " );
        }
        if( exampleCriteria.getEmail() != null ) {
            sql.append( "email = '" );
            sql.append( exampleCriteria.getEmail() );
            sql.append( "' AND " );
        }
        sql.append( "'A' = 'A'" );
        resultSet = statement.executeQuery( sql.toString() );
        if( resultSet.next() ) {
            employee = newEmployeeFrom( resultSet );
        }
        return employee;
    }
    catch( SQLException e ) {
        e.printStackTrace();
        throw new FindException( e.getMessage() );
    }
    finally {
        closeAll( connection, statement, resultSet );
    }
}
```

A second implementation would include a parallel hierarchy. For instance, you could have an Employee class and an EmployeeCriteria class that has many of the same methods. The hierarchy is parallel because you generally need one Criteria object for each significant domain object.

An advantage of the parallel hierarchy is that you can add methods that make sense for querying that would not be part of a domain object. For instance, to query by last name, you could have a setLastNameEquals method and a setLastNameLike method. The first would match all exact matches, while the second could do fuzzier wild card matching.

It also gives you the ability to search for null values. If you use an actual business object for querying, any null value is ignored. With a Criteria object, you can find all employees whose last name is not set by calling setLastNameNull(). This method would set a flag that your DAO could use to look for null values.

```java
public class EmployeeCriteria {
    String lastNameEquals = null;
    String lastNameLike = null;
    boolean lastNameNull = false;

    public String getLastNameEquals() {
        return lastNameEquals;
    }

    public void setLastNameEquals(String lastNameEquals) {
        this.lastNameEquals = lastNameEquals;
    }

    public String getLastNameLike() {
        return lastNameLike;
    }

    public void setLastNameLike(String lastNameLike) {
        this.lastNameLike = lastNameLike;
    }

    public boolean isLastNameNull() {
        return lastNameNull;
    }

    public void setLastNameNull(boolean lastNameNull) {
        this.lastNameNull = lastNameNull;
    }
}
```

The DAO's code would create SQL just as before, but could check for very clear indicators of what it is to search for. If the lastNameEquals property is set, then you need to add last_name = 'value' to your query. If the lastNameLike property is set, then you need to add last_name LIKE '%value%' to your query. If lastNameNull is set to true, then you simply add last_name IS NULL to the query.

```java
public Employee findFor( EmployeeCriteria exampleCriteria ) throws FindException {
    Connection connection = null;
```

```
        Statement statement = null;
        ResultSet resultSet = null;
        Employee employee = null;
        try {
            connection = getConnection();
            statement = connection.createStatement();

            StringBuffer sql = new StringBuffer( "SELECT employee_id, first_name, "
                + "last_name, email "
                + "FROM employees "
                + "WHERE " );
            if( exampleCriteria.getLastNameEquals() != null ) {
                sql.append( "last_name = '" );
                sql.append( exampleCriteria.getLastNameEquals() );
                sql.append( "' AND " );
            }
            if( exampleCriteria.getLastNameLike() != null ) {
                sql.append( "last_name LIKE '%" );
                sql.append( exampleCriteria.getLastNameLike() );
                sql.append( "%' AND " );
            }
            if( exampleCriteria.isLastNameNull() ) {
                sql.append( "last_name IS NULL AND " );
            }
            sql.append( "'A' = 'A'" );
            resultSet = statement.executeQuery( sql.toString() );
            if( resultSet.next() ) {
                employee = newEmployeeFrom( resultSet );
            }
            return employee;
        }
        catch( SQLException e ) {
            e.printStackTrace();
            throw new FindException( e.getMessage() );
        }
        finally {
            closeAll( connection, statement, resultSet );
        }
    }
```

Softly Typed Example

Another type of search by example uses a softly typed criteria object. In this case, you use a map of name value pairs that is passed to the DAO for lookup. An implementation of this type gives a lot of flexibility in what can be added to the criteria. You could add new searchable fields without ever changing the criteria object itself. The downside is that there is no compile time checking, so it is possible to set names that the DAO is not looking for; this problem can be solved by using static variables for names.

As with all implementations, you can do a simple version or a more complete version. With simple criteria, any value that is in the criteria is an "=" match in SQL; in other words, if the value is included, then it must be an exact match. In order to handle fuzzy matching and nulls, you need a more complete implementation.

For a simple implementation, you could simply extend a map, adding public final static constants.

```java
public class SimpleSoftEmployeeCriteria extends HashMap {
    public final static String OID = "oid";
    public final static String LAST_NAME = "lastName";
    public final static String FIRST_NAME = "firstName";
    public final static String EMAIL = "email";
}
```

A more complete implementation could take into account concepts such as setting values that will match a NULL or giving a collection of values that a valid match must be a part of. Allowing the specification of fuzzy logic is easy too. You can use specifiers such as LIKE and BETWEEN. All of this can be done while using a variable criteria.

```java
public interface Criteria {
    /**
     * Adds a value that the attribute must match
     *
     *@param  attribute  Attribute to compare
     *@param  value      Value it must be equal to
     */
    public void addEquals(String attribute, Object value);

    /**
     * Adds a value that the attribute must be like (globbing with % for sql)
     *
     *@param  attribute  Attribute to compare
     *@param  value      Value to compare to
```

```
    */
    public void addLike(String attribute, Object value);

    /**
     *  Sets values that the attribute must be between
     *
     *@param  attribute  Attribute to compare
     *@param  from       Low end of comparison
     *@param  to         High end of comparison
     */
    public void addBetween(String attribute, Object from, Object to);

    /**
     *  Sets a list of values that the attribute must be contained in
     *
     *@param  attribute  Attribute to compare
     *@param  values     Attribute must match one of the values included
     */
    public void addIn(String attribute, Collection values);

    /**
     *  Adds a feature to the Null attribute of the Criteria object
     *
     *@param  attribute  The feature to be added to the Null attribute
     */
    public void addNull(String attribute);
}
```

Creating a concrete implementation of this type of criteria could allow you to still have some compile time checking through constant values. Much like the previously demonstrated soft criteria, you can extend the criteria and add constants.

```
public class EmployeeCriteria extends AbstractCriteria {
    public final static String OID = "oid";
    public final static String LAST_NAME = "lastName";
    public final static String FIRST_NAME = "firstName";
    public final static String EMAIL = "email";
}
```

A final addition to such criteria that you could include is a collection of rules. You could add rules for each attribute that is set. This would allow runtime checking of values being set. In other words, if you wanted to write a rule for numDependants and wanted to enforce that only integers are added to the criteria, you could write a rule that would only allow adding of integers. If a consumer of your criteria tried to add an attribute that is not listed in the rules, you could throw an exception.

Search Languages

The last method of specifying what you want your DAOs to return is through a search language. In this situation, you define a language other than SQL that allows consumers to query for objects they need. The reason you create a new language is to allow separation between your consumers and the underlying persistence layer. If you allowed SQL to be handed in, the consumers would immediately be coupled to the database server, and you would have nullified much of the value you obtain from a separate Data Management Tier.

How you implement the search language is up to you. You could use the Interpreter pattern that is listed in the Gang of Four's *Design Patterns: Elements of Reusable Object-Oriented Software* (Gamma, Helm, Johnson, and Vlissides. Addison-Wesley Publishing Company. ISBN: 0-20163-361-2). You could also use a tool such as the Java Compiler Compiler (JavaCC). You could brute force a language using the `java.util.StringTokenizer` and a lot of work.

Another possible search language solution would be to use XML. By defining your search language in XML, you can leverage one of the many XML parsers that have already been written. This allows you to not worry about the reading of the language, just how the language is built.

Because there are so many different ways to define a search language, I will leave the ultimate implementation up to you. Although it is sometimes necessary to create your own language to use as a search language, I recommend against it for DAO queries. I have seen projects implement these languages, and they are difficult and error prone. Using one of the previous methods of implementing querying will probably work very well for most projects.

The Rest of the CRUD

Most database interaction can be broken down into Create, Read, Update, and Delete (CRUD) processes. Of the four, reading is usually the most complex. Implementing the other processes will almost always consist of making a database connection, reading from objects and writing to objects, and communicating with the database. This doesn't change very much between different designs of a Data Management Tier.

In the Create, Update, and Delete processes of CRUD, a JDBC statement is created, values are set, and the statement is executed.

Inserting New Objects

Inserting a new object consists of creating the object, interacting with it, usually setting values, executing business methods, and then storing the object to the database, all of which is very easy.

One issue with persistence layers is you need to identify which objects are the same even if they contain different values. For instance, one part of an application can read the record for employee Dave Glyzewski and legally change his name to Homer Simpson. Another part of the application can have a separate copy of the record for Dave Glyzewski without the name change. It is often necessary to uniquely identify an object without taking into account business-relate attributes.

You can change Dave Glyzewski's name, his number of dependants, e-mail address, and phone number. It is even possible to not initially have and later obtain a Social Security number. Because all of these things are changeable but do not change the entity the object is referring to, I suggest coming up with a simple unique identifier. This is usually called an *object identifier* (OID).

In many cases, you will not want to issue the OID until right before you store the object in the persistence layer. That allows for generation of temporary objects without excess work.

Generating Universally Unique Object Identifiers

There are many ways to generate OIDs. You can use a sequence from a database, which will keep track of issued OIDs and increment the sequence when issuing another. It is possible to implement a similar process on your own by creating a table that will contain a row for each business object and a column containing that class's last issued ID.

Another idea is to create a Global Unique Identifier (GUID) or a Universal Unique Identifier (UUID). Both of these take into account the address of the computer the identifier is generated on and the time it was generated. Often other ingredients will go into the mix to make everyone feel safer about the generated number, like the hash code of an object in the VM to ensure that two objects weren't created at the same time.

Similar to a GUID and easier to obtain is a java.rmi.dgc.VMID, which is intended to be unique across all Java Virtual Machines. The conditions for a VMID to be unique are that the system it is generated on takes more than one millisecond to boot, the clock is not moved backwards, and the IP address is obtainable from Java and does not change for the life of the object.

While a VMID promises to be unique, it does not conform to the definition of UUID or GUID, which requires the use of a hardware identifier from the network card. Access to that information is not available from Java at this time. So VMID is the best we have in Java currently without implementing native calls to the underlying operating system.

The code to generate a VMID is very simple. Unfortunately, there is not a simple type to convert it to store it in the database other than String. For that reason, your business objects would need to have their OIDs be strings.

```
String vmid = new VMID().toString();
```

With all that being said, most applications do not need GUIDs. One of the arguments is that they allow sharing of objects between systems. While Web services make this more likely than ever, most systems will not trust even GUIDs and will find other ways to uniquely identify objects coming from other systems rather than rely on a promise of another system.

Another simple way to generate an OID is to get the highest currently stored OID and increment it by one. In this situation, you go to the table that contains the object to be stored and simply select the max number in that column. For this to work, you need to give up some performance by synchronizing both the nextOid method and the insert method.

```
private synchronized long nextOid( Statement statement ) throws SQLException {
    String sql = "SELECT MAX( employee_id ) FROM employees";
    ResultSet resultSet = statement.executeQuery( sql );
    resultSet.next();
    long lastOid = resultSet.getLong( 1 );
    return lastOid + 1;
}
```

A variation of this method is to create a separate table to contain all the OIDs, then issue one every time one is requested. That way you will not need to synchronize your methods. One downside is that you could be issuing a lot of unused numbers.

Inserting the Object

Now that you have a unique identifier for the object, let's insert it into the database. This is a fairly straightforward proposition. You simply create an INSERT SQL statement and populate it with the values from the object to be inserted. In a situation like inserting an employee object, you create an INSERT statement for your Employees table that lists all of the attributes you will be storing.

Oftentimes when inserting an object, you will want to return a different object from the one that was handed in. This is due to side effects caused by inserting the object. An example is the creation of an OID. The employee object that is handed into the `insert` method does not have an OID, but the one returned should. It is a judgment call as to whether to return the same object with side effects enacted or to return a different object. In the following example, I show you how to create a new employee object:

```java
/**
 * This method inserts an employee into the database. It is a different
 * employee object that is returned from this method. The new employee object
 * contains all the data of the original as well as a unique object identifier.
 */
public synchronized Employee insert( Employee employee )
    throws PersistenceException {
    Connection connection = null;
    Statement statement = null;
    long oid = 0;
    int results = 0;
    try {
        connection = getConnection();
        statement = connection.createStatement();

        oid = nextOid( statement );

        String sql = "INSERT INTO employees "
            + "(employee_id, first_name, last_name, email) "
            + "VALUES "
            + "("
            + oid + ", "
            + "'" + employee.getFirstName() + "', "
            + "'" + employee.getLastName() + "', "
            + "'" + employee.getEmail() + "' "
            + ")";
        results = statement.executeUpdate( sql );

        if( results == 1 ) {
            Employee newEmployee = new Employee( oid );
            newEmployee.setFirstName( employee.getFirstName() );
            newEmployee.setLastName( employee.getLastName() );
            newEmployee.setEmail( employee.getEmail() );
            return newEmployee;
        }
        else {
            throw new PersistenceException( "Unable to insert Employee" );
        }
    }
```

```
catch( SQLException e ) {
    e.printStackTrace();
    throw new PersistenceException( e.getMessage() );
}
finally {
    closeAll( connection, statement, null );
}
}
```

One final note on the preceding code is that it does not throw an SQLException. It instead creates a PersistenceException. I would recommend having the PersistenceException wrap the SQLException in order to retain valuable troubleshooting data.

Updating the Business Object

Oftentimes values on business objects change. An example with our HR application would be when employees change the number of dependants they have or change their names after marriage. Because of interdependencies of objects, it is rarely a good policy to delete data from the database and reinsert it when changes are needed. Instead you update the data.

Updating an object's data is very similar to inserting the object originally, you just use different SQL. Instead of the insert statement, you use an update statement. Because you are updating an object's data in the database, you do not need to issue a new OID, nor do you need to return an object because there should be no side effects of the update.

```
public void update( Employee employee ) throws PersistenceException {
    Connection connection = null;
    Statement statement = null;
    int results = 0;
    try {
        connection = getConnection();
        statement = connection.createStatement();

        String sql = "UPDATE employees SET "
        + "first_name = '" + employee.getFirstName() + "', "
        + "last_name = '" + employee.getLastName() + "', "
        + "email = '" + employee.getEmail() + "' "
        + "WHERE employee_id = " + employee.getOid();
        results = statement.executeUpdate( sql );
```

```
            if( results != 1 ) {
                throw new PersistenceException( "Unable to update Employee" );
            }
        }
        catch( SQLException e ) {
            e.printStackTrace();
            throw new PersistenceException( e.getMessage() );
        }
        finally {
            closeAll( connection, statement, null );
        }
    }
```

As with the insert method, this method throws a PersistenceException. This helps keep the rest of your application independent of the underlying persistence mechanism. Another point to note is that you throw an exception if the number of affected rows returned from your executeUpdate is not 1. That is because only one row should be affected; if it isn't, then either the object was deleted or it never existed.

Deleting Business Objects

The simplest of the CRUD features is deleting. The SQL is simple and so is the method. You simply hand in an object you want removed from persistence; once this is done you move on. The delete method will delete all values that are associated with the OID of the object passed in.

```
public void delete( Employee employee ) throws PersistenceException {
    if( employee == null ) {
        return;
    }

    Connection connection = null;
    Statement statement = null;
    int results = 0;
    try {
        connection = getConnection();
        statement = connection.createStatement();

        String sql = "DELETE FROM employees WHERE employee_id = "
        + employee.getOid();
        results = statement.executeUpdate( sql );
```

```
            if( results != 1 ) {
                throw new PersistenceException( "Unable to delete Employee" );
            }
        }
        catch( SQLException e ) {
            e.printStackTrace();
            throw new PersistenceException( e.getMessage() );
        }
        finally {
            closeAll( connection, statement, null );
        }
    }
```

As with the update method, one row should be affected by the delete method. Otherwise the method needs to throw an exception. After all the work is done, the connection and statement are closed in a finally block.

Summary

In this chapter, I covered many features of a basic persistence layer. Specifically I showed you several ways to query for data from a persistence layer. I talked about ways to create unique identifiers for objects. The chapter addressed inserting objects into the database and updating existing objects. Finally I covered deleting objects from storage.

For querying Data Management Tiers, find methods provide a simple mechanism that will cover all needs for most uses. If a more robust process for querying is required, then searching by example can be used. There are a few ways to implement this, but using a soft criteria object gives a lot of versatility and allows for searching for the same attribute in different ways.

Most objects should have some type of unique identifier to ensure that changes to attributes can happen without changing the referenced object. In establishing a unique identifier, be aware of the specific needs of the application. Some systems need identifiers that are unique across systems and even unique across the globe. Others simply increment a counter for that type of object.

Inserting, updating, and deleting objects is simply a matter of taking business objects and converting them into SQL. Once that happens, the underlying database will reflect the state of the objects.

CHAPTER 6

Persistence-Related Design Patterns

ALICE WAS BEGINNING to get very tired of sitting by her sister on the bank, and of having nothing to do: Once or twice she had peeped into the book her sister was reading, but it had no pictures or conversations in it, "and what is the use of a book," thought Alice "without pictures or conversation?" In this chapter, I will talk about *design patterns*, which are as great a way to communicate as pictures and conversation. Design patterns are documents that contain instructions for solving a specific problem within a specific context. Software designers write down patterns to give other designers a path or recipe to follow to solve recurring design problems. In other words, design patterns are conceptual templates you can apply to areas of your application or system as appropriate.

Object-oriented design patterns are ever evolving; as new languages and new technologies come forward, so too will new patterns. As an example, Sun's J2EE BluePrints contain patterns that are relevant to that platform (see `http://java.sun.com/blueprints` for more on Java BluePrints).

By definition, the following need to be included in a pattern:

- Definition of a problem

- Considerations for the problem or the context of the problem

- A general solution

- Sample code for the solution

- Good and bad consequences of the pattern

- Related patterns

- Code examples

One thing to keep in mind is that design patterns are meant to be flexible. You generally won't find the exact chunk of code you need in a design pattern, but you will find some sign posts and directions to help guide you. For example, a design pattern will not tell you where to put your curly braces or exactly what to call your class, but it will suggest that an object that fulfills the Strategy pattern provide behavior to the object that wraps it. You are free to develop your own implementations of the design pattern. One measurement of success in implementing a design pattern is how recognizable the pattern in the code is to those who come after you to maintain or enhance the code. This evolution of usefulness and efficiency are what make design patterns so valuable.

The Value of Patterns

Patterns are often used for communication. They help communication between the designers actively working on a project and the designers and developers who come later. The pattern creates a pathway to follow to help interpret the code that was written. A pattern is also useful for communicating to someone outside the immediate design team. With a pattern, you don't need to know everything about the application in order to help with the design. A designer can say, "The Strategy pattern is a good fit for this problem," and in that simple sentence the designer has conveyed many ideas concerning the properties and implementation of the object or component.

Patterns give some design assurance when developers clearly name objects that conform to the pattern. For example, if I see classes named SQLServerStrategy, MySQLStrategy, and OracleStrategy, I can surmise that it is possible to add support for PostgreSQL by following the Strategy pattern. This gives developers a common ground to work from regardless of the project state when they come in. It also helps to ensure the integrity of the design, by providing that continuity. Always keep in mind that names that makes sense today may not be clear to you or others tomorrow. Ensure that you keep some level of documentation and comments in all of your classes.

A designer's toolbox can be extended with the use of design patterns. When a designer sees a requirement that fits a pattern, the designer can move on knowing the solution for the requirement. For example, if a designer receives a requirement that the application shall allow the use of a simple query language, the designer knows he can use the Interpreter pattern for creating the language. The designer does not need to come up with a new, elegant solution to the problem.

Another use of patterns is to convey experience from an experienced designer to a less experienced designer. A designer who has not seen a problem before can read design patterns relevant to that problem and essentially build on the experience of others. The simple language of patterns makes for a shared knowledge base. However, I have seen many projects where developers who were learning patterns succumb to the "pattern of the week" syndrome. This is where the developer learns the Command pattern, and everything looks like a command to her.

In this chapter, I will discuss some design patterns that I feel strongly lend themselves to object-relational persistence: the Builder, Strategy, and Facade patterns. I will give example implementations of these patterns, and it is important to remember that there are more ways for you to implement these than I will show you. Patterns are to be taken as guideposts only.

The History of Design Patterns

Design patterns originated with Christopher Alexander, a building architect, who recognized architectural patterns and began writing about them in the 1960s and 1970s. He wrote several books, including *The Timeless Way of Building* (Oxford University Press. ISBN: 0-19502-402-8) and *A Pattern Language* (Oxford University Press. ISBN: 0-19501-919-9). In these books, he laid out elegant solutions to common design problems. A novice architect could take these patterns and apply them to his own designs. The novice could thereby create a design that exceeded his own experience.

Software design patterns were first recognized in the late 1980s. Two gentlemen named Ward Cunningham and Kent Beck had been looking at Christopher Alexander's work and recognized several software patterns from their own experience. They wrote these patterns down to help junior designers produce better designs. Ward and Kent then brought these patterns to the Object-Oriented Programming, Systems, Languages, and Applications (OOPSLA) Conference in 1987 where they shared them.

Erich Gamma, at about this same time, began documenting patterns with Richard Helm, another designer. Ralph Johnson and John Vlissides were added to the mix, and *Design Patterns: Elements of Reusable Object-Oriented Software* (Addison-Wesley Publishing Company. ISBN: 0-20163-361-2) was created. You may have heard this book being called the "Gang of Four book," or the "GOF book." In their book they cover many patterns, including all of the ones I will cover in this book.

In 1993 Kent Beck and Grady Booch sponsored a mountain retreat in Colorado that signaled the beginning of the Hillside Group. This group, which put on the first Patterns Languages of Programs Conference (PLOP), has furthered the use of patterns by espousing their benefits.

If you find you have more interest in design patterns, I highly recommend you pick up a copy of the Gang of Four book and form a patterns study group. You can also receive a lot of good direction from the Web on how to facilitate such a group. I also suggest you check out the Portland Patterns Repository off of Ward's site at http://www.c2.com.

Using the Builder Pattern for SQL Generation

The first pattern I will discuss is known as a *creational pattern,* which is used in creating objects. This pattern is named the *Builder pattern.* The Builder pattern is useful when you have several complex objects that follow similar steps in their construction.

First, I need to acknowledge I am not a database administrator. I am an object-oriented designer/developer, so SQL can feel foreign to me. When I look at SQL statements, I see complex objects.

Secondly, I have seen a lot of errors introduced into code in which someone tries to edit SQL that is embedded in Java code. Developers need to keep track of quotes and break the SQL up in such a way as to make the code readable in Java. There are often issues with missing spaces in the SQL. Pulling the SQL out and putting it into property files is a partial solution, but it doesn't solve the problem when you are dealing with dynamically generated SQL. The problem becomes worse when you need to add conditional portions to the SQL, resulting in the SQL statement being scattered throughout a method or class.

SQL Statements As Objects

A SQL UPDATE statement consists of a Command section, a Table section, a list of columns and their data, and finally, a Criteria section. An INSERT statement consists of a Command section, a Table section, a list of columns and their data, but no Criteria section. A DELETE statement consists of a Command section, a Table portion, and a Criteria section, but no columns or their data. Each of these statements is different in their content, but not so different in how they are built.

The Builder pattern itself consists of taking those parts of the construction and pulling them out into a Builder object, then creating a Director that will execute those parts on the Builder. It is the Director's job to do the creating; it is the Builder's job to make that creation available to the Director. Figure 6-1 illustrates these relationships.

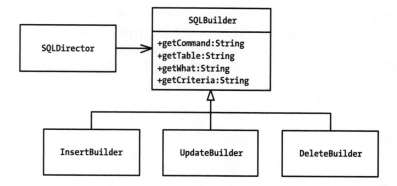

Figure 6-1. Conceptual model of Director and Builders

In this figure, you can see that the Director has a reference to a SQLBuilder, really any subclass of SQLBuilder. The InsertBuilder extends the SQLBuilder and implements the methods on the SQLBuilder. It is the InsertBuilder that is going to do the work directed by the Director.

Director of the Construction

The Director portion of the pattern has one method that works on the Builder (see Listing 6-1). In this case, it makes calls to the Builder, takes the results, and puts them together in the final object. You could also have the Director simply be a method on the Builder superclass.

Listing 6-1. Director.java

```java
public class Director {
  ...
  public static String buildSQL( SQLBuilder builder ) {
    StringBuffer buffer = new StringBuffer();
    buffer.append( builder.getCommand() );
    buffer.append( builder.getTable() );
    buffer.append( builder.getWhat() );
    buffer.append( builder.getCriteria() );
    return buffer.toString();
  }
  ...
}
```

Note there is one method here that the Director uses to build the SQL. It takes the Builder as an input argument. This could be any type of Builder: InsertBuilder, UpdateBuilder, DeleteBuilder, etc. The Director then calls the same series of methods on whatever Builder it has a reference to. The Builder itself knows how to build those different objects based on the Builder's type.

The Builder's Superclass

Next, you need to create an abstract superclass that all of the SQL Builders will inherit from, as shown in Listing 6-2. This class will simply list the methods that the Director is expecting.

Listing 6-2. SQLBuilder.java

```
public abstract class SQLBuilder {
  public abstract String getCommand();
  public abstract String getTable();
  public abstract String getWhat();
  public abstract String getCriteria();
}
```

I use an abstract superclass here, but for this simple example, an interface would work fine. One reason you may want to use an abstract superclass is that you will most likely find code that is shared across your Builders. The getTable() method could easily be shared across Builders by implementing it in this superclass, because it does not change. All Builders return the table name.

Creating an InsertBuilder

Listing 6-3 shows the first part of an implementation of the SQLBuilder for creating an INSERT SQL statement. I will first show you the easy portions and progress to the more difficult portions of the InsertBuilder.

Listing 6-3. InsertBuilder.java, Part One

```
public class InsertBuilder extends SQLBuilder {
  private String table;

  public void setTable( String table ) {
    this.table = table;
  }
```

```
public String getTable() {
  return table;
}

public String getCommand() {
  return "INSERT INTO ";
}

public String getCriteria() {
  return "";
}
...
}
```

Here the `getTable` method is fulfilled through a simple `get`/`set` pair for an attribute. The `getCommand` method simply returns a string. By looking at this small portion of the complex SQL statement, you can see how the Builder is useful. The Director does not know or care what is returned by the Builder. It is the Builder's responsibility to create an `Insert` statement.

The `getCriteria` method is the most controversial of the three methods. The `Insert` statement is the one of the three statements I listed previously that will never have any criteria. You will never have a `Where` clause for an `Insert` statement. This is what Martin Fowler calls the *Refused Bequest smell* in his excellent book, *Refactoring: Improving the Design of Existing Code* (Addison-Wesley Publishing Company. ISBN: 0-20148-567-2). By *smell*, Martin is referring to the "odor" that emanates from bad code. The `InsertBuilder` implements a method that it does not need or want. By making this object-oriented design concession, you can greatly simplify the design. Another option here is to have the superclass contain methods that return empty strings. You need only override applicable methods this way. With a little creativity, you could extend this pattern to handle `SELECT` and `JOIN` operations.

The next part of this class handles all of the columns and data for those columns (see Listing 6-4). As was already covered earlier in this book, the "what" portion of this Builder needs to produce a string that contains columns first, followed by values:

```
(column1, column2, column3) VALUES (value1, value2, value3 )
```

Listing 6-4. InsertBuilder.java, Part Two

```java
import java.util.*;

public class InsertBuilder extends SQLBuilder {
  private Map columnsAndData = new HashMap();
  ...
  public void addColumnAndData( String columnName, Object value ) {
    if( value != null ) {
      columnsAndData.put( columnName, value );
    }
  }
  ...
  public String getWhat() {
    StringBuffer columns = new StringBuffer();
    StringBuffer values = new StringBuffer();
    StringBuffer what = new StringBuffer();

    String columnName = null;
    Iterator iter = columnsAndData.keySet().iterator();
    while( iter.hasNext() ) {
      columnName = (String) iter.next();
      columns.append( columnName );
      values.append( columnsAndData.get( columnName ) );
      if( iter.hasNext() ) {
        columns.append( ',' );
        values.append( ',' );
      }
    }

    what.append( " (" );
    what.append( columns );
    what.append( ") VALUES (" );
    what.append( values );
    what.append( ") " );
    return what.toString();
  }
  ...
}
```

Here you add two new methods and an attribute. The first method adds columns and data to the Builder. Notice that you do not need to bother adding a column if the value is null, because the column in the database already contains a null. This can also help catch bugs where code tries to set primary keys to null. The database will complain that you skipped the column entirely. An UpdateBuilder would have a very similar method for adding columns and data. The only difference between the InsertBuilder and UpdateBuilder's add method is that you will want nulls to make it through to clear fields in the database for the UpdateBuilder.

In order to execute the code, I have included part of a BuilderMain class in Listing 6-5. This shows how to create an InsertBuilder, set the table, and add columns and values.

Listing 6-5. BuilderMain.java

```
InsertBuilder builder = new InsertBuilder();
builder.setTable( "employees" );
builder.addColumnAndData( "employee_id", new Integer( 221 ) );
builder.addColumnAndData( "first_name", "'Shane'" );
builder.addColumnAndData( "last_name", "'Grinnell'" );
builder.addColumnAndData( "email", "'al@yahoo.com'" );
String sql = buildSQL( builder );
```

This will generate the following SQL:

```
INSERT INTO employees (first_name, last_name, email) VALUES
('Shane','Grinnell','al@yahoo.com')
```

Adding additional columns to this SQL statement becomes very easy. You can just add new calls to addColumnAndData(). This is particularly useful early in development when the database is less than stable and you are constantly editing SQL. Using a pattern like this, you never have to leave the Java mindset for SQL. Later, if you find that the auto-generated SQL is a bottleneck, you can optimize those methods that present a problem.

Using the Strategy Pattern to Handle Different Databases

The Strategy pattern is useful when you have an object that needs to behave differently depending on the situation. It removes the need to add a lot of if/else or switch statements to every method. The class instead delegates the call to the current Strategy.

For example, you could write a JDBCHelper to simplify your creating of connections. The JDBCHelper could also format strings and dates correctly for creating dynamic SQL.

Another requirement you may have is that the class must work for both Microsoft Access and Microsoft SQL Server. You have a few choices for a situation like this. You can create a different JDBCHelper for each database you will support. You can add a lot of conditional logic to pretty much every method to take into account the differences between the databases, or you can use a Strategy pattern.

I once had a very smart Smalltalk programmer suggest to me that you could write code without ever using an if statement. He acknowledged that though you could, you probably would never want to. There is, however, a general object-oriented belief that switch statements and conditional logic have problems, because anytime you implement a switch statement, there is a high probability that another part of the code will need to know the difference between the different cases as well. Then if you change one switch statement, you will have to change them all. This is the problem the Strategy pattern solves, because it takes all behavior that differs between the databases and puts it into one object that you can switch in and out, depending on the database you are working with.

In Figure 6-2, you can see the JDBCHelper and its relationship to the strategies. The helper class does not need to constantly test to see which database is being used to do work. Whenever work is meant for MS Access, MSAccessStrategy will be used.

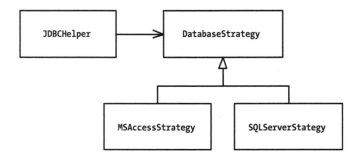

Figure 6-2. Conceptual model of JDBCHelper and its Strategies

Let's consider how you would use such a JDBCHelper if you had an employee object that you wanted to insert into the database. You would use the JDBCHelper to get the database connection, and then you could use the InsertBuilder to create your INSERT SQL statement. It is important to note that there was a problem with the InsertBuilder used in Listing 6-5, as I had to add single quotes around my string values as I handed them into the addColumnAndData method. This is a very SQL thing to do in Java code. You could use your JDBCHelper to handle that formatting for you, since it is your translator between Java and the database (see Listing 6-6).

Listing 6-6. JDBCHelper.java

```java
Employee employee = buildTestEmployee();
Connection con = null;
Statement statement = null;
try {
  DatabaseStrategy strategy
      = new SQLServerStrategy("GEMINI", "strategy_pattern", "sa", "" );
  JDBCHelper helper = new JDBCHelper( strategy );

  InsertBuilder builder = new InsertBuilder();
  builder.setTable( "employees" );
  builder.addColumnAndData( "oid",
      helper.format( employee.getGuid() ) );
  builder.addColumnAndData( "first_name",
      helper.format( employee.getFirstName() ) );
  builder.addColumnAndData( "last_name",
      helper.format( employee.getLastName() ) );
  builder.addColumnAndData( "employed",
      helper.format( employee.getEmployed() ) );
  builder.addColumnAndData( "date_of_birth",
      helper.format( employee.getDateOfBirth() ) );
  builder.addColumnAndData( "num_dependants",
      helper.format( employee.getNumDependants() ) );

  con = helper.getConnection();
  statement = con.createStatement();
  statement.executeUpdate( SQLDirector.buildSQL( builder ) );
}
catch( Exception e ) {
  e.printStackTrace();
}
finally {
  if( statement != null ) {
```

```
    try { statement.close(); }
    catch( SQLException e ) {}
  }
  if( con != null ) {
    try { con.close(); }
    catch( SQLException e ) {}
  }
}
```

In Listing 6-6, I show you how to create the JDBCHelper with all the information it will need to use the database. The helper is used for creating connections. It also is used for formatting values before adding them to the SQL statement. Now the only SQL-specific part of the code is the column names. Also note that this listing reuses the InsertBuilder and SQLDirector from the last section (shown in Listings 6-4 and 6-1, respectively).

The next thing I want to describe is the JDBCHelper. This is the object that will wrap the Strategies, and it will change behavior based on what Strategy is used (see Listing 6-7).

Listing 6-7. JDBCHelper.java That Provides Formatting

```
import java.sql.*;

public class JDBCHelper {
  private DatabaseStrategy strategy;

  public JDBCHelper( DatabaseStrategy strategy ) throws ClassNotFoundException {
    this.strategy = strategy;
    strategy.loadDriver();
  }

  public Connection getConnection() throws SQLException {
    String url = strategy.generateURL();
    return DriverManager.getConnection( url );
  }

  public String format( Object value ) {
    return strategy.format( value );
  }
```

```
  public String format( boolean value ) {
    return format( new Boolean( value ) );
  }

  public String format( int value ) {
    return format( new Integer( value ) );
  }
  ...
}
```

Here you start to see the value of the Strategy pattern. In the JDBCHelper's constructor, you see the Strategy used for loading the database driver. This is a perfect use of the Strategy, since every database can have a different driver class. In this example, this method will load either Sun's sun.jdbc.odbc.JdbcOdbcDriver or Microsoft's com.microsoft.jdbc.sqlserver.SQLServerDriver, depending on the Strategy. It could load any other SQL Server driver as well.

The Strategy is then used to create a URL for connecting to the database. This is useful because the URL for connecting to Access through the Type 1 JDBC-ODBC bridge is very different from the URL for connecting to SQL Server through Microsoft's Type 4 JDBC driver.

The last thing the Strategy is used for is to format values for the specific database. This is important because not all databases support the same types. Sometimes, even when they do support the same types, they may require the values be formatted differently. An example of this is dates. MS Access accepts a literal date formatted with pound signs: #10-13-1970 00:00:00# (#MM-dd-yyyy HH:mm:ss#); SQL Server cannot handle that format but can accept "1970-10-13 00:00:00" (yyyy-MM-dd HH:mm:ss). The format method can also help to translate to types that do not exist in a database. For instance, you can convert a Boolean to a bit for SQL Server.

You can add some helper format methods that take primitives and wrap them in objects to hand off to the Strategy's format method. This makes the use of the JDBCHelper easier because you do not need to worry about what return type a method has, as it is just handed off to a format method.

Now implement some Strategies of your own. First create an abstract superclass for all of the Strategies (see Listing 6-8). Once again, an interface would be fine, but you can most likely abstract out functionality that can be shared across Strategies. For instance, strings are always formatted by putting single quotes around them.

*Listing 6-8. DatabaseStrategy.java—the Superclass of All Example Database
Strategies*

```java
import java.sql.*;

public abstract class DatabaseStrategy {
  protected String server;
  protected String databaseName;
  protected String user;
  protected String passwd;
  public DatabaseStrategy(String server,
      String databaseName,
      String user,
      String passwd ) {
    this.server = server;
    this.databaseName = databaseName;
    this.user = user;
    this.passwd = passwd;
  }
  public abstract void loadDriver() throws ClassNotFoundException;
  public abstract String generateURL();
  public abstract String format( Object value );
}
```

The first implementation of the Strategy will be for Microsoft Access, and
this is shown in Listing 6-9. Allow for loading the Type 1 JDBC-ODBC driver, generate the URL for an ODBC source, and add the method to format objects for
Access's SQL.

Listing 6-9. MSAccessStrategy.java—Strategy That Helps with Microsoft Access

```java
import java.text.*;

public class MSAccessStrategy extends DatabaseStrategy {
  public MSAccessStrategy (String server,
      String databaseName,
      String user,
      String passwd ) {
      super( server, databaseName, user, password );
  }
  private static final SimpleDateFormat dateFormat =
      new SimpleDateFormat( "#MM-dd-yyyy HH:mm:ss#" );

  public void loadDriver() throws ClassNotFoundException {
```

```
    Class.forName( "sun.jdbc.odbc.JdbcOdbcDriver" );
  }

  public String generateURL() {
    return "jdbc:odbc:" + database;
  }

  public String format( Object value ) {
    if( value == null ) {
      return null;
    }
    Class clazz = value.getClass();
    if( Character.class.equals( clazz ) || char.class.equals( clazz ) ) {
      value = value.toString();
    }
    if( value instanceof String ) {
      StringBuffer stringVal = new StringBuffer( (String) value );
      for( int i = 0; i < stringVal.length(); i++ ) {
        if( stringVal.charAt( i ) == '\'' ) {
          stringVal.insert( i, '\'' );
          i++;
        }
      }
      return "\'" + stringVal + "\'";
    }
    if( value instanceof java.util.Date ) {
      return dateFormat.format( value );
    }
    return value.toString();
  }
}
```

Notice that at the top, you create a SimpleDateFormat that conforms to Access's expectations for dates. Then you list the loadDriver method that loads the JdbcOdbcDriver class. The JdbcOdbcDriver class will register itself when it is loaded. The next method builds a very simple URL prefixed with jdbc:odbc for the JdbcOdbcDriver.

Finally, there is the format method. This method first gets the class from the object handed in. If that class is either Character.class or char.class, then you simply convert it to a string. If the method receives a string, it wraps the object in single quotes. If it receives a Date object, it uses the SimpleDateFormat to lay it out for the database.

Working with Primitive Types

You will note that in the MSAccessStrategy's format method in Listing 6-9, you test not only for Character.class but also for char.class. You might be surprised that the code even compiles. Primitive classes are not often talked about because few people come across them.

I became aware of primitive classes when I was writing a reflection-based persistence toolkit for a project I was working on. I had my Strategies in place, and they were working well when I was manually mapping objects to SQL by calling format for every attribute I wanted added to the SQL, but they failed when I used reflection to get an array of attributes and hand that off to the format method. The class that was returned from the object's getClass method was not the Character.class I expected, but the char.class.

You do not need to check for the char.class or any other primitive class, the way I demonstrate how to use Strategies in this chapter. If you use reflection, though, be aware of them.

Listing 6-10. SQLServerStrategy.java—Strategy for Working with Microsoft SQL Server

```java
import java.text.*;

public class SQLServerStrategy extends DatabaseStrategy {
  public SQLServerStrategy (String server,
      String databaseName,
      String user,
      String passwd ) {
      super( server, databaseName, user, password );
  }
  private SimpleDateFormat dateFormat =
      new SimpleDateFormat( "''MM-dd-yyyy HH:mm:ss''" );

  public void loadDriver() throws ClassNotFoundException {
    Class.forName( "com.microsoft.jdbc.sqlserver.SQLServerDriver" );
  }

  public String generateURL() {
    StringBuffer buffer = new StringBuffer( "jdbc:microsoft:sqlserver://" );
    buffer.append( server );
    buffer.append( ":1433;databasename=" );
```

```
      buffer.append( database );
      buffer.append( ";user=" );
      buffer.append( user );
      if( passwd != null && passwd.length() != 0 ) {
        buffer.append( ";password=" );
        buffer.append( passwd );
      }
      return buffer.toString();
  }


  public String format( Object value ) {
    if( value == null ) {
      return null;
    }
    Class clazz = value.getClass();
    if( Character.class.equals( clazz ) || char.class.equals( clazz ) ) {
      value = value.toString();
    }
    if( value instanceof String ) {
      StringBuffer stringVal = new StringBuffer( (String) value );
      for( int i = 0; i < stringVal.length(); i++ ) {
        if( stringVal.charAt( i ) == '\'' ) {
          stringVal.insert( i, '\'' );
          i++;
        }
      }
      return "\'" + stringVal + "\'";
    }
    if( value instanceof java.util.Date ) {
      return dateFormat.format( value );
    }
    if( Boolean.class.equals( clazz ) || boolean.class.equals( clazz ) ) {
      if( ( (Boolean) value ).booleanValue() ) {
        return "1";
      }
      else {
        return "0";
      }
    }
    return value.toString();
  }
}
```

The Strategy pattern simplifies your class's ability to work with multiple databases. Instead of checking a flag to find out what database the object is working with and acting appropriately, the class simply trusts the Strategy to do the right thing. This also vastly simplifies adding new databases. Now instead of having to go into every method and adding a new database type to check for and act differently for, you can add a new Strategy that handles the new database.

One topic I didn't cover in this section is creation and selection of the Strategy to use. There are many ways you can select a strategy. Your application or system could use a property file and read the Strategy class name from that, and then create an instance of that class using reflection. You can use a Factory object, which is another pattern I did not cover but is described in the book *Design Patterns: Elements of Reusable Object-Oriented Software*. I leave the selection and creation of the Strategy up to you.

Using the Facade Pattern to Simplify Queries

The Facade pattern is a structural pattern. That means its purpose is to help the designer simplify the relationship between objects. This pattern is particularly useful when the system being designed needs to access or use a complex subsystem or library. Essentially, the Facade pattern puts a simple "false front" on the subsystem or library.

The problem arises when you have several classes that make calls to several classes in a library. Each of your classes needs to know the composition of the library in order to do its job. Oftentimes you may be using a fraction of the functionality of the library, but you need to pour through all of the documentation and interfaces to get the work done.

The Facade pattern consists of putting a class or component in front of the library or subsystem. That class or component is the Facade. The Facade makes available the functionality your classes need from the library or subsystem without making everything available. From the outside the Facade looks like a simpler implementation of the library.

By putting a Facade in front of the library, you simplify your interaction with it. You also decouple your classes from the internals of the library. That makes it easier to change libraries at a later date. The Facade also protects your classes from having to change if the library itself changes; you can just update and recompile the Facade.

You can see in Figure 6-3 that the interaction with the library before the Facade was complex and in a sense violated encapsulation. By putting a Facade in front of the library, the classes only need to know about the Facade, not the contents of the library.

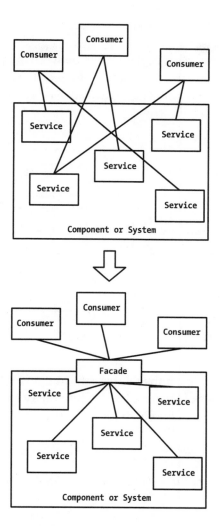

Figure 6-3. System before and after adding the Facade

Using a Facade That Wraps JDBC Queries

Normally when you want to make a call through JDBC to access a database, you need to interact with several JDBC objects. Usually there is a Connection, a Statement, and a ResultSet. This can lead to a lot of redundant code to open and maintain all of these connections. It can also lead to an intimate knowledge about the driver class being used.

One solution to this problem is to create a Facade that will sit in front of the JDBC library and simplify queries to the database. Client classes will interact with the Facade rather than directly with JDBC. With a clean Facade design, you should be able to change from JDBC to another data access library with minimal or no changes to the client classes.

In Figure 6-4, you can see the relationship between the QueryFacade and the Connection, Statement, and ResultSet classes. The QueryFacade will sit in front of these classes, allowing access only through itself. The QueryFacade provides encapsulation of the library.

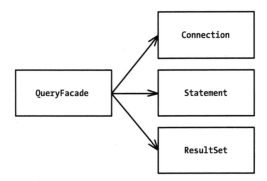

Figure 6-4. Conceptual model for the QueryFacade

The ideal Facade would completely hide the underlying library. You should be able to create an instance of the Facade, execute a query on it, and then iterate through the objects stored in the database (see Listing 6-11).

Listing 6-11. FacadeMain.java

```
QueryFacade facade = new QueryFacade( new EmployeeResultSetMap() );
try {
  Iterator iterator = facade.execute( "SELECT * FROM EMPLOYEES" );
  Employee employee = null;
  while( iterator.hasNext() ) {
    employee = (Employee) iterator.next();
    System.out.println( employee.getGuid() );
  }
}
catch( SQLException e ) {
  e.printStackTrace();
}
finally {
  facade.close();
}
```

Here a QueryFacade is created. A SQL query is handed to the QueryFacade and an Iterator is returned. The Iterator knows how to map the result set to an object through the EmployeeResultMap object that was part of the Facade's constructor. In this way, you can run through the results of a query without dealing with JDBC.

In Listing 6-11, JDBC is not entirely hidden. This is easily remedied. You could have created a Facade-related exception to wrap the SQLException. You could also have created a dynamic mapping between the result set and the employee object either through an XML mapping or reflection.

Inside the QueryFacade

The QueryFacade itself, shown in Listing 6-12, will wrap JDBC work. It will hide the connection, statement, and result set. This will also help to ensure that connections are always closed correctly.

Listing 6-12. QueryFacade.java Wrapping JDBC

```java
import java.sql.*;
import java.util.*;

public class QueryFacade {
  private ResultSetMap map;
  private String query;
  private Connection connection;
  private Statement statement;
  private ResultSet resultSet;

  public QueryFacade( String query, ResultSetMap map ) {
    this.query = query;
    this.map = map;
    try {
      Class.forName( "com.microsoft.jdbc.sqlserver.SQLServerDriver" );
    }
    catch( ClassNotFoundException e ) {
      e.printStackTrace();
    }
  }

  public Iterator execute() throws SQLException {
    connection = getConnection();
    statement = connection.createStatement();
    resultSet = statement.executeQuery(query);
    return new FacadeIterator();
```

```
      }

    public void close() {
      if( resultSet != null ) {
        try {
          resultSet.close();
        }
        catch( SQLException e ){}
      }
      if( statement != null ) {
        try{
          statement.close();
        }
        catch( SQLException e ) {}
      }
      if( connection != null ) {
        try {
          connection.close();
        }
        catch( SQLException e ){}
      }
    }

    private Connection getConnection() throws SQLException {
      String url =
"jdbc:microsoft:sqlserver://gemini:1433;databasename=strategy_pattern;user=sa";
      return DriverManager.getConnection( url );
    }
    ...
}
```

The first part of the listing should be fairly clear after the coverage of JDBC. The constructor loads the Driver class. The constructor also takes the query and ResultSetMap as arguments. The next part is the execute method. This executes the query, and then returns an Iterator. I will discuss the Iterator in a moment. The third part of this listing is the close method, which closes the connection, statement, and result set. This greatly simplifies the maintenance of connections outside of this class. Finally, there is the private getConnection method. This method is pretty straightforward: It obtains a JDBC connection for the execute method.

The QueryFacade sits in front of the JDBC Connection, Statement, and ResultSet classes. Instead of interacting with these classes, client code makes calls to the QueryFacade. This reduces the classes that the client code needs to know about from three to one.

Supporting the QueryFacade

There are two parts necessary for this Facade that I have not talked about yet: the ResultSetMap, shown in Listing 6-13, and the FacadeIterator. Neither of these classes are part of the Facade pattern, but they do help to create a clean object-oriented QueryFacade.

Listing 6-13. ResultSetMap.java

```java
import java.sql.*;

public interface ResultSetMap {
  public Object convert( ResultSet resultSet ) throws SQLException;
}
```

The ResultSetMap is an interface that has one method. The purpose of the method is to convert the current location in the result set to a business object. This piece could be replaced with any kind of mapping. I chose a simple class to keep the example clean.

The way the ResultSetMap works is a JDBC result set is handed in to the convert method. The convert method will create a new instance of the business object, and then call the various getType(columnName) methods on the result set to get the values and set them on the business object. The business object will then be returned. The ResultSetMap object will be used exclusively by the FacadeIterator.

The FacadeIterator shown in Listing 6-14 acts as an adapter. The FacadeIterator wraps the result set and makes it appear as an Iterator. This helps remove coupling to JDBC. This can be a great advantage if you need to switch relational databases.

Listing 6-14. QueryFacade.java That Provides a Custom Iterator

```java
import java.sql.*;
import java.util.*;

public class QueryFacade {
  ...
  private class FacadeIterator implements Iterator {
    private Object next;
    FacadeIterator() {
      next();
    }

    public boolean hasNext() {
      return next != null;
    }
```

```
    public Object next() {
      Object current = next;
      try {
        if( resultSet.next() ) {
          next = map.convert( resultSet );
        }
        else {
          next = null;
        }
        return current;
      }
      catch( SQLException e ) {
        throw new NoSuchElementException( e.getMessage() );
      }
    }

    public void remove() {
      throw new UnsupportedOperationException();
    }
  }
}
```

The FacadeIterator is a private inner class to the QueryFacade. The class relies on the QueryFacade's resultSet and map instance variables to work. When the class is instantiated, it calls its own next method so it knows how to respond to hasNext. Every call to next moves the result set by one, then it uses the map object to obtain the business object from the database row.

The hasNext method simply responds with whether the previous call to next turns up another object. The remove method is not supported, which is not uncommon in Iterators and appropriately throws an UnsupportedOperationException.

Summary

I have shown how to apply design patterns for object persistence. The Builder is a great pattern for creating SQL. The Strategy pattern helps in making applications or systems flexible and extensible. The Facade pattern can help to hide the internals of JDBC to simplify queries.

This is just a beginning—there are many more patterns that you may find helpful. Go to http://www.c2.com and look around in the Portland Patterns Repository, which features a lot of good material on this subject. As I mentioned at the beginning of the chapter, patterns can help you improve your design beyond your level of experience.

CHAPTER 7

Unit Testing Persistence Layers

ONCE UPON A MIDNIGHT DREARY, while I pondered, weak and weary, fearing my code changes had caused more problems than they fixed, I ran my unit tests and checked it all in. There is no feeling of confidence like that provided by good unit tests. Unfortunately, too many people still believe that it is too much work to create unit tests. I believe unit tests save time and code.

First off, let me talk about what a unit test is. A *unit test* is a type of white box testing. *White box testing* is when you know how the thing being tested works, as compared to black box testing and gray box testing. In *black box testing*, you have no idea how the thing being tested works, so you can only test inputs and outputs. *Gray box testing* is when you test from the outside like black box testing, but you understand how the code works and that guides your tests. All three types of tests are important.

In white box testing, the person who writes the code is the same person who writes the test. Specifically, this person is testing known units of the system. This gives an advantage because the author of the functionality knows exactly how it is supposed to act. The downside is the author can only test the unit in ways he expects the unit to be used. Often a second person will try to use the unit in ways that are unexpected by the author of the code.

While unit testing is not a complete testing solution, it is very valuable in the development of a system. Unit testing complemented with functional or system testing will significantly reduce bugs in that system. Parts of the system the functional testers should not be concerned with such as valid arguments to a method are the parts of the system best covered by the unit test. Functional testing covers how the units work together.

Because unit tests are largely automatic, they give a wonderful sense of security to bug fixing and refactoring existing code. There really is no feeling on earth like making a huge change across 20 or 30 classes in order to fix a bug, then running the unit tests and seeing that the system is still stable after the fix. It is with confidence that you then check the code into the version control system. Anyone who has experienced this once will know how important the tests are. Anyone who experiences it twice will know there is no better way to code.

I cannot count the number of times I have made a simple change to some code that I thought no one else was dependent on. Ran the unit tests and been amazed by the things that broke. My first instinct is that someone checked in bad code, but more often than not my simple change broke code that I thought was unrelated. Since I didn't know about the relationship, it would have taken quite a bit of time and energy to debug it.

Another great use of unit tests is to document a system for other developers. Code is organic and during development changes constantly. Maintaining method comments, while important, can be cumbersome, particularly when those comments explain the inner workings of a method. Those types of comments often get overlooked when a "quick fix" is applied.

Unit tests, on the other hand, need to be up to date with the method in order to pass. Very often a quick fix is applied, the developer runs the tests, and the tests fail because the unit test is out of date. Since she cannot check the code in until the unit test works, she fixes the test, thereby fixing the documentation.

Now when another developer wants to know how to use a method, he looks at the unit tests. Good unit tests will show valid input values and valid returns from the tested method. The tests will show both how to use the method and how not to use it.

JUnit: A Java Unit-Testing Framework

JUnit is not the only unit-testing framework for Java. It is, however, the most commonly used one. It is so common, in fact, that for many people it has become synonymous with unit testing.

JUnit has spawned children in many different languages. There is NUnit for .NET, PhpUnit, and many more. Most people think exclusively of JUnit when Java unit testing is discussed. For that reason, in this chapter I will focus on using JUnit. First I will give a unit testing overview showing you how to write and run unit tests. Then I will discuss various ways to unit test persistence layers.

Dissecting JUnit

JUnit, like all Java-based frameworks, is simply a collection of classes. The way you use JUnit is to extend a class and add your own tests. JUnit also comes with many test running tools including a Java Swing–based user interface, an AWT user interface, and a console-based user interface.

The smallest part of unit testing with JUnit is an assertion. An *assertion* is how the test knows whether it passed or failed. Essentially an assertion is a method call that either receives a true value or throws an exception. So in a test, you would tell the assertion call that either the value being passed is equal to an expected value or an exception needs to be thrown.

Because assertions work at as low a level as true values from comparisons, anything can be tested. You could test the Java Virtual Machine's addition functionality by executing an assertion comparing an expected value with the addition result:

```
assertTrue( 5 == ( 3 + 2 ) );
```

Assertions can also be used to test an object's equals methods:

```
assertTrue( obj1.equals( obj2 ) );
```

Assertions are contained within tests. In JUnit, the test is a method on a class. The purpose of the test is to test some unit of functionality in an application or system. Often the unit being tested is a business method on a domain or process object. For example, if I had a method that summed all the integers in a collection, I would write a test method that exercised the sum method and verified it was working correctly. Listing 7-1 shows the simple object I want to test.

Listing 7-1. Object That Calculates the Sum of Integers

```
package com.apress.javapersistence.chapter07;

public class IntegerSum {
    public int sum(int[] integers) {
        int result = 0;

        for(int i = 0; i < integers.length; i++) {
            result += integers[i];
        }

        return result;
    }
}
```

In Listing 7-2, you can see a very simple JUnit unit test that works on the object in Listing 7-1. I am placing this code here simply to show a basic unit test. All of the parts of a JUnit test will be covered later in this chapter.

Listing 7-2. Simple Unit Test for Summing Object

```java
package com.apress.javapersistence.chapter07;

import junit.framework.TestCase;

public class TestIntegerSum extends TestCase {
    public void testSum() {
        int integer0 = 10;
        int integer1 = 12;
        int integer2 = 14;
        int expected = integer0 + integer1 + integer2;

        int[] integers = new int[3];
        integers[0] = integer0;
        integers[1] = integer1;
        integers[2] = integer2;

        IntegerSum calculator = new IntegerSum();

        int result = calculator.sum(integers);

        assertEquals(expected, result);
    }
}
```

Tests in JUnit are methods of a subclass of TestCase. A *test case* is a class that holds a group of related tests. While related tests are methods on one class, instances of that class will only execute one method for their entire life. For example, if I had a test case named TestShoppingCart and it had three tests on it—testAddItem, testCalculateTotal, and testGetItem—in order to run all three tests I would need to create three instances of the TestShoppingCart class. Each instance would reflect one of the tests.

The way this is enforced is that the constructor takes a String argument. If the constructor's argument is the name of a method on the class, then that is the test that will be run by the test case. A second way to run a specific test is to override the runTest method on TestCase. This approach is a little less flexible.

In most uses of JUnit, a test case is directly related to a single class in the application or system. So for every significant business object or process there would be a corresponding test case. All the tests on the test case would exercise and test the methods on the related object.

It is often desirable to run multiple tests together. In order to do this, you group your tests in a TestSuite. A *test suite* is a Java object whose purpose is to group related tests, possibly in a specified order, which can be helpful if you want to run an "add" test followed by a "delete" test.

The next section will show an example of creating a unit test, including a test case and a test suite. All of this will be wrapped in describing a procedure called *test-driven development*.

Test-Driven Development

The first thing I will show you with JUnit is how to use it to minimize the amount of code you need to write. The way this works is by writing your tests first. Then you write just enough code to make your tests pass. Once your unit tests pass, you move on to the next part of the system.

Parts of this way of testing and coding can seem counterintuitive for two reasons: First, it often feels to people new to unit testing that they are writing more code by writing unit tests, and second, it is unfamiliar because most of us feel that we don't get off track very often and know exactly what is needed for the task at hand. So the argument becomes, "I will just implement this part because we are under a tight deadline, and I will write unit tests on the next part."

These are both incorrect assumptions. On various projects, I have personally written much more code than I needed because I didn't fully understand the problem. I have also spent much time troubleshooting and debugging code that I didn't fully understand. If I had had unit tests to keep me on track, I would have done a better job on those projects.

You don't have to test your code into existence to get the full advantage of unit testing. I do, however, suggest you try it a couple times. You may find you like it.

The first step in test-driven development is writing a test case. A test case in JUnit is a Java class that extends `junit.framework.TestCase` and follows a couple of conventions. The first convention is that you should implement a constructor that takes a string as an argument. Secondly, all the unit test methods should begin with a lower case "test" followed by the name of the method being tested. Thirdly, you will often want to implement a static "suite" method that returns a `junit.framework.TestSuite` object. In current versions of JUnit, you no longer need to implement a separate `suite` method, but it does provide you with the ability to order your tests.

The test methods will do work with the business objects and run various "assert" calls to ensure that the results returned from those business methods are what were expected. The assert methods are inherited from the `TestCase` super-class. In the current JUnit implementation, the assert method names have been changed from `assert`, which is a keyword and part of Java 1.4, to `assertEquals`, `assertNotNull`, `assertNull`, `assertSame`, and `assertTrue`. The way it works is if an assert fails, the test stops, a test failure is logged, and then the rest of the tests are run. In the end, JUnit produces a report showing how many tests passed and which tests failed.

In test-driven development, or "testing into existence," you first write a test case for the functionality you want to implement. For these examples, I will walk you through unit testing a very basic shopping cart.

Your first decisions are what the name of the class you are testing will be, where it will reside, and what the first functionality you want from the class to be. For this example, assume you are testing a class name ShoppingCart. It will reside in a package named com.apress.javapersistence.chapter07.bo, and the first thing you want to test is adding items to the cart.

Because of these decisions, you know that your first test case will be named TestShoppingCart. It will also reside in the com.apress.javapersistence. chapter07.bo package. Finally, the first test method on the class will be testAddItem.

The convention of prefixing test cases with "Test" is just that—a convention. You could suffix your test class names or come up with your own naming strategy. I would suggest following one convention, though, to make it easier to remove those classes from any deployed JAR files. If you do decided to prefix your test cases with "Test", you will quickly notice that your tests are grouped together in your package.

Let's look at a unit-test test case. Listing 7-3 shows a Java class that extends a superclass named TestCase. Defined within that class is a method that is prefixed with the word "test". Below that is a suite method and a main method that will be explained in a moment.

Listing 7-3. Example of a Basic JUnit Unit Test

```java
package com.apress.javapersistence.chapter07.bo;

import junit.framework.*;

public class TestShoppingCart extends TestCase {
    public TestShoppingCart(String testName) {
        super(testName);
    }

    public void testAddItem() throws Exception {
        ShoppingCart cart = new ShoppingCart();
        Item item = new Item();
        cart.addItem(item);
        assertEquals(1, cart.getNumberItems() );
        assertEquals(item, cart.getItem( 0 ) );
    }
```

```
public static Test suite() {
    TestSuite suite = new TestSuite(TestShoppingCart.class);
    return suite;
}

public static void main(String[] args) {
    junit.textui.TestRunner.run(suite());
}
}
```

As this listing shows, you extend `TestCase` to create a unit test. You implement the required constructor that takes a string, and add your first test method. Keep in mind that neither the `ShoppingCart` object nor the `Item` object exists yet. This method shows how you will use them when they are written.

You have a `suite` method that simply returns a suite containing all tests on this class. A suite is a bundle of tests. Each test can be explicitly added to the suite, or you can simply add a class to the suite, in which case all methods that begin with the word "test" will be added to the suite.

Finally, you have a `main` method that allows you to run this unit test alone. Running individual unit tests is one of the most powerful features of JUnit. You can write very little code, and then test it independently of the rest of the system. Adding a `main` method to the test class gives you a finer-grained testing mechanism.

Now that you have your first unit test, you can see exactly how the `ShoppingCart` object will be used. If you had an incorrect understanding of the problem it would quickly manifest itself before any business logic was written. This is kind of like looking at code that does not exist yet. You can look into the future and see how the shopping cart will work.

Your next step, believe it or not, is to try to compile the unit test. This probably sounds insane, since you have not implemented a `ShoppingCart` class or `Item` class, but imagine how hard it would be to troubleshoot if it did somehow compile. You might as well compile it and make sure that you haven't missed something basic. The reason this might compile is because the classpath could include someone else's `ShoppingCart` and/or `Item` class.

The next step is to implement just enough code to let the unit test compile but not run. For this, you will create a stub class. All methods shall throw an `UnsupportedOperationException` or return null if you prefer. Listing 7-4 shows a basic stub class meant to allow the test to compile but not run.

Listing 7-4. Stub Class to Support Unit Test Compiling

```java
package com.apress.javapersistence.chapter07.bo;

public class ShoppingCart {
    public void addItem( Item item ) {
        throw new UnsupportedOperationException( "todo" );
    }

    public int getNumberItems() {
        throw new UnsupportedOperationException( "todo" );
    }

    public Item getItem( int index ) {
        throw new UnsupportedOperationException( "todo" );
    }
}
```

Now you try to compile again. The first error you should see is that you forgot to create an Item object. Quickly remedy this by creating a class called Item with no methods or attributes. Once again, you are trying to get your test to compile first.

When you compile the test class this time, it should compile without error. The next step is to run the test. This is an important step. I have run tests against stub classes and had them pass. This is because I was comparing incorrect values in my assert calls. The important thing is that those same tests would have passed with a broken implementation as well. Run your test just to be sure. On running the test, you should see a message like the one in Listing 7-5.

Listing 7-5. JUnit Unit Test Output

```
.E
Time: 0.054
There was 1 error:
1) testAddItem(com.apress.javapersistence.chapter07.bo.TestShoppingCart)
java.lang.UnsupportedOperationException: todo
...
com.apress.javapersistence.chapter07.bo.TestShoppingCart.main(TestShoppingCart.
java:54)
FAILURES!!!
Tests run: 1,   Failures: 0,   Errors: 1
```

This is a good failure. If you didn't see this message, then you were interacting with another ShoppingCart, or your test was bad. Perhaps you had reversed your test's logic or made some other basic mistake. If that had been the case and you had not tried to run the test, you might not have found the bad test for quite a while. Just recently I found a unit test that had passed for months that was testing broken code; obviously it was not my unit test ;^). Since you did see this message, it is now time to implement the ShoppingCart class.

Here is where the big time savings comes in. Since you have decided exactly how the class should act, and since you have written tests for every contingency you expect the class to face, you now only have to write enough code to make the tests pass. Then you stop. Let me repeat that: Only write enough code to make the tests pass then *stop*. If you write anything more than the minimum amount of code to support the tests, you are wasting your time and possibly someone else's money.

The reason this works is because if your code is to be used in a mission-critical or life-or-death situation, you write a lot of unit tests. The unit tests will help make your critical software more robust. You determine the level you will test to. Also keep in mind that you can add tests later. If a bug is found a month from now, you can add a test to your test case and ensure that bug does not rear its ugly head again.

Just enough code in your shopping cart would consist of adding a collection of items to the class. You then have the addItem method add to the items collection. The getNumberItems method returns the size of the collection. The getItem method returns an item for the given index. These additions appear in Listing 7-6.

Listing 7-6. Complete Shopping Cart

```
package com.apress.javapersistence.chapter07.bo;

public class ShoppingCart {
    private List items = new ArrayList();

    public void addItem( Item item ) {
        items.add( item );
    }

    public int getNumberItems() {
        return items.size();
    }

    public Item getItem( int index ) {
        return (Item) items.get( index );
    }
}
```

Now when you run your unit tests, they should pass. If a test does not pass, you need to either look at the unit test itself or the class's implementation. Fix any problems you find and run the test again. Keep fixing the bugs and running the test until the test passes.

Based on my experience I have decided for myself and the projects that I lead that unit tests do provide value. Therefore I now write the test first and get this extra bonus of not writing the wrong class or extra code. This reduces bugs and helps my productivity, far offsetting any time spent writing the tests themselves.

Run All Tests with a TestPackage Unit Test

Test suites are great, but they are and should be limited to one class. For this reason, it is desirable to create a test case that reflects an entire package. A natural name for this test is TestPackage, though I have seen this same concept with many different names. The suite method on a TestPackage would contain all of the suite methods of all of the test cases in that package. It would also contain all of the suites of all of the subpackage's TestPackages.

In this way, you can run an entire package and all of its subpackages very quickly and easily. This becomes more important as the system grows. Listing 7-7 shows a basic TestPackage class. This same basic class should exist in every package; only the added tests in the suite method should change.

Listing 7-7. TestPackage for Testing All Classes in a Package

```
package com.apress.javapersistence.chapter07.bo;

import junit.framework.*;

public class TestPackage extends TestCase {
    public TestPackage(String s) {
      super(s);
    }

    public static Test suite() {
      TestSuite suite = new TestSuite();

      suite.addTest( TestShoppingCart.suite() );
      suite.addTest( TestUSMoney.suite() );

      return suite;
    }
```

```
public static void main(String[] args) {
    junit.textui.TestRunner.run(suite());
}
}
```

Now you have a mechanism for running one test in the system or all tests in all systems. In any project, all tests should be run at least once a day. Developers should run tests on the code they are working on before every check in.

You can also use unit tests to help with debugging. Because unit tests are self-contained, you do not need to debug the entire application before getting to the code that is giving you trouble. Using your favorite IDE, put break points in your unit tests and then step into the code that is giving you trouble.

Unit Testing Data Access Objects and Persistence Layers

Unit testing Data Access Objects (DAOs) or any type of persistence layer is not really any different from testing any other type of Java object. The main issue to be aware of is the state of the database at any given point in the testing. If for instance you have a test that adds a new shopping cart with a unique identifier of "34673", the second time you run that test you should get an exception because the primary key uniqueness would be violated.

There are several ways to maintain the state of your database for unit testing. The first and least recommended is manually. You can rebuild the database before you run your unit tests. Finally, you can ensure that all objects added are removed and any objects removed are re-added.

The first method is the least likely to be successful. Trying to manually correct the database after unit testing is in direct conflict with the principles of automated unit testing. Oftentimes this is the method that is used initially in unit testing though.

There are many ways you can rebuild the database before running unit tests. You can manually copy a database into place depending on the database you are going against. You can write tools that will drop all tables and rebuild them. Another option is to delete all records from the table and then add the records the test is interested in.

These processes can be added to the unit tests themselves. JUnit provides a facility to run methods before and after tests run. These are called setUp and tearDown. It is possible to build the database in a TestCase's setUp method.

There is a great open source framework, named DbUnit, that supports this type of building and clearing the database, and it's available at http://dbunit.sourceforge.net. DbUnit can be very helpful, but the downside is that it is very relational in concept and not very object oriented. With DbUnit you create in memory data sets and tables that your tests run against.

It is also possible to wrap all the tests in a suite with a call to methods that will build the database to an expected state for the tests to run. This, however, still has the problem of tests affecting the state of the database for other tests.

If possible I suggest running the tests with a clean insert. What I mean is that the setUp method first deletes the contents of the tables, and then adds records. The tearDown method does nothing in this case. The positive of this approach is that the tests are not affected by the state of the database. If you do this you may want to have multiple copies of the database so that any sample data you have is not lost.

The final way I suggest is to create methods that insert and delete objects from the database. These methods can be called by tests when they are needed. Usually I create these tests by first writing a test for the insert functionality. I then break the actual inserting code out into a separate method that the test calls. The same thinking goes for the delete functionality. I then change my insert test to call the delete method at the end to restore the database.

This will not work in many situations where there are foreign key constraints or referential integrity, but for simple testing it is the easiest to maintain—particularly since rebuilding the database in any way can be very time consuming and deter developers from running tests.

More on JUnit

The first part of this chapter is meant to be an introduction to JUnit. There is much more to learn and many more best practices that I have not covered here. For more good information concerning JUnit, check out the framework's site at http://www.junit.org. There are even links on the site for similar unit testing tools for other languages.

The original JUnit framework was written by Kent Beck and Erich Gamma; the product is released under the IBM Common Public License, which means it is free to use. The project is hosted at Source Forge, and anyone can contribute code or suggestions.

Testing JDBC Using Mock Objects

Mock Objects is a testing framework that is intended for very fine-grained unit testing. The general principal behind the framework is to run complex tests in a very controlled environment. Often the tests are intended to be run out of container. What that means is that services are emulated for the tests to run. For this book, that would mean running tests without needing a real database to run against. This can be particularly useful if developers are limited in the databases they can work against.

Basically with Mock Objects, instead of creating a real database connection to test, you create a mock connection. This connection not only returns the data you tell it to, it also can verify that requests were made to it correctly.

For example, if you have some code that uses a prepared statement, you can ensure that all the arguments were passed to the prepared statement. Now, instead of ensuring that the correct objects get returned from your DAOs, you can ensure that your DAOs are behaving exactly as expected.

Let's take a step back. Mock Objects is a framework, and more than that a concept that you can learn more about at http://www.mockobjects.com. The idea is that you can create fake (mock) objects to run your tests against. In doing this, you can obtain a great deal of control over how your tests run.

All that the Mock Objects framework provides is a bunch of objects that implement existing Java interfaces. In reference to Java persistence, they provide a `MockConnection`, `MockStatement`, `MockPreparedStatement`, `MockResultSet`, and many more classes. These classes make it easy to write tests against Mock Objects.

There are many ways in which this provides value when unit testing. For instance, it can be very difficult to simulate a database disconnection in a standard unit test. With Mock Objects, you can throw exceptions whenever you wish to. This allows you to make your code very robust.

As I mentioned before, another value of using Mock Objects is to ensure that the expected JDBC objects are references. Say, for instance, you expect your business objects to be built from the results of three different prepared statements. With Mock Objects, you can verify that all three prepared statements were actually used.

Writing Tests with Mock Objects

The first thing you need to think about when using Mock Objects is exactly what you want to test and how to best get to that functionality. For example, you may want to change the structure of your DAO methods to be more granular. While this may seem like a bad idea because you are considering changing your code to support testing, it actually makes sense in the long run.

By making your methods more granular and passing objects like connections into those methods, you actually create very clear separation between different parts of your DAOs. Each method ends up being focused on one task. This will help with long term maintenance and can often help reduce bugs.

How does this work? In regular unit testing, you would test coarse-grained methods. You might have a method that simply tests for finding a shopping cart. In Listing 7-8, you can see a test that calls the `findFor` method on a DAO and ensures that the cart contains its expected values.

Listing 7-8. Coarse-Grained Unit Test for Finding a Shopping Cart

```java
public void testFindFor() throws Exception {
    String cartUid = "1";
    int expectedItems = 2;
    ShoppingCart cart = dao.findFor( cartUid );
    assertEquals( expectedItems, cart.getNumberItems() );
}
```

While this test is important, if it fails, you have no idea why it failed. This code tests the DAO very broadly; either it passes or fails—you get no information regarding why it failed. Sometimes the logic can be sufficiently complex that you want to perform much more specific unit testing.

An example is writing a test that ensures that a shopping cart is created correctly with values from the result set. In Listing 7-9, you see a test where a mock result set is created. The result set is passed to a fine-grained method on your DAO, which creates a shopping cart from its values. Finally, you verify that all expected values are retrieved from the result set. If the uid is not retrieved from the result set, the unit test will fail at the verification call.

Listing 7-9. Fine-Grained Unit Test for Creating a Shopping Cart

```java
public void testCreateShoppingCart() throws Exception {
    String uid = "1";
    MockSingleRowResultSet resultSet = new MockSingleRowResultSet();
    resultSet.addExpectedNamedValues( new String[]{ "uid" },
        new Object[]{ uid } );

    ShoppingCart cart = dao.createShoppingCart(resultSet);
    assertNotNull(cart);
    assertEquals( uid, cart.getUid() );

    resultSet.verify();
}
```

Summary

This chapter has addressed unit testing for data access objects and persistence layers. Specifically, I talked about using JUnit to help with test-driven development. I talked about the time savings and confidence that can be achieved with good unit testing practices. This chapter discussed how to test a Java persistence layer. I even talked about using frameworks such as Mock Objects to gain greater depth in your unit testing.

By writing your unit tests, you can change code safely and quickly. It is easier to experiment with different solutions if you know that you are not breaking other code. You will also find that writing less and simpler code is a result of writing unit tests. This value is very important and cannot be emphasized enough.

In test-driven development, it is important to remember to go through all the steps. Write the test and watch the compile fail. Write just enough code to compile the test and run it and watch the test fail. Write just enough code to make the test pass and then stop. In running the tests that you know will fail, you increase your safety net. The one time that you don't run those tests against stubs is the time that you will spend a lot of effort debugging code that should never have passed in the first place.

Choosing your strategy for unit testing your persistence layer is particularly important. Select a method that best fits your project and your project team. Pick a method that is easiest to implement and will be most likely used by project team members.

When using Mock Objects, realize that the intention is toward a very granular unit test. Use the verify feature in the framework. These guidelines can lead to very comprehensive unit testing, and can lead to a good design in your persistence layer.

Look for ways to integrate unit testing into your development cycle. Some people have tests automatically run before adding code to version control. Many teams have processes automatically run every day that tests entire systems. Look at other frameworks that can help with your unit testing. Products like Cactus can test servlets and EJBs in your system. HttpUnit can find problems in the output of JSPs. Be creative, you will feel more confident in your code.

CHAPTER 8

Enterprise JavaBeans: Container Managed Persistence 2.0

ON JANUARY 6, 1482, THE PEOPLE of Paris were awakened by the tumultuous clanging of all the bells in the city. Container Managed Persistence had reached maturity. Actually, the specification was finalized August 14, 2001, but who cares about dates. We finally have a specification that allows for complex automatic persistence of our entity beans. And we are about to get another revision in the EJB 2.1 specification.

To talk about Container Managed Persistence (CMP), we first need to put it in context. CMP is part of Sun's Enterprise JavaBeans (EJB) specification. Enterprise JavaBeans are distributed components, which means that you can share functionality between different applications. EJBs are broken down into three different types: *session beans* do work and contain business logic, *message beans* react to messages and perform work, and *entity beans* represent data.

Since entity beans represent data in an application, Container Managed Persistence applies specifically to entity beans. As there are many good books on the topic of Enterprise JavaBeans, including *Enterprise JavaBeans 2.1* by Rob Castaneda, Stefan Denninger, Ingo Peters (Apress. ISBN: 1-59059-088-0), I will therefore focus primarily on CMP with just a brief and high-level overview of EJBs.

Unlike previous chapters, CMP is not a specification in itself; it is instead a part of a larger specification. The EJB specification defines Enterprise Java components. Often EJBs are distributed components. The EJB specification defines how these components should be written, how they are deployed, and how these objects can interact. The specification also specifies how data from entity beans can be stored.

In the beginning, entity beans had one type of persistence, called Bean Managed Persistence (BMP). The code covered in Chapter 5 shows what Bean Managed Persistence is: code in which persistence is handled by the developers.

In the EJB specification 1.1, CMP was finalized. With the release of the EJB 2.0 specification, there have been many improvements and changes to the specification. In fact, so many changes have been made that the current specification is not backwards compatible with the 1.1 specification. All new development of entity beans should be done using the 2.0 specification, and that is what this chapter will focus on.

CMP provides a great deal of flexibility in the way entity beans are stored. Like all of the J2EE specifications, Sun has spent a lot of time defining specific roles with specific responsibilities. The developer of the component does not need to know exactly where or how the object will be stored. She can trust that the data will make it into a persistent storage mechanism.

Where and how the object is stored is specified through the application server's deployment tools at deployment time. It is in the deployment tools that the deployer decides what database to use, what relationships are available, and whether there are dependencies. Often the deployer is able to modify the tool-generated SQL to conform to deployment requirements.

The way this information is conveyed at deployment time is in deployment descriptors. A *deployment descriptor* is an XML file that describes how the EJB shall be persisted. The deployment descriptor has the responsibility to describe a lot more about the EJB than just the persistence.

The CMP abstraction further allows for storage in many different types of storage mechanisms. An application server can use an object database, or even XML flat files. Most often you will find CMP being used to store objects to relational databases.

The rest of this chapter will cover a brief introduction to EJBs. I will then delve into the specifics of CMP 2.0. Finally, the chapter will show some concrete examples of CMP using Sun's J2EE Reference Implementation.

Parts of an Entity Enterprise JavaBean

Before I go too far, I want to give a basic introduction of Enterprise JavaBeans and what they consist of. This will give us a common point of reference as we move forward in the chapter. A typical entity EJB consists of at minimum four parts: home (`EJBHome`) and remote (`EJBObject`) interfaces, the bean itself, and the deployment descriptor. A fifth part that is optional, but important for CMP, are the local interfaces, which I will talk about a little later in this chapter.

The first part of an entity bean is the home interface. The home interface is a factory interface that is used for creating, finding, and removing entity beans. Developers will create a Java interface and define it in the deployment descriptor. Upon deployment, the application server creates objects that support that interface.

The remote interface is a Java interface that used by consumers of an entity bean to interact with it. As with the home interface, the developer creates a simple Java interface and indicates its role in the deployment descriptor. The application server in turn generates actual objects to support the interface. Although an object implementing the interface is created, it is simply a remote proxy to the actual bean class.

Next there is the bean class, which functionally implements the prior two interfaces. Where the home interface will have a create method, the bean class will have a corresponding ejbCreate method. Where the remote interface will have business methods, the bean will have matching business methods. A call to the home and remote interfaces actually trigger method calls on this underlying bean class.

Finally, the deployment descriptor is an XML file that ties all of the preceding interfaces and bean class together. Additionally, the deployment descriptor describes to an application server and deployment tool various properties of the entity bean. Transaction management for methods will be described here. This is also where Container Managed Persistence is described for the EJB.

There are two more optional but very important interfaces for the EJB: local (EJBLocalObject) and local home (EJBLocalHome). These interfaces are used within the same runtime environment. A remote client will access the remote and home interfaces, but locally running classes will rely on the local and local home interfaces; this includes other EJBs and even servlets running on the application server.

In Figure 8-1, you can see how these interfaces relate. Specifically, you can see that external clients use the remote interfaces to interact with the entity bean. Consumers of the bean that exists inside the container will use the local interfaces.

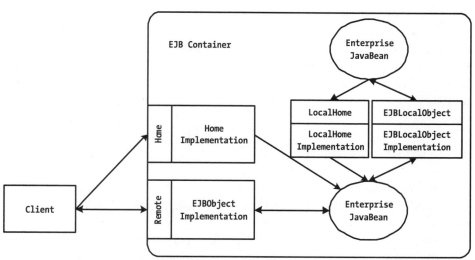

Figure 8-1. Parts of an entity Enterprise JavaBean

Once again, this is not meant to be a comprehensive explanation of EJBs. For that I suggest reading any of the many good books on EJBs. This section should simply give an overview to help you understand the context to which CMP is pertinent.

Container Managed Persistence Contracts

Many parts of the specification dictate how the EJB needs to be written to utilize Container Managed Persistence. These include how persistent fields are defined, what interfaces can provide access to relationships, and how the finder methods need to be written. In this section, I will cover these parts of the specification.

One of the first aspects that differentiates a CMP entity bean from a Bean Managed Persistence entity bean is that a CMP entity bean is an abstract class, whereas a fully implemented BMP entity bean cannot be an abstract class. The reason for this is that the application server creates the concrete class with which all client code will interact. When the application server creates the concrete class, all of the persistence-related abstract methods are fulfilled.

In the same vein, it is not possible for the abstract class to interact directly with persistent fields. Instead, the bean will interact with the abstract accessor methods representing these fields. In other words, if I want my bean to contain a property called `name`, I would create abstract methods named `getName` and `setName` per the JavaBean specification. Specify all fields by adding `cmp-field` elements to the deployment descriptor.

Another important part of the class contract is that only local interfaces and the bean itself can work with relationships. Remote interfaces shall not contain any relationship methods. What this means is that helper methods need to be provided for remote clients to work with relationships. We will look at this more in a little bit.

Persistent Fields

Persistent fields are fields that will be stored in the database. Obviously not all fields need to be stored. For those that do there are several requirements, some of which we have seen already.

One important requirement for persistent fields is that they must be either Java primitives or classes that implement `java.io.Serializable`. This shouldn't be too surprising, since this is the same sort of data that can be persisted through serialization. While it is possible to store serializable objects, I don't recommend it. The reason is that while primitives are easily and consistently stored in most any sort of data store, there is no way to know how the serialized objects will be stored. They could be stored as blobs, or in some database-specific object store.

Objects and fields returned from the EJBs are copies of the data; modifying the value does not affect the data store. To change a value in the data store, you need to set new values on the bean itself.

In some cases it may be desirable to have persistent data that is available to the bean while not being made available to clients. So while the persistent fields need to be defined on the bean and in the deployment descriptor, they do not need to be on the remote interface. This gives the ability to add concrete methods on the bean that use the persistent fields, which in turn are made available to the client.

This becomes valuable when you want to group multiple fields together into a value object. For example, if your database stores zip code data in two fields, and you want to return the data in a single call, you would create a class called ZipCode. Your bean would have methods called getZipCodeFirstFive, getZipCodeLastFour, and getZipCode. The first two methods would be abstract and described as container managed in your deployment descriptor. The last method would be concrete and use the first two to create a ZipCode object. In your remote interface, you would list only the getZipCode method of the three.

Primary Keys

The *primary key* is a special persistent field. It can be either a single value or a compound value. If you want a compound key, you need to place the parts of the key in a single class that can be used. Regardless, the key must be a serializable value. The primary key cannot be a primitive type.

This is the field that is used to uniquely identify an entity bean. All of the discussions in earlier chapters apply here as well. You need to be aware of your uniqueness requirement for these keys.

Relationships

Relationships are situations where beans are connected in some way. The connection between an employee and his address is an example of a relationship. Container Managed Persistence allows many different types complex relationships between entity beans. One entity bean can be related to another through a one-to-one, a one-to-many, or even a many-to-many relationship. This allows you to model your applications any way you need to.

First, let's take a better look at what these relationships mean. In a *one-to-one relationship,* a single object is related to one and only one other object. In a *one-to-many relationship,* a single object can be related to any number of different objects; this is typically considered a *parent-child relationship.* In a *many-to-many relationship,* the objects are loosely tied together. Any one object can be related to any number of other objects, and vice versa. You can see these relationships in Figure 8-2.

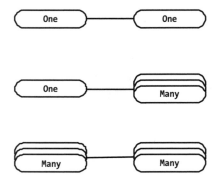

Figure 8-2. Types of relationships

The only way to interact with the relationships is through the local interfaces or through the abstract methods on the bean itself. It is illegal to try to add a remote interface to the "many" side of a relationship. Only the local interface can be used. In order to interact with the relationships through the remote interface, you will need to create helper methods that in turn interact with the local interfaces.

Say, for example, I want my remote client to be able to set a new address for an employee. Instead of allowing the client to simply assign an address, the client will instead need to pass all of the address's values. The bean will then take those values and create a new address and apply the values.

Another requirement placed on related beans is that they must be deployed with the same deployment descriptor. They need to be part of the same conceptual unit. This may change in future specifications, but for today you need to keep the components together.

Deployment Descriptor

I mentioned before that the parts of the Enterprise JavaBean are tied together with the deployment descriptor. A deployment descriptor is an XML file that contains descriptions of all the parts of the bean. The deployment descriptor is important to Container Managed Persistence because this is the primary definition of how CMP will work.

All classes and interfaces and their roles are defined in the deployment descriptor. There is a lot more information that can be set, but much of it is outside the scope of this book. For CMP, the elements we are interested in include the cmp entries, the relationship entries, and finder entries.

While all EJBs have entries for the bean class, local and remote interfaces, transactions, and security, CMP beans also have entries for persistence-type, cmp-version, cmp-fields, and prim-key-class at minimum. These entries tell the system what to persist and how.

Listing 8-1 contains a chunk of XML that we will look at in more detail later in the chapter when I show you how to create CMP beans. Notice the declaration of cmp-version–this differentiates between CMP 1.1 and CMP 2.0; as I stated before, the two are very different. Also notice the numerous cmp-field entries. Each cmp-field tag defines a field that the container will manage for you. Finally, the prim-key-class field tells the container how to track the instances stored.

Listing 8-1. Minimal Container Managed Persistence Deployment Descriptor

```
<entity id="Address">
    <ejb-name>Address</ejb-name>
    <home>com.apress.javapersist.chapter08.ejbs.address.AddressHome</home>
    <remote>com.apress.javapersist.chapter08.ejbs.address.Address</remote>
    <local-home>com.apress.javapersist.chapter08.ejbs.address.AddressLocalHome
    </local-home>
    <local>com.apress.javapersist.chapter08.ejbs.address.AddressLocal</local>
    <ejb-class>com.apress.javapersist.chapter08.ejbs.address.AddressBean
    </ejb-class>
    <persistence-type>Container</persistence-type>
    <prim-key-class>java.lang.Long</prim-key-class>
    <reentrant>False</reentrant>
    <cmp-version>2.x</cmp-version>
    <abstract-schema-name>Address</abstract-schema-name>
    <cmp-field>
        <field-name>id</field-name>
    </cmp-field>
    <cmp-field>
        <field-name>streetLine1</field-name>
    </cmp-field>
    <cmp-field>
        <field-name>streetLine2</field-name>
    </cmp-field>
    <cmp-field>
        <field-name>city</field-name>
    </cmp-field>
    <cmp-field>
        <field-name>state</field-name>
    </cmp-field>
    <primkey-field>id</primkey-field>
</entity>
```

Also within this same section of XML, between the entity tags, is where local references are listed. These become important for relationships. Listing 8-2 illustrates a local reference. Remember, Listing 8-2 would exist between the entity tags in the preceding XML.

Listing 8-2. Local Reference XML

```
<ejb-local-ref id="EJBLocalRef_1044729389599">
    <ejb-ref-name>ejb/Employee</ejb-ref-name>
    <ejb-ref-type>Entity</ejb-ref-type>
    <local-home>com.apress.javapersist.chapter08.ejbs.employee.EmployeeLocalHome
    </local-home>
    <local>com.apress.javapersist.chapter08.ejbs.employee.EmployeeLocal</local>
    <ejb-link>Employee</ejb-link>
</ejb-local-ref>
```

Queries are also defined within the deployment descriptor. Later in this chapter, I will discuss EJB QL, but for now let's look at the XML related to querying. Listing 8-3 shows a single finder method. Notice that the method and parameters are described. The final part of this section of code is the EJB QL itself. For now, simply notice how similar to SQL it looks. Also notice that the location the query is expecting to obtain data from is the same as the abstract-schema-name defined in our basic deployment descriptor.

Listing 8-3. EJB QL Finder Method Defined in XML

```
<query>
    <description>Find by street</description>
    <query-method>
        <method-name>findByStreet</method-name>
        <method-params>
            <method-param>java.lang.String</method-param>
        </method-params>
    </query-method>
    <ejb-ql>select object(a) from Address a where a.street = ?1</ejb-ql>
</query>
```

The last part of the deployment descriptor I want to show is the relationship portion. Specifically this section of code shows a one-to-many relationship where one address can be shared by multiple employees. Notice explicitly the XML defining roles, multiplicity, and even the cmp-fields that will be available to interact with the relationship in Listing 8-4.

Listing 8-4. Relationships Defined in the Deployment Descriptor

```
<ejb-relation>
    <description>Employees to Addresses</description>
    <ejb-relation-name>Residents Relationship</ejb-relation-name>
    <ejb-relationship-role>
        <ejb-relationship-role-name>employee</ejb-relationship-role-name>
        <multiplicity>One</multiplicity>
        <relationship-role-source>
            <ejb-name>Address</ejb-name>
        </relationship-role-source>
        <cmr-field>
            <cmr-field-name>employee</cmr-field-name>
            <cmr-field-type>java.util.Collection</cmr-field-type>
        </cmr-field>
    </ejb-relationship-role>
    <ejb-relationship-role>
        <ejb-relationship-role-name>address</ejb-relationship-role-name>
        <multiplicity>Many</multiplicity>
        <relationship-role-source>
            <ejb-name>Employee</ejb-name>
        </relationship-role-source>
        <cmr-field>
            <cmr-field-name>address</cmr-field-name>
        </cmr-field>
    </ejb-relationship-role>
</ejb-relation>
```

Now we have covered the basics of CMP in an EJBs Deployment Descriptor. I will show a complete deployment descriptor later in the chapter. For now, let's keep in mind that all persistent fields must be declared in the deployment descriptor as well as relationships.

Life Cycle of a CMP Entity Bean

Obviously, there is a life cycle that an object goes through in an application. This life cycle can be broken down into creating, modifying, and deleting. This section will discuss how these things happen for a Container Managed Persistence bean.

Creating Objects

Creation of a CMP bean from a client's view is no different from that of a Bean Managed Persistence EJB. In both cases, the client invokes a create method on the home interface. This in turn invokes the ejbCreate method on the bean itself. Here is where CMP becomes much simpler than BMP.

In a BMP bean, all values handed to the ejbCreate method must be manually added to the database—usually through JDBC, possibly through a DAO, as discussed in Chapter 5. In either case, there is quite a bit of work that goes into the data storage.

In CMP all the developer needs to do is call the appropriate setter methods for each of the arguments passed in. This in turn causes the container to write the data to the data store. It is far less code than with BMP.

One requirement imposed on developers using CMP is that all fields in the primary key must be set in the ejbCreate method. If the primary key consists of a unique identifier, that value must either be passed in or obtained by the ejbCreate method. This would need to be done for a BMP bean as well.

Modifying Objects

Modifying objects with CMP is very straightforward. The container maintains synchronization with the data store. Upon setting a value, you can assume that it is stored, unlike with BMP, where calls to ejbStore and ejbLoad are required.

So to modify a persistent field, you simply call the set method. This in turn will result in the ejbStore method being called. This makes persistence almost transparent.

Removing Objects

There are two different ways to remove an object from storage using CMP. The first is using the object to remove itself by calling the remove method. The second is using the bean's home interface, which contains a remove method that takes a primary key.

Removing the object first removes all references to itself from other objects. If you remove an address object, it will first have all of its references removed from all related employee objects. Lastly, the record itself is removed from the database.

Cascading Deletes

In some situations child objects should not exist without their parents. When an employee is removed, all associated personnel records should be removed too. Having a personnel record in the database does not make sense with out an employee associated with it.

CMP handles this situation through an additional property in the deployment descriptor element for relationships. When a cascading delete is appropriate, simply add a `cascade-delete` element to the relationship part of the deployment descriptor.

The effect of this is that when the employee record is removed, all related personnel records will automatically be removed as well. This functionality makes it very easy to manage dependencies.

EJB QL

EJB QL is short for the Enterprise JavaBean Query Language. Since the introduction of entity beans, querying has been done through `findBy` methods. In BMP, these are methods that wrap SQL queries through JDBC. In CMP, the `findBy` methods exist only in the home interfaces and tied to EJB QL that is defined in the deployment descriptor.

The first part of EJB QL is the `findBy` methods in the local home or remote home interfaces. These methods are always named `findBy<qualifier>`. So to create a method that will find an employee by last name, you would declare a method called `findByLastName` that would take a string as an argument.

Similar to `findBy` methods are `ejbSelect` methods. These methods are used by an EJB to persistent data or related entities. These methods must be prefixed with "ejbSelect". They can return either a collection of or a single `EJBObject` or `EJBLocalObject` instance. The bean class itself must define a public abstract method. The container will provide the implementation based on information in the deployment descriptor. The `ejbSelect` methods are not added to the interfaces. These methods are for the bean itself to use.

The next part of EJB QL we will talk about is the actual queries themselves. Along with the finder method signature, a CMP query must be defined in the deployment descriptor. The parts consist of the finder method the query applies to, the arguments for that method, and the EJB QL query.

The one finder method that does not need to be associated with a query in the deployment descriptor is the `findByPrimaryKey`. This method returns either a local or remote interface depending on the home interface where it is defined. The method takes a single argument of the type the primary key is defined as. Both the remote and local home interfaces must define this method.

The syntax for EJB QL is very similar to SQL. Unlike SQL, EJB QL is based on an abstract definition that is defined in the deployment descriptor. Often this will and should look like Java objects. You query against the name listed in the `abstract-schema-name` tag for properties that are listed in the `cmp-field` tags.

For example, if you have an abstract schema named Employee and a `cmp-field` named lastName, you can write a query based on the last name that would look like this: `select object(e) from Employee e where e.lastName = ?1`. This query in turn would be placed in `ejb-ql` tags within a query element of the deployment descriptor.

If you break this last statement down, you can see that it contains all of the parts you have come to expect from a query language. You declare what you are selecting, and you state where to find the data. Finally, you have a `filter where` clause that ensures you get only those employees you are interested in. The `?1` parameter is tied to the arguments passed into the `findBy` method. There needs to be a numbered parameter for each argument to that method.

Besides this basic query functionality, EJB QL also supports more complex expressions such as IN, DISTINCT, BETWEEN, IS NULL, and LIKE that act very much like their SQL counterparts. Some additional expressions include IS EMPTY and MEMBER OF. The language also provides some simple functions including CONCAT, LENGTH, and SUBSTRING for manipulating strings as well as ABS and SQRT for arithmetic.

Using Sun's Reference Implementation

Now that we have discussed Container Managed Persistence in the abstract, it is time to show how to implement and use it. For this part of the chapter, I will be using Sun's J2EE Reference Implementation (RI). The J2EE Reference Implementation can be obtained from Sun at `http://java.sun.com/j2ee/`.

One problem with using Sun's Reference Implementation is that the SQL generated is not compatible with MySQL directly. You can edit the generated SQL, but for this chapter rely on the Cloudscape RDBMS that comes built into the RI.

While you are going to deploy to Sun's RI, most of your work is not application server–specific. This includes your EJBs and unit tests to ensure that your EJBs are valid—all of which will be packaged together in an Enterprise Archive (EAR).

In Chapter 7 you learned about unit testing. For this example, you will use an extension to the JUnit framework called Cactus. Cactus allows for in-container testing of EJBs. What I mean by that is your unit tests will run within the application server, allowing you to use the local interfaces.

Cactus actually runs as a servlet. All I will show in this chapter are the actual test cases that look very similar to straight JUnit test cases. To actually deploy the unit tests, you will need to download and create a Web application using Cactus. Cactus can be downloaded from `http://jakarta.apache.org/cactus/`. The site also has good documentation unit testing EJBs. You can also download all of the code for this chapter from the Apress site at http://www.apress.com.

Now it is time to get down to business. For this example, you will focus on the sample HR application. You will create two Enterprise JavaBeans, an employee bean and an address bean. Both EJBs are Container Managed Persistence entity beans. I will show how to create relationships between the objects. Finally, you will unit test them and ensure everything works correctly. Your unit tests will also show how a client would interact with the EJBs.

Local Home Interfaces

In order to do any work at all with an EJB, you need to be able to create, find, and remove them. This functionality is provided by the home interfaces. Since you are working within the application server, we will focus on the local home interfaces.

Listing 8-5 shows the EmployeeLocalHome interface that extends the javax.ejb.EJBLocalHome interface. There are only a few methods defined: one create method and two finder methods. Notice the one finder method is the primary key finder, the other is by employee's last name. We will see in a little bit the deployment descriptor where the EJB QL is defined for the last name finder, but not necessary for the primary key finder.

Listing 8-5. EmployeeLocalHome

```
package com.apress.javapersist.chapter08.ejbs.employee;

import javax.ejb.CreateException;
import javax.ejb.EJBLocalHome;
import javax.ejb.FinderException;

public interface EmployeeLocalHome extends EJBLocalHome {

    public EmployeeLocal create(Long id) throws CreateException;

    public EmployeeLocal findByPrimaryKey(Long primaryKey)
        throws FinderException;

    public EmployeeLocal findByLastName(String lastName)
        throws FinderException;
}
```

The AddressLocalHome in Listing 8-6 is simpler than the EmployeeLocalHome. Still it serves the same purpose. This is where you create all addresses you will interact with. This interface contains the single create method and a single find by primary key method. This is the minimum number of methods an entity bean home interface can contain.

Listing 8-6. AddressLocalHome

```
package com.apress.javapersist.chapter08.ejbs.address;

import javax.ejb.CreateException;
import javax.ejb.EJBLocalHome;
import javax.ejb.FinderException;

public interface AddressLocalHome extends EJBLocalHome {

    public AddressLocal create(Long id) throws javax.ejb.CreateException;

    public AddressLocal findByPrimaryKey(Long primaryKey)
        throws FinderException;
}
```

Now you have defined the factory interfaces where all instances will be created and found. One method you don't see in these interfaces is the remove method. This is defined in the EJBLocalHome interface that both of these extend. The remove method takes a primary key as an argument and has no return type.

Local Interfaces

Now let's look at the interfaces you will interact with after you have created or found an instance through the home interfaces. It is with the local interfaces that you will do almost all of your work. While you will define an actual class to support these interfaces, clients will never interact directly with that class. Clients will always interact either with the local or remote interfaces.

In Listing 8-7, you can see the EmployeeLocal interface. It is desirable for all clients running within the application server to interact with this interface rather than the remote interface. The remote interface is available to classes within the application server, but the local interface offers more functionality and in many implementations can have performance benefits as well.

Listing 8-7. EmployeeLocal

```
package com.apress.javapersist.chapter08.ejbs.employee;

import com.apress.javapersist.chapter08.ejbs.address.AddressLocal;

public interface EmployeeLocal extends javax.ejb.EJBLocalObject {

    public String getFirstName();
    public void setFirstName(String newFirstName);

    public String getLastName();
    public void setLastName(String newLastName);

    public String getEmail();
    public void setEmail(String newEmail);

    public AddressLocal getAddress();
    public void setAddress(AddressLocal anAddress);
}
```

For the most part, this interface simply contains getters and setters for properties that will be stored in the database. The exceptions to this rule are the getter and setter for the AddressLocal interface. These two methods actually represent a relationship rather than a persistent field.

In Listing 8-8, you can see the AddressLocal interface that was referenced in the EmployeeLocal interface. For the most part it is another simple collection of getters and setters for accessing persistent data. Here the interesting part is the getter and setter for the Employee property.

Listing 8-8. AddressLocal

```
package com.apress.javapersist.chapter08.ejbs.address;

import java.util.Collection;
import com.apress.javapersist.chapter08.ejbs.employee.EmployeeLocal;

public interface AddressLocal extends javax.ejb.EJBLocalObject {

    public String getStreetLine1();
    public void setStreetLine1(String newStreetLine1);

    public String getCity();
    public void setCity(String newCity);
```

```
    public String getState();
    public void setState(String newState);

    public String getStreetLine2();
    public void setStreetLine2(String newStreetLine2);

    public void addEmployee(EmployeeLocal employee);
    public int getNumberEmployees();

    public Collection getEmployee();
    public void setEmployee(Collection anEmployee);
}
```

Notice that the getter and setter for the Employee property actually deal with a collection. This indicates that there is a one-to-many relationship between the employee and address. For this example, plan on setting this up so that an employee has one primary address, but an address can be shared by multiple employees.

Container Managed Persistent Entity Beans

So far everything we have seen could apply to a BMP entity bean as well as the CMP entity bean. It is in this next part that the differences start to show. In this section we will look at the actual entity bean classes themselves.

In Listing 8-9 you can see the EmployeeBean. As discussed earlier, this is an abstract class; all of the persistent fields are indicated by abstract methods for getters and setters. Also available on the class are abstract methods that are used for managing the relationship with the address.

Listing 8-9. EmployeeBean

```
package com.apress.javapersist.chapter08.ejbs.employee;

import javax.ejb.CreateException;
import javax.ejb.EntityBean;
import javax.ejb.EntityContext;
import javax.ejb.RemoveException;

import com.apress.javapersist.chapter08.ejbs.address.AddressLocal;
```

```java
public abstract class EmployeeBean implements EntityBean {
    private EntityContext myEntityCtx;

    public abstract Long getId();
    public abstract void setId(Long newId);

    public abstract String getFirstName();
    public abstract void setFirstName(String newFirstName);

    public abstract String getLastName();
    public abstract void setLastName(String newLastName);

    public abstract String getEmail();
    public abstract void setEmail(String newEmail);

    public abstract AddressLocal getAddress();
    public abstract void setAddress(AddressLocal anAddress);

    public void setEntityContext(EntityContext ctx) {
        myEntityCtx = ctx;
    }

    public EntityContext getEntityContext() {
        return myEntityCtx;
    }

    public void unsetEntityContext() {
        myEntityCtx = null;
    }

    public Long ejbCreate(Long id)
        throws CreateException {
        setId(id);
        return null;
    }

    public void ejbPostCreate(Long id) throws CreateException {}
    public void ejbActivate() {}
    public void ejbLoad() {}
    public void ejbPassivate() {}
    public void ejbRemove() throws RemoveException {}
    public void ejbStore() {}
}
```

Also in this class are life cycle methods that are necessary for any entity bean. The life cycle methods are all listed at the end of the class. These methods are related to the home interface, while the field and relationship methods are related to the remote and local interfaces.

The code for the AddressBean in Listing 8-10 is actually more interesting than that for the EmployeeBean. The AddressBean also has abstract getters and setters for persistent fields, as well as life cycle–related methods. Where the AddressBean gets interesting is in the relationship methods.

Listing 8-10. AddressBean

```
package com.apress.javapersist.chapter08.ejbs.address;

import java.util.Collection;
import javax.ejb.CreateException;
import javax.ejb.EntityBean;
import javax.ejb.EntityContext;
import javax.ejb.RemoveException;

import com.apress.javapersist.chapter08.ejbs.employee.EmployeeLocal;

public abstract class AddressBean implements EntityBean {
    private EntityContext myEntityCtx;

    public abstract Long getId();
    public abstract void setId(Long newId);

    public abstract String getStreetLine1();
    public abstract void setStreetLine1(String newStreetLine1);

    public abstract String getCity();
    public abstract void setCity(String newCity);

    public abstract String getState();
    public abstract void setState(String newState);

    public abstract String getStreetLine2();
    public abstract void setStreetLine2(String newStreetLine2);

    public abstract Collection getEmployee();
    public abstract void setEmployee(Collection anEmployee);
```

```
    public void addEmployee(EmployeeLocal employee) {
        getEmployee().add(employee);
    }

    public int getNumberEmployees() {
        return getEmployee().size();
    }

    public void setEntityContext(EntityContext ctx) {
        myEntityCtx = ctx;
    }

    public EntityContext getEntityContext() {
        return myEntityCtx;
    }

    public void unsetEntityContext() {
        myEntityCtx = null;
    }

    public Long ejbCreate(Long id) throws CreateException {
        setId(id);
        return null;
    }

    public void ejbPostCreate(Long id) throws CreateException {}
    public void ejbActivate() {}
    public void ejbLoad() {}
    public void ejbPassivate() {}
    public void ejbRemove() throws RemoveException {}
    public void ejbStore() {}
}
```

Besides the abstract get/setEmployee methods, there are also two helper methods that clients can interact with for affecting the relationship. There is an addEmployee method that is not abstract. This method is very important to easily allow clients to associate employees with addresses. A very similar method could be used with the remote interface, but instead of passing a AddressLocal the address's data could be passed.

Finally the getNumberEmployees method is a helper method that allows clients to know how many employees are associated with a particular address. Again, this method can be made available through the remote interface.

A Deployment Descriptor Example

Here Listing 8-11 shows the complete deployment descriptor. Most parts have been described earlier in this chapter. Unfortunately, some lines in the deployment descriptor were too long for the printed page. In those cases, I have either moved the closing tag to the next line, or had to move the value between the tags and the closing tag to lines of their own. In order to make this work, you will need to put all tags with a single value on a single line.

Listing 8-11. ejb-jar.xml

```xml
<?xml version="1.0" encoding="UTF-8"?>
<!DOCTYPE ejb-jar PUBLIC
"-//Sun Microsystems, Inc.//DTD Enterprise JavaBeans 2.0//EN"
"http://java.sun.com/dtd/ejb-jar_2_0.dtd">
<ejb-jar id="ejb-jar_ID">
    <display-name>Chapter 8</display-name>
    <enterprise-beans>
        <entity id="Address">
            <ejb-name>Address</ejb-name>
            <home>com.apress.javapersist.chapter08.ejbs.address.AddressHome
            </home>
            <remote>com.apress.javapersist.chapter08.ejbs.address.Address
            </remote>
            <local-home>
            com.apress.javapersist.chapter08.ejbs.address.AddressLocalHome
            </local-home>
            <local>com.apress.javapersist.chapter08.ejbs.address.AddressLocal
            </local>
            <ejb-class>com.apress.javapersist.chapter08.ejbs.address.AddressBean
            </ejb-class>
            <persistence-type>Container</persistence-type>
            <prim-key-class>java.lang.Long</prim-key-class>
            <reentrant>False</reentrant>
            <cmp-version>2.x</cmp-version>
            <abstract-schema-name>Address</abstract-schema-name>
            <cmp-field>
                <field-name>id</field-name>
            </cmp-field>
            <cmp-field>
                <field-name>streetLine1</field-name>
            </cmp-field>
            <cmp-field>
```

```xml
            <field-name>streetLine2</field-name>
        </cmp-field>
        <cmp-field>
            <field-name>city</field-name>
        </cmp-field>
        <cmp-field>
            <field-name>state</field-name>
        </cmp-field>
        <primkey-field>id</primkey-field>
        <ejb-local-ref id="EJBLocalRef_1044729389599">
            <ejb-ref-name>ejb/Employee</ejb-ref-name>
            <ejb-ref-type>Entity</ejb-ref-type>
            <local-home>
            com.apress.javapersist.chapter08.ejbs.employee.EmployeeLocalHome
            </local-home>
            <local>
            com.apress.javapersist.chapter08.ejbs.employee.EmployeeLocal
            </local>
            <ejb-link>Employee</ejb-link>
        </ejb-local-ref>
    </entity>
    <entity id="Employee">
        <ejb-name>Employee</ejb-name>
        <home>com.apress.javapersist.chapter08.ejbs.employee.EmployeeHome
        </home>
        <remote>com.apress.javapersist.chapter08.ejbs.employee.Employee
        </remote>
        <local-home>
        com.apress.javapersist.chapter08.ejbs.employee.EmployeeLocalHome
        </local-home>
        <local>com.apress.javapersist.chapter08.ejbs.employee.EmployeeLocal
        </local>
        <ejb-class>
        com.apress.javapersist.chapter08.ejbs.employee.EmployeeBean
        </ejb-class>
        <persistence-type>Container</persistence-type>
        <prim-key-class>java.lang.Long</prim-key-class>
        <reentrant>False</reentrant>
        <cmp-version>2.x</cmp-version>
        <abstract-schema-name>Employee</abstract-schema-name>
        <cmp-field>
            <field-name>id</field-name>
        </cmp-field>
        <cmp-field>
```

```xml
            <field-name>firstName</field-name>
        </cmp-field>
        <cmp-field>
            <field-name>lastName</field-name>
        </cmp-field>
        <cmp-field>
            <field-name>email</field-name>
        </cmp-field>
        <primkey-field>id</primkey-field>
        <ejb-local-ref id="EJBLocalRef_1044729389619">
            <ejb-ref-name>ejb/Address</ejb-ref-name>
            <ejb-ref-type>Entity</ejb-ref-type>
            <local-home>
            com.apress.javapersist.chapter08.ejbs.address.AddressLocalHome
            </local-home>
            <local>
            com.apress.javapersist.chapter08.ejbs.address.AddressLocal
            </local>
            <ejb-link>Address</ejb-link>
        </ejb-local-ref>
        <query>
            <description></description>
            <query-method>
                <method-name>findByLastName</method-name>
                <method-params>
                    <method-param>java.lang.String</method-param>
                </method-params>
            </query-method>
            <ejb-ql>select object(e) from Employee e where e.lastName = ?1
            </ejb-ql>
        </query>
    </entity>
</enterprise-beans>
<relationships>
    <ejb-relation>
        <description></description>
        <ejb-relation-name>Residents Relationship</ejb-relation-name>
        <ejb-relationship-role>
            <ejb-relationship-role-name>employee
            </ejb-relationship-role-name>
            <multiplicity>One</multiplicity>
            <relationship-role-source>
                <ejb-name>Address</ejb-name>
            </relationship-role-source>
```

```
            <cmr-field>
                <cmr-field-name>employee</cmr-field-name>
                <cmr-field-type>java.util.Collection</cmr-field-type>
            </cmr-field>
        </ejb-relationship-role>
        <ejb-relationship-role>
            <ejb-relationship-role-name>address</ejb-relationship-role-name>
            <multiplicity>Many</multiplicity>
            <relationship-role-source>
                <ejb-name>Employee</ejb-name>
            </relationship-role-source>
            <cmr-field>
                <cmr-field-name>address</cmr-field-name>
            </cmr-field>
        </ejb-relationship-role>
    </ejb-relation>
</relationships>
</ejb-jar>
```

Points of interest in this deployment descriptor are the `cmp-fields`, relationship entries, and finders. Notice that there is a `cmp-field` for every abstract getter and setter defined in the bean.

In the `finderByLastName` declaration you can see both the method description and the EJB QL. Once again, see how similar to SQL it is. This query simply looks to the `cmp-field` lastName and filters on the passed in parameter.

The relationships are very explicit in their multiplicity, property names, and return types. Notice that the `java.util.Collection` for the employee side of the relationship is declared here. One other collection type is possible here, and that is the `java.util.Set`. For a situation like this, the set would probably have been more applicable since it would not allow for duplicate entries.

Unit Test Client

In this section, I provide unit tests for the preceding code to show how a client would interact with a CMP entity bean. As I mentioned in Chapter 7, unit tests can be a great source of documentation for classes. In this case, you can see exactly how to create, modify, and remove instances of the entity beans. These tests also show how to use the finders and manage relationships.

The tests extend `org.apache.cactus.ServletTestCase`, which is the only difference from standard JUnit tests. By using Cactus, you are able to test in container. There are other frameworks, such as JUnitEE, that allow similar in-container testing.

Listing 8-12 shows exactly how your employee CMP bean works. You have testCreateEmployee, which tests the creation of the bean, ensures that it is indeed in the data store by requesting it and verifying the data is correct. The test finishes by removing the created employee, setting the data store back to its original state.

Listing 8-12. EmployeeBeanTest

```
package com.apress.javapersist.chapter08.ejbs.employee;

import java.rmi.NoSuchObjectException;
import javax.ejb.FinderException;
import javax.ejb.NoSuchObjectLocalException;
import javax.ejb.ObjectNotFoundException;
import javax.naming.InitialContext;
import javax.naming.Context;
import javax.rmi.PortableRemoteObject;

import org.apache.cactus.ServletTestCase;

import com.apress.javapersist.chapter08.ejbs.address.*;


import junit.framework.TestCase;
import junit.framework.TestSuite;

public class EmployeeBeanTest extends ServletTestCase {
    public static final Long KEY = new Long(5);
    public static final String FIRST_NAME = "Damon";
    public static final String LAST_NAME = "Payne";
    public static final String EMAIL = "dpayne@mybusiness.com";
    public static final Long ADDRESS_KEY = KEY;

    private EmployeeLocalHome employeeHome;

    public EmployeeBeanTest(String arg0) {
        super(arg0);
    }

    protected void setUp() throws Exception {
        super.setUp();
        if (employeeHome == null) {
            Context initial = new InitialContext();
            Object objref = initial.lookup("java:comp/env/ejb/Employee");
            employeeHome
```

```
            = (EmployeeLocalHome) PortableRemoteObject.narrow(objref,
                EmployeeLocalHome.class);
    }
}

public static void setTestDataOn(EmployeeLocal employee) {
    employee.setFirstName(FIRST_NAME);
    employee.setLastName(LAST_NAME);
    employee.setEmail(EMAIL);
}

public void testCreateEmployee() throws Exception {
    EmployeeLocal employee = employeeHome.create(KEY);
    setTestDataOn(employee);

    employee = employeeHome.findByPrimaryKey(KEY);
    assertNotNull(employee);
    assertEquals(FIRST_NAME, employee.getFirstName());
    assertEquals(LAST_NAME, employee.getLastName());
    assertEquals(EMAIL, employee.getEmail());

    employeeHome.remove(employee.getPrimaryKey());

    try {
        employee = employeeHome.findByPrimaryKey(KEY);
        fail();
    }
    catch(FinderException e) {
        // Good, we want this.
    }
}

public void testModifyEmployee() throws Exception {
    String newEmail= "damon.payne@mybusiness.com";

    EmployeeLocal employee = employeeHome.create(KEY);
    setTestDataOn(employee);

    employee.setEmail(newEmail);

    EmployeeLocal storedEmployeeLocal = employeeHome.findByPrimaryKey(KEY);
    assertEquals(newEmail, storedEmployeeLocal.getEmail());
```

```java
        storedEmployeeLocal.remove();
    }

    public void testRemoveEmployee() throws Exception {
        EmployeeLocal employee = employeeHome.create(KEY);
        setTestDataOn(employee);

        EmployeeLocal storedEmployeeLocal = employeeHome.findByPrimaryKey(KEY);

        employeeHome.remove(storedEmployeeLocal.getPrimaryKey());

        try {
            employee.getLastName();
            fail();
        }
        catch(NoSuchObjectLocalException e) {
            // Should have thrown exception.
        }
    }

    public void testRelationship() throws Exception {
        AddressLocalHome addressHome = AddressBeanTest.createAddressHome();
        AddressLocal address = addressHome.create(AddressBeanTest.KEY);
        AddressBeanTest.setTestDataOn(address);

        EmployeeLocal employee = employeeHome.create(KEY);
        setTestDataOn(employee);

        employee.setAddress(address);
        address.addEmployee(employee);

        AddressLocal storedAddress
            = addressHome.findByPrimaryKey(AddressBeanTest.KEY);
        assertEquals(1, storedAddress.getNumberEmployees());

        EmployeeLocal storedEmployee = employeeHome.findByPrimaryKey(KEY);
        assertEquals(storedEmployee.getAddress(), storedAddress);

        address.remove();
        employee.remove();
    }
```

```java
public void testFindByFirstName() throws Exception {
    EmployeeLocal employee = employeeHome.create(KEY);
    setTestDataOn(employee);

    try {
        employee = employeeHome.findByLastName("INVALID");
        fail();
    }
    catch(ObjectNotFoundException e) {
        // Should have thrown exception.
    }

    employee = employeeHome.findByLastName(LAST_NAME);
    assertNotNull(employee);
    assertEquals(FIRST_NAME, employee.getFirstName());

    employee.remove();
}

public static TestSuite suite() {
    return new TestSuite(EmployeeBeanTest.class);
}
}
```

The testModifyEmployee test creates an employee, sets values on it, then modifies one value. The test then retrieves the employee and ensures that the modified value was retrieved from the database. There is a testRemoveEmployee test that ensures employees are actually removed by removing them via the home interface.

The testRelationship test ensures that addresses and employees can be associated as expected. This method ties an address to an employee and an employee to the address. The test further retrieves new references from the data store and ensures that the relationships are actually there.

The final test is testFindByLastName. This test creates an employee and stores it in the data store. Then the test retrieves the employee based on the last name. This method tests the EJB QL defined in the deployment descriptor.

Listing 8-13 shows many of the same tests this time for the address entity bean. This test case tests the creation, modification, and removal of addresses. Relationships aren't addressed because they were covered in the employee tests.

Listing 8-13. AddressBeanTest

```java
package com.apress.javapersist.chapter08.ejbs.address;

import java.rmi.NoSuchObjectException;
import javax.ejb.FinderException;
import javax.ejb.NoSuchObjectLocalException;
import javax.naming.InitialContext;
import javax.naming.Context;
import javax.rmi.PortableRemoteObject;

import org.apache.cactus.ServletTestCase;

import junit.framework.TestCase;
import junit.framework.TestSuite;
import junit.textui.TestRunner;

public class AddressBeanTest extends ServletTestCase {
    public static final Long KEY = new Long(10);
    public static final String STREET_LINE1 = "123 N. West St.";
    public static final String STREET_LINE2 = "Apt. 204";
    public static final String CITY = "Milwaukee";
    public static final String STATE = "WI";

    private AddressLocalHome addressHome;

    public AddressBeanTest(String arg0) {
        super(arg0);
    }

    protected void setUp() throws Exception {
        super.setUp();
        if (addressHome == null) {
            addressHome = createAddressHome();
        }
    }

    public static AddressLocalHome createAddressHome() throws Exception {
        Context initial = new InitialContext();
        Object objref = initial.lookup("java:comp/env/ejb/Address");
        return (AddressLocalHome) PortableRemoteObject.narrow(objref,
            AddressLocalHome.class);
    }
```

```java
public static void setTestDataOn(AddressLocal address) {
    address.setStreetLine1(STREET_LINE1);
    address.setStreetLine2(STREET_LINE2);
    address.setCity(CITY);
    address.setState(STATE);
}

public void testCreateAddress() throws Exception {
    AddressLocal address = addressHome.create(KEY);
    setTestDataOn(address);

    address = addressHome.findByPrimaryKey(KEY);
    assertNotNull(address);
    assertEquals(STREET_LINE1, address.getStreetLine1());
    assertEquals(STREET_LINE2, address.getStreetLine2());
    assertEquals(CITY, address.getCity());
    assertEquals(STATE, address.getState());

    addressHome.remove(address.getPrimaryKey());

    try {
        address = addressHome.findByPrimaryKey(KEY);
        fail();
    }
    catch(FinderException e){
    }
}

public void testModifyAddress() throws Exception {
    String newStreetLine1 = "345 W. North St.";

    AddressLocal address = addressHome.create(KEY);
    setTestDataOn(address);
    address.setStreetLine1(newStreetLine1);

    AddressLocal storedAddress = addressHome.findByPrimaryKey(KEY);
    assertEquals(newStreetLine1, storedAddress.getStreetLine1());

    storedAddress.remove();
}
public void testRemoveAddress() throws Exception {
    AddressLocal address = addressHome.create(KEY);
    setTestDataOn(address);
```

```
        AddressLocal storedAddress = addressHome.findByPrimaryKey(KEY);

        addressHome.remove(storedAddress.getPrimaryKey());

        try{
            address.getStreetLine1();
            fail();
        }
        catch(NoSuchObjectLocalException e) {
            // Should have thrown exception.
        }
    }

    public static TestSuite suite() {
        return new TestSuite(AddressBeanTest.class);
    }

    public static void main(String[] args) {
        TestRunner.run(AddressBeanTest.class);
    }
}
```

Deploying and Running

Now that you have written and understand your two EJBs and their tests, it is time to deploy them. The first step is getting and setting up an application server. As I mentioned before, you will be using Sun's Java 2 Enterprise Edition Reference Implementation. You will need to download and install the RI to be able to follow along with this exercise.

Once you have installed the Reference Implementation, you need to start the various services. The first service to start is the Cloudscape database. This is achieved by running cloudscape -start from the RI's bin directory. The next service is the application server itself. This is achieved by running j2ee -verbose from the RI's bin directory. If you don't receive a message on starting the RI saying "J2EE server startup complete," you will need to go back to the installation instructions.

The next step is to start the deployment tool. This is accomplished by running deploytool from the RI's bin directory. Upon startup the deployment tool should be visible and look like the window shown in Figure 8-3.

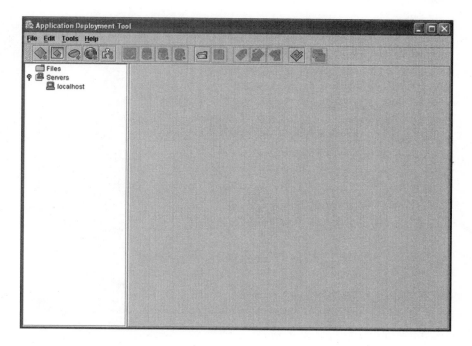

Figure 8-3. Reference Implementation deployment tool

Now that you have the deployment tool running, you need to set up a data source that your EJBs will use. For this you will need to go into the Tools menu and select Server Configuration. You should see a dialog box that looks like Figure 8-4. In this screen you will want to go to the Standard Data Sources section and add a new data source. For your data source name use `jdbc/Chapter08` with a URL of `jdbc:cloudscape:rmi:CloudscapeDB:create=true`, which will match all of the existing data sources defined.

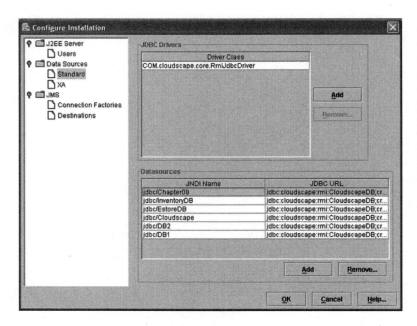

Figure 8-4. Configuring a new data source

Next you need to create your Enterprise Archive for deployment. This step is outside the scope of this book, but essentially consists of creating the EJB JAR file using Java's jar utility. Next, the JAR file is put into another archive using the jar utility, this time with an .ear extension. This same EAR file will contain your Cactus unit tests if you create them in the form of a Web Archive (WAR) file.

Once you have created your EAR file, you open it with the deployment tool. For this simply select the File | Open menu item, and then choose your EAR file from the file system. Upon loading the EAR, the deployment tool will look like Figure 8-5. Notice that your EJBs are now visible in the deployment tool.

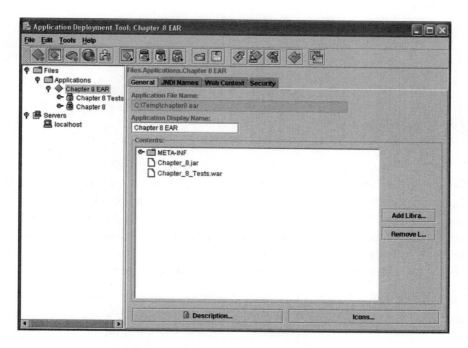

Figure 8-5. Opened Enterprise Archive

Next comes the wonderful step where your application server does all of the work you would have had to do if you were using Bean Managed Persistence. You now have the deployment tool generate your SQL. In order to do this, you select either one of your EJBs. Next, select the Entity tab. Toward the bottom on the right-hand side of the screen is a button that says Deployment Settings; click this button.

On the dialog box that comes up is a button for Database Settings. These must be set before any SQL can be generated. By clicking this button, you see the dialog box shown in Figure 8-6. Here you set the database JNDI name to the same value you gave your data source in the server configuration. When using Cloudscape, the User Name and Password fields can be left blank. Then click OK. On returning to the previous screen, click Generate Default SQL. This will create the SQL for your Container Managed Persistence.

Figure 8-6. SQL generation

Now you are ready to deploy your EAR. In this step, right-click the EAR you had opened in the deployment tool and select Deploy from the context menu. You will be presented with the deployment introduction screen. Simply click Next to go to the next screen. Now you should see a screen that looks like Figure 8-7. You need to set the JNDI names for your entity beans here. Set the address bean to `ejb/Address` and the employee bean to `ejb/Employee`. After this, you can click Next to configure your WAR file for testing, or finish if you have another way to test the beans.

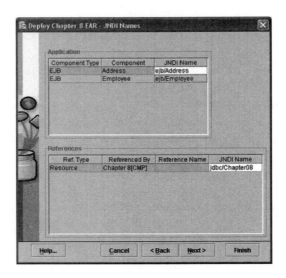

Figure 8-7. Deploying the beans

Now your Container Managed Persistence beans are deployed. You can test them and ensure everything is working correctly.

Summary

This chapter has covered a lot of material related to Container Managed Persistence for entity beans. We have seen how to write CMP beans, including what interfaces and classes are required. We have also looked into the deployment descriptor for a CMP entity bean and written unit tests to see how the beans work.

In writing a CMP bean, you need to remember that all persistent fields are represented by abstract accessors. Those fields also need to be serializable or primitives. Each persistent field also needs a `cmp-field` entry in the deployment descriptor.

Relationships are connections between entity beans. Two related beans must exist within the same deployment descriptor. Relationships can be one-to-one, one-to-many, or many-to-many. Relationships can only be directly interacted with through the local interfaces or by the bean itself. To manage a relationship through a remote interface, you will need to provide helper methods.

Rather than using SQL, you have the opportunity to use the object-oriented container managed EJB Query Language. This is the best way to obtain your objects from your data source. EJB QL is comprised of both methods and a SQL-like query language. There are two different types of query methods for EJB QL, finder and select methods. All finder and select methods need to be defined in the deployment descriptor and are fulfilled by the container.

CHAPTER 9

Writing to the ODMG 3.0

WHEN ON BOARD H.M.S. BEAGLE, as naturalist, I was much struck with certain facts in the distribution of the organic beings inhabiting South America, and in the geological relations of the present to the past inhabitants of that continent. These facts, as will be seen in the latter chapters of this volume, seemed to throw some light on the origin of species—particularly I want to address an object-relational specification that has been a contributor to many other frameworks and systems, the Object Data Management Group. This in turn will throw some light on other frameworks that I will cover in the next chapters.

The Object Data Management Group (ODMG) is a committee that was formed in 1991 to create a specification that would allow developers to write objects that could be persisted transparently: independent of language and independent of mechanism. The ODMG's belief is that a specification can be defined that both an object database and an object-to-relational layer can implement.

This would allow software to be developed that could change from a relational database storage mechanism to object database storage. The reverse would also be true. Essentially the goal is write once, store anywhere. By writing applications to the ODMG, a system should not be bound to one storage mechanism.

In order to achieve this goal, the ODMG has come up with several specifications. The specifications are all grouped together under the ODMG 3.0 standard, and they are implemented by many object databases and object-relational frameworks. The ODMG is also a reference for technologies like Java Data Objects (JDO) and similar technologies.

For this chapter, since we are discussing the ODMG, and the underlying storage mechanism should be irrelevant, I am going to primarily refer to Object Data Management Systems (ODMSs). By this, I mean that your objects will be stored in either a relational database or object database. The ODMG frees you from worrying about which it is. For the code in this chapter, I used both the commercial Poet FastObjects object database and the open source Jakarta ObJectRelationalBridge (OJB) product, which I cover in more detail in Chapter 11.

I will not go too far in depth into the ODMG because it is a large topic and implementations vary a great deal. For more information on the ODMG, I suggest going to their Web site at http://www.odmg.org. The ODMG specification is also available in book form from their site. The reason I want to address the ODMG is not only because it can be useful for Java persistence, but also because many persistence products are either based on it or claim compatibility with it.

Object Model

The ODMG's object model is based on the model defined by the Object Management Group (OMG), which is the creator of the Common Object Request Broker Architecture (CORBA) and is intended to be compatible with that specification. What this means is that they took a well-established object model (CORBA) and modified it as little as possible to use it for persistence. This in turn gives developers an easy path to incorporate this technology into their already existing distributed applications.

The object model really specifies how objects can relate to each other and how they interact. In addition, things like relationships, locking, and transactions are also defined in the ODMG's object model. This is particularly important to the ODMG since the specification is used across more languages than Java. An object stored using ODMG in Java should theoretically be retrievable from C++ or Smalltalk.

How objects relate and interact is already taken care of for you by the Java language itself. And this relationship is compatible with the ODMG's requirements. One object can contain references to another. You can use references to objects' call methods on other related objects to perform work.

As an example, Figure 9-1 shows an OMDG object model that contains an Employee class with two subclasses, Manager and Developer. The Java object model is exactly the same. That is because Java naturally supports the basic object model.

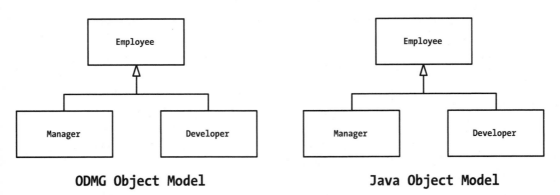

ODMG Object Model   **Java Object Model**

Figure 9-1. ODMG vs. Java's basic object model

Inheritance works the same way in the OMDG's object model as in Java's. Figure 9-2 illustrates that an interface can inherit from any number of interfaces but cannot inherit from a class. A class, however, can inherit not only from any number of interfaces, but also from one other class. This is the same as Java's normal inheritance model.

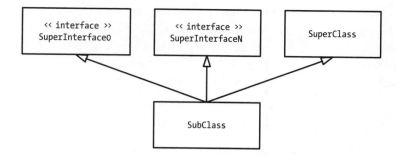

Figure 9-2. Class and interface inheritance in the ODMG's object model

A concrete example of this is shown in Figure 9-3, where you can see a SportsCar interface that can inherit from both the TwoSeater and Turbo interfaces, but cannot inherit from the ChevroletCar or HondaCar classes. The Corvette class, however, can inherit from both the TwoSeater and Turbo interfaces as well as the ChevroletCar class, but not the HondaCar class as well.

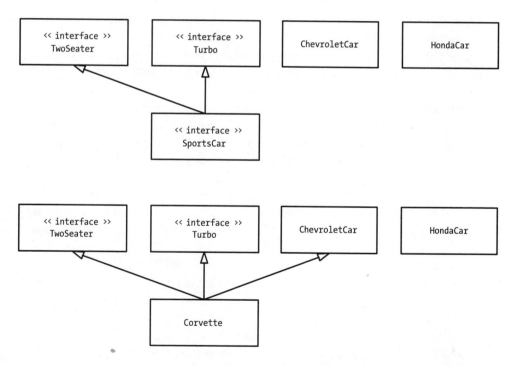

Figure 9-3. Concrete example of interface and class inheritance rules for the ODMG object model

As I mentioned before, all of this may seem redundant to Java programmers, but it is important because data stored in many ODMG data sources can be made available to other programming languages. This depends on the underlying implementation, but it is important to address. Languages like C++ support multiple inheritance of classes, which the ODMG does not allow.

Working with Objects

While specifications are great, it is now time to see how you can use the ODMG to do actual work. In this section, I am going to show how to add objects to the ODMS. I will show how to name objects in the ODMS and retrieve them by those names. I will show how to persist objects without having to name them, and how to delete persisted objects. Finally, I will show how to modify and update objects already stored.

Object Identity and Names

Every object stored in an ODMS has its own unique identity. There should be no accessible attribute that can be used to duplicate an object's identity; in other words, the get/setId methods you added to your business object cannot be the ODMG unique identifier. If you clone an object and duplicate all its fields, the clone is still not considered the same object by the ODMS because when it is added to the system, the clone will receive its own unique identifier.

How unique identifiers are implemented is not defined by the ODMG specification. It is left up to the implementers. However, the specification does state that application code should not be able to specify the unique identifier or value.

This is actually very liberating to you as a developer. You no longer need to worry about creating unique identifiers in the way you did in Chapter 5. The system takes care of that for you. You can also compare two different objects and know whether they are the same or different. Often, however, your applications require you to define application-based unique identifiers.

It would be helpful if you could access an object you know of by name. If you do need some name to identify an object, you can name it. To name an object is to give it an arbitrary string, which can be used to retrieve the object. The string used must be unique throughout the ODMS. It is not possible to assign the name "John Smith" to two different employees regardless of their real names. Not all objects in the ODMS need to have a name. Addresses, for instance, will rarely be accessed except through the entity they are associated with. Usually, you are looking for a specific person or place's address. Whether an object has a name depends on how the objects are going to be used. If you are writing geographical mapping software, you will probably want to name your addresses in order to make them easier to retrieve.

It is the key objects that are at the base of a hierarchy that will normally get a name. A department from which you can get a list of employees is a good example of an object to name. Naming projects in order to retrieve all of the associated documents would make sense.

The code for binding an object is shown in Listing 9-1. The code accesses a database, and a transaction is started. Employees are bound to names in the database. Finally, the transaction is committed and the database connection is closed.

Listing 9-1. Binding an Object to a Name in ODMG 3

```
package com.apress.javapersist.chapter09;

import com.apress.javapersist.chapter09.bo.*;
import org.odmg.*;

public class BindEmployees {

    public static void main(String[] args) {
        try {
            persistEmployees();
        }
        catch( Exception e ) {
            e.printStackTrace();
        }
    }

    private static void persistEmployees() throws Exception {
        Implementation impl = ODMGStrategy.getImpl();
        Database db = impl.newDatabase();
        db.open(ODMGStrategy.getDbIdentifier(), Database.OPEN_READ_WRITE);

        Transaction txn = impl.newTransaction();
        txn.begin();
        try {
            Employee employee1 = ODMGStrategy.createEmployee1();
            Employee employee2 = ODMGStrategy.createEmployee2();
            db.bind(employee1, "CEO");
            db.bind(employee2, "CTO");
            txn.commit();
        }
```

```
        catch (Exception e) {
            txn.abort();
            throw e;
        }
        finally {
            db.close();
        }
    }
}
```

There are actually two implementation-specific parts defined by the ODMG. I have wrapped the two implementation-specific parts in one strategy object called ODMGStrategy. The first thing that will change between each implementation of the strategy is the actual class that is the starting point for ODMG work. This class must implement the org.odmg.Implementation interface. The second part that is specific to the implementation is exactly how a database is referenced. The actual argument to db.open() is of type java.lang.Object. For most ODMG implementations, this will be some type of string reference, URL, or identifier from their configuration.

Once the objects have been bound to the database, it is easy to look up the objects. You simply follow similar procedures as binding, but make a call to lookup instead. In Listing 9-2, you see that a database is obtained and a transaction is started. A call to lookup is made, and then the transaction is committed.

Listing 9-2. Performing a Lookup of Bound Objects with ODMG

```
package com.apress.javapersist.chapter09;

import com.apress.javapersist.chapter09.bo.*;
import org.odmg.*;

public class LookupEmployees {

    public static void main(String[] args) {
        try {
            lookupEmployees();
        }
        catch( Exception e ) {
            e.printStackTrace();
        }
    }

    private static void lookupEmployees() throws Exception {
```

```
Implementation impl = ODMGStrategy.getImpl();
Database db = impl.newDatabase();
db.open(ODMGStrategy.getDbIdentifier(), Database.OPEN_READ_WRITE);

Employee employee1 = null;
Employee employee2 = null;

Transaction txn = impl.newTransaction();
try {
    txn.begin();
    employee1 = (Employee) db.lookup("CEO");
    employee2 = (Employee) db.lookup("CTO");
    System.out.println( "CEO: " + employee1 );
    System.out.println( "CTO: " + employee2 );
    txn.commit();
}
catch (Exception e) {
    txn.abort();
    throw e;
}
finally {
    db.close();
}
}
}
```

You can also unbind names from an object stored in an ODMG repository.
For this you connect to the database and simply call the unbind method (see
Listing 9-3). This does not delete the objects from the ODMS, it simply removes the
shortcut for accessing the object. Once an object is unbound, you must query to
obtain a reference to it. I will discuss querying through ODMG in the section
"Object Query Language" later in this chapter.

Listing 9-3. Unbinding Objects from an ODMS

```
package com.apress.javapersist.chapter09;

import com.apress.javapersist.chapter09.bo.*;
import org.odmg.*;

public class UnbindEmployees {

    public static void main(String[] args) {
        try {
```

```
                    unbindEmployees();
            }
            catch( Exception e ) {
                e.printStackTrace();
            }
        }


        private static void unbindEmployees() throws Exception {
            Implementation impl = ODMGStrategy.getImpl();
            Database db = impl.newDatabase();
            db.open(ODMGStrategy.getDbIdentifier(), Database.OPEN_READ_WRITE);

            Employee employee1 = null;
            Employee employee2 = null;

            Transaction txn = impl.newTransaction();
            try {
                txn.begin();
                employee1 = (Employee) db.lookup("CEO");
                employee2 = (Employee) db.lookup("CTO");
                System.out.println( "CEO: " + employee1 );
                System.out.println( "CTO: " + employee2 );
                db.unbind( "CEO" );
                db.unbind( "CTO" );
                txn.commit();
            }
            catch (Exception e) {
                txn.abort();
                throw e;
            }
            try {
                txn.begin();
                employee1 = (Employee) db.lookup("CEO");
                employee2 = (Employee) db.lookup("CTO");
                System.out.println( "Wrong, shouldn't have reached this" );
            }
            catch( ObjectNameNotFoundException e ) {
                // Good, shouldn't be found
                txn.commit();
            }
            finally {
                db.close();
            }
        }
    }
}
```

It is important to note that objects are not bound or unbound until the transaction commits. This allows easy rollback. So if an exception is thrown while working with the object, changes will not be persisted. This gives confidence in the state of the objects.

Adding Objects to and Removing Objects from Persistence

While binding makes an object persistent and adds it to the database, you don't always need to tie a name to an object. Many objects will simply be added to the persistence layer and later retrieved using regular queries, which I discuss later in this chapter.

In order to make an object persistent, you simply call the makePersistent method on the ODMG Database object. Listing 9-4 shows that it is simply a call to makePersistent, which adds the object to the database.

Listing 9-4. Making an Object Persistent in ODMG

```
package com.apress.javapersist.chapter09;

import com.apress.javapersist.chapter09.bo.*;
import org.odmg.*;

public class PersistEmployee {

    public static void main(String[] args) {
        try {
            persistEmployees();
        }
        catch( Exception e ) {
            e.printStackTrace();
        }
    }

    private static void persistEmployees() throws Exception {
        Implementation impl = ODMGStrategy.getImpl();
        Database db = impl.newDatabase();
        db.open(ODMGStrategy.getDbIdentifier(), Database.OPEN_READ_WRITE);

        Transaction txn = impl.newTransaction();
```

```
            txn.begin();
            try {
                Employee employee3 = ODMGStrategy.createEmployee3();
                db.makePersistent(employee3);
                txn.commit();
            }
            catch (Exception e) {
                txn.abort();
                throw e;
            }
            finally {
                db.close();
            }
        }
    }
```

Once the object is added to the database, it will stay there until it is deleted from the persistence mechanism. Notice that removing an object from persistence does not in any way delete that object from application memory. It simply removes the object from the ODMS.

Another point to note is that while binding an object does make a transient object persistent, unbinding does not remove that object from persistence. Only calling the deletePersistent method on the Database does that. In Listing 9-5, you see an object being removed from persistence.

Listing 9-5. Removing an Object from Persistence

```
package com.apress.javapersist.chapter09;

import com.apress.javapersist.chapter09.bo.*;
import org.odmg.*;

public class DeleteEmployees {

    public static void main(String[] args) {
        try {
            deleteEmployees();
        }
        catch( Exception e ) {
            e.printStackTrace();
        }
    }
```

```
private static void deleteEmployees() throws Exception {
    Implementation impl = ODMGStrategy.getImpl();
    Database db = impl.newDatabase();
    db.open(ODMGStrategy.getDbIdentifier(), Database.OPEN_READ_WRITE);

    Employee employee1 = null;
    Employee employee2 = null;

    Transaction txn = impl.newTransaction();
    try {
        txn.begin();
        employee1 = (Employee) db.lookup("CEO");
        employee2 = (Employee) db.lookup("CTO");
        System.out.println( "CEO: " + employee1 );
        System.out.println( "CTO: " + employee2 );
        db.unbind( "CEO" );
        db.unbind( "CTO" );
        db.deletePersistent(employee1);
        db.deletePersistent(employee2);
        txn.commit();
    }
    catch (Exception e) {
        txn.abort();
        throw e;
    }
    try {
        txn.begin();
        employee1 = (Employee) db.lookup("CEO");
        employee2 = (Employee) db.lookup("CTO");
        System.out.println( "Wrong, shouldn't have reached this" );
    }
    catch( ObjectNameNotFoundException e ) {
        // Good, shouldn't be found
        txn.commit();
    }
    finally {
        db.close();
    }
}
}
```

Once again, until the commit method is called on the transaction, no changes are made to the underlying database. So making a call to makePersistent and deletePersistent has no lasting effect until the transaction commits.

Modifying Persisted Objects

In order to modify an object that is already registered with the ODMS, you need to lock it for modification. In this way you avoid conflicts with other users in the system. You lock an object through the associated transaction.

In Listing 9-6, you see an object being obtained from the database by lookup. Once the object is available, it is locked with the lock state of Transaction.WRITE. While the object is locked, no one else can obtain the lock and modify that same object. After the lock is obtained, any changes made to the object are tracked and will be persisted when the transaction commits.

Listing 9-6. Modifying an Object Using ODMG

```
package com.apress.javapersist.chapter09;

import com.apress.javapersist.chapter09.bo.*;
import org.odmg.*;

public class ModifyEmployee {

    public static void main(String[] args) {
        Implementation impl = ODMGStrategy.getImpl();
        Database db = impl.newDatabase();
        try {
            db.open(ODMGStrategy.getDbIdentifier(), Database.OPEN_READ_WRITE);

            Employee employee1 = null;

            Transaction txn = impl.newTransaction();
            txn.begin();
            employee1 = (Employee) db.lookup("CEO");
            System.out.println( "CEO: " + employee1 );
            txn.lock(employee1, Transaction.WRITE);
            employee1.setEmail("dglyzewski@centare.com");
            txn.commit();

            txn.begin();
            employee1 = (Employee) db.lookup("CEO");
            System.out.println( "CEO: " + employee1 );
            txn.commit();
        }
        catch (Exception e) {
            e.printStackTrace();
        }
```

```
        finally {
            try {
                db.close();
            } catch (ODMGException e) {}
        }
    }
}
```

In this code, you find the object bound to the name CEO. You then change the e-mail address of the employee and commit the change. Once the transaction is committed, you obtain a second transaction and look up the CEO again. From there, you ensure that the change has taken effect.

As with other ODMG interaction, no changes are written to the ODMS until the transaction is committed. You are still protected from leaving the persistence mechanism in an inconsistent state in that way.

Querying for Objects

Not all objects are bound, nor should they all be. For this reason, you need a way to find objects that are stored in the ODMS but do not have a name tied to them. For this purpose the ODMG has defined the Object Query Language (OQL).

OQL is a query language much like Structured Query Language. In fact, the language is taken from SQL-92 with extensions and omissions that are appropriate for working with objects. For this reason, it is fairly easy to learn.

Object Query Language

As I said before, the language for OQL is very similar to SQL. With it, you can query your ODMS for objects stored within. The main difference between OQL and SQL is the difference between objects and tables. With SQL, you extract data from tables; with OQL, you extract objects. In SQL, your criteria is based on columns in tables; in OQL, your criteria is based on attributes of objects stored in your data store. The data store can be an object database, a relational database that can natively store objects, or an ODMG-compliant OR framework.

So where in SQL you would query for a row of data that has a column that matches a value, in OQL you query for an object with an attribute that matches a value. Rather than looking for a row of data, you are searching for an instance of an object. The huge savings of time is in not trying to turn a row of data into an object.

Basic OQL would consist of a select statement followed by the class name and optional query criteria.

```
SELECT objectName
FROM className AS className
WHERE className.attribute1 = value1 AND className.attribute2 = value2
```

For example, to query for an employee whose last name is Glyzewski and first name is Dave, you would write a query like this:

```
SELECT emp
FROM com.apress.javapersist.chapter09.bo.Employee AS emp
WHERE emp.lastName = 'Glyzewski' AND emp.firstName = 'Dave'
```

This is fairly generic OQL. Today there are few products that support a complete OQL implementation. Most of those are in the object database arena. Some products such as the open source Jarkarta project ObJectRelationalBridge (OJB) do support a limited OQL. Many other products that claim ODMG compliance also have limited or missing OQL support.

The point is that you should be prepared to modify your OQL if you go from one ODMG implementation to another. The problem is very similar to that experienced when switching from one relational database to another—the SQL often needs to change.

For a complete OQL syntax and description, I suggest referencing the ODMG's Web site at http://www.odmg.org. They also have a sample grammar available for download.

Querying from Java

Now that you have an idea of the basic syntax of OQL, let's see how to use it with a Java ODMG implementation. In Listing 9-7, you obtain a reference to your ODMG implementation, from which you obtain a reference to a database object. You also obtain a transaction to work within. Next, you obtain an instance of an OQLQuery object. To this object you pass the OQL to execute and bind any variables. Finally, you execute the query, which returns any matching results in a collection.

Listing 9-7. Select Employees Using OQL

```
package com.apress.javapersist.chapter09;

import com.apress.javapersist.chapter09.bo.*;
import org.odmg.*;

public class SelectEmployees {
```

```java
public static void main(String[] args) {
    Implementation impl = ODMGStrategy.getImpl();
    Database db = impl.newDatabase();
    try {
        db.open(ODMGStrategy.getDbIdentifier(), Database.OPEN_READ_WRITE);

        Transaction txn = impl.newTransaction();
        txn.begin();
        OQLQuery query = impl.newOQLQuery();
        String oql = "select emp from "
                + Employee.class.getName()
                + " where firstName = $1";
        query.create( oql );
        query.bind(args[0]);
        System.out.println( query.execute() );
        txn.commit();
    }
    catch( Exception e ) {
        e.printStackTrace();
    }
    finally {
        try {
            db.close();
        }
        catch(ODMGException e){}
    }
}
}
```

Summary

This chapter has been an introduction to the large and complex topic of the Object Data Management Group and their specification. The purpose of the ODMG is to provide write once, store anywhere. The specification theoretically allows stored Java objects to be retrieved and used by Smalltalk applications.

The ODMG simply releases specifications. Many products, ranging from object databases to off-the-shelf persistence layers, implement the ODMG's specifications. This is what gives a system the ability to write the ODMG and change the underlying persistence framework. This can also be considered a weakness because they do not provide a reference implementation that can be compared against.

Using the ODMG, you saw in this chapter how to bind objects to arbitrary strings for easy referral and retrieval. You also saw how to look those objects up and modify them. I talked about deleting objects from the underlying persistence layer and, briefly, using transactions within ODMG.

Finally, this chapter covered basic OQL. The language is an offshoot of SQL and intended for object retrieval based on object attributes. In OQL you write the queries directly for the objects, not against a table row. When you want all employees with a certain birthday, that is exactly what you ask for. In a more traditional OR method, you would have to figure out exactly how to obtain all employee data you need to instantiate the Employee object yourself.

CHAPTER 10

Persistence with Java Data Objects (JDO)

BUT THE BASIN OF THE MISSISSIPPI is the BODY OF THE NATION. All the other parts are but members, important in themselves, yet more important in their relations to this. So, too, with how Java Data Objects (JDO) relates to our applications. The goal in software development is to write a piece of software to solve some problem. The tools are primarily important in relation to that solution. JDO is not meant to be the focus, but a transparent, helping framework.

Java Data Objects is Sun's answer to write once, store anywhere. The idea is to remove the need for any type of data storage knowledge and allow Java developers to store their data in any relational database, object database, or file-based storage without having to know any of the underlying details. This is actually very similar to the goals of the Object Data Management Group (ODMG) discussed in Chapter 9.

There has been much cross-pollination of ideas between the ODMG and the JDO design team. In fact, the ODMG's Java binding was submitted as a basis for JDO. They both provide transparent persistence, object querying, and extents. Even with these similarities, there are still many differences.

You may wonder why there is a need for yet another standard with JDBC for hand-built persistence and ODMG for transparent persistence. The primary reason given by Sun is a need for simplification. There are many parts of the ODMG specification that are not necessary for developers who want to focus exclusively on writing software in the Java language.

A second reason for another specification is because the ODMG has had some trouble getting consistent and complete implementations. Many products claim ODMG compliance while only providing a part of the specification. Creating the JDO specification allows Sun to define what should be available for a product to be compliant.

Because of the similarity between ODMG and JDO, many of the Java products that are ODMG compliant were first to become JDO compliant. This applies both to commercial and open source products.

The goal of this chapter is not to be a definitive guide to JDO. This chapter is intended to introduce JDO in a way that should help people to get up and running in a basic way very fast. For in-depth coverage, I suggest getting *Using and Understanding Java Data Objects* by David Ezzio (Apress. ISBN: 1-59059-043-0), or even reading the specification from Sun, which can be found at `http://java.sun.com/products/jdo`.

What Is a JDO Implementation?

There are three conceptual parts to any JDO implementation, much like a JDBC implementation. There is Sun's JDO API, the classes that implement that API, and the specification that spells out how the implementation should act. The API is freely available from Sun, but has very little value without an implementation behind it.

Like they do with all of their Java APIs, Sun makes available enough interfaces and classes that developers can count on how they will use the implementation. Developers can download the JDO API and write software that uses JDO without any JDO implementation behind it; they will not be able to test it, but they can write it. One way that Sun made this easier is by moving all implementation-specific configuration information into a property file that is loaded at runtime.

So unlike in JDBC where you need to write the code that pulls the driver name from a configuration file and to either have a call to `Class.forName` or explicitly reference the driver class, in JDO you specify the driver class in the properties file, which is easily loaded and passed into JDO. This wonderful feature also allows code to easily move from one implementation to another, hopefully without any recompiling.

While it is true that Sun does not freely distribute a commercially usable JDO implementation, they do make available a Reference Implementation. The Reference Implementation is a way for Sun to prove that the specification is viable. The Reference Implementation is file based: Instead of using a relational database, it uses the file system for storage and the file system context for Java Naming and Directory Interface (JNDI). The code in this chapter was written using Sun's Reference Implementation.

While there are many interfaces and classes in the JDO API, the primary parts consist of `PersistenceManager`, `Query`, and `Transaction`. Most JDO work will be done with these interfaces. In the next section I will discuss how these classes relate.

Overview of the JDO Architecture

I said before that JDO consists primarily of a few important interfaces. Let's talk about what those are. Figure 10-1 shows the basic players in using JDO. The `JDOHelper` class is used to gain a reference to an implementing instance of the `PersistenceManagerFactory`. The persistence manager factory is used to obtain an instance of a `PersistenceManager`. It is from the persistence manager that you will perform most of your work. Specifically, you will use the persistence manager to obtain references to Transactions, which you need for persisting and removing objects, and Queries that you use for finding objects.

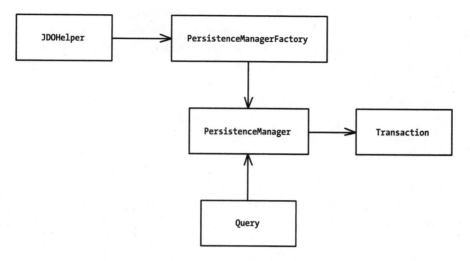

Figure 10-1. The main interfaces and classes of JDO

Of the objects shown, only the JDOHelper is an actual class. All others are interfaces. Each of those classes would be implemented by the underlying JDO implementation. It is for this reason that JDO helper is your starting point in working with JDO.

How JDO Works

In general, Sun has left the specifics of how a JDO implementation works to the JDO providers. Sun does not care how or where the implementers store their data. There are, however, commitments that any JDO implementation must fulfill.

Source and Byte-Code Enhancing

While a developer can create persistable classes for JDO by hand, I don't recommend it. There are many dependencies that would be easy to miss or introduce bugs into. While it may seem like a violation of Java to "enhance" either a source or class file, it is actually the best solution that could be arrived at.

The reason that a class needs to be enhanced is because Java does not provide enough hooks in the language to allow a persistence mechanism to know when work has been done to the persistable class. In other words, there is no way for a

JDO implementation to know that a value has been changed on an object retrieved from the data store.

In a handwritten persistence layer, it can be permissible to write data to the database that has not been modified or to load entire object graphs; these only work because the developers have complete control over the application and usage. Developers quickly notice a major performance problem introduced by loading the entire object graph. When writing a framework, you cannot control how developers will use it. For this reason you need to know exactly what is going on in the code.

In turn, the fine-grained control achieved through enhancement gives JDO the ability to provide complex functionality. It is possible in this way to provide lazy loading of data. In other words, it is possible to have a reference to an object that is not wholly loaded from the database.

So Sun decided on recommending class enhancement. There are two types of enhancement discussed in the specification: one is source code enhancement, the other is byte-code enhancement. In the first, the Java class's source code is modified before it is compiled. In the second, the post-compiled class file is modified.

The second method has a few benefits, such as the version-controlled source does not contain any non–developer-added code. Finally, a compiled then enhanced class will still contain valid debug information (provided one isn't trying to debug code the implementation added to the class). This is because the debug information is placed in the class file on the first compile and is not touched by the enhancement.

One aspect that the specification dictates is a binary compatibility; a class that is enhanced by the Reference Implementation must be usable by all compliant JDO implementations. Classes enhanced by any JDO-compliant enhancer must be usable by any other JDO-compliant implementation. This feature allows you to move enhanced JAR files and compiled classes from one implementation to another.

A class enhanced with one implementation's enhancer should work with another implementation. Since you can use any enhancer with any implementation, it is the implementation-specific features that separate the enhancers such as caching or anything else they use to differentiate themselves.

Be careful when using any implementation-specific features; this is the candy that gets organizations hooked on one specific vendor. Many times it seems prudent to use the features, but when the vendor raises its prices, changes its licensing fees, or goes out of business completely, it can be a very costly venture to refactor all your code to another implementation that does not have the same features.

JDO Transactions and What Happens After the Rollback

Transactions in JDO are similar to all the other transactions we have discussed in this book. They conform to the ACID properties. The JDO Transaction interface has begin, rollback, and commit methods. There isn't much mystery in how these work. Before modifying an object that is contained within persistent storage, the code needs to begin a transaction. When the work is done committing, the transaction will write the modified data to the data store.

Besides these expected functions, there are some additional helpful features of JDO transactions. One feature is the ability to tell the implementation to restore values to their original state after a commit or rollback. This gives developers the freedom to modify and work with objects knowing that if there is a problem, not only will the data store not be left in an instable state, but neither will the object being worked on.

One aspect of transactions in JDO that may not be immediately apparent is the fact that a persistence manager is tied to a single transaction at a time. This gives you the ability to easily access the current transaction from the persistence manager.

Querying with JDOQL

Stored objects are of little value without a way of querying, kind of like write-only memory. JDO has a very nice query mechanism. Essentially, querying in JDO relies on yet another query language, this one called JDOQL. Fortunately, it is a very simple language that is object based, similar to OQL.

Unlike OQL and SQL, JDOQL is a combination of objects, method calls, and filter strings. The entire query process is composed of creating a specific Query object, setting attributes of the query, and then executing the query and retrieving the results.

Queries are created from the persistence manager by making calls to the newQuery method. The idea of this method is to specify what class the query applies to. Optionally, in creating the query you can specify a list of objects that can be part of the results and/or indicate a filter that each part of the result must match.

Complex queries can contain parameters, variables, and filtering all specified through methods. Parameters can be specified to the query through calls to declareParameters. Variables are specified through declareVariables. Result ordering is specified through setOrdering.

The filtering language is very simple object and boolean based. This means that filtering is based on matching object attributes, either an object's attribute matches the filter or it does not. So to filter on employee information you create the query with an `Employee` class. Then filter based on employees' attributes. The code for this can be as simple as that in Listing 10-1.

Listing 10-1. Employee Query Example

```
Query query = persistenceManager.newQuery(Employee.class, "firstName==\"John\"");
```

This query will return all employees whose first name is "John". The query itself will not be run until the `execute` method is called. At that time an unmodifiable collection will be returned containing all employees with the first name of John. By making the collection unmodifiable, Sun prevents confusion between the collection and the data store. Otherwise developers might believe they are adding objects to the data store if they could add the object to the collection.

Notice that the filter uses JavaBean property names very much like those used in OQL. You don't need to specify `getFirstName`, you simply use the attribute name "firstName". JDOQL also supports nested properties. You could use something like `address.zipCode.firstFive == "22333"` to find all employees in the 22333 zip code.

Getting All Instances in Extents

An extent is the way to obtain a reference to all instances of classes within the data store. The extent facility is different from a query in the fact that there is no ability to filter within the extent. The actual interface returned from the extent is that of a `java.util.Iterator`, which makes it very easy to run through the contents.

Often it is desirable to retrieve all instances of a class and its subclasses. An extent can optionally contain all instances of subclasses of the specified class. Whether to include subclasses is specified by the second argument, which is a boolean.

An extent can be extremely large. Once again, depending on the object graph, it could be prohibitively large to load all instances of a class. For this reason, many implementations support loading *hollow objects*. This refers to code that can have a reference to an object, but none of its data has been retrieved from the database. When data for the hollow object is accessed for the first time, it is loaded from the database.

JDO Class Restrictions and Requirements

There are very few restrictions placed on classes that can be persisted by JDO. Some of the restrictions are helped by JDO enhancers. Other restrictions you simply need to be aware of such as inheritance and attribute types.

For inheritance, persistence classes can inherit from nonpersistent classes. Nonpersistent classes can inherit from persistent classes. Persistent classes can inherit from persistent classes. However, persistent classes cannot inherit from natively implemented classes, e.g., java.net.Socket and java.lang.Thread.

That was a mouthful. Let's walk through that one more time. If you have a non-persistent class named Person, you can create a persistent class named Employee that extends it. You can create a second persistent class named Manager that extends Employee. You cannot, however, create a subclass of java.lang.Thread and persist it.

Any fields in a nonpersistent superclass cannot be persisted, which means that any attributes of nonpersistent class Person cannot be saved when you save an Employee object.

All classes in the hierarchy must use the same JDO identity type. So your Employee and Manager class must both use the same identity type. This is important for supporting extents.

Arrays are a concern when it comes to JDO. Arrays cannot be subclassed, so no specialized tracking class can be implemented. It is impossible to create a specialized array wrapper that would notice and track changes to an array. Therefore, a developer must use JDOHelper's makeDirty method to indicate that an array's values have changed.

Different Types of JDO Identity

If two objects represent the same data in the JDO repository, they are said to share the same JDO identity. This is different from Java identity exposed through the "==" operator or the equals method. While JDO uniqueness is not dependent on these Java methods of comparison, if the same persistence manager is used, these tests can be true.

It is very important to maintain object uniqueness with JDO—this is how you can maintain data integrity. If two objects could have the same identity, they could end up having different state or data. The question would then arise as to which one would be considered the definitive source of data for the data store.

There are three types of identity in JDO: application, data store, and nondurable. *Application identity* is analogous to a primary key. It is maintained by the application and often required by the data store. A *data store identity* is maintained between JDO and the data store; the application does not know or care about it. *Nondurable identity* is intended for an implementation to track objects within the JVM.

JDO XML Metadata

One of the requirements of the JDO specification is that a persistable object must have a metadata file associated with it. JDO's metadata files are XML files with a .jdo extension. The purpose of the file is to tell the enhancer and implementation what objects to persist and how.

If only one class is defined in the metadata file, then the filename should be the same as the class but with the .jdo extension. If multiple classes are defined in the file, then the metadata file should have the name of the shared package. A metadata file for com.apress.javapersist.bo.Employee could be named Employee.jdo, bo.jdo, javapersist.jdo, apress.jdo, or com.jdo. The enhancer will look for the metadata file in that order.

The contents of the metadata files are very simple, containing only a few tags. The structure of the file is as follows:

- *XML declaration:* Defines the file as an XML file.

- *DTD:* Indicates the Document Type Definition, which describes how the document needs to be put together.

- *jdo tag:* Starts the definition of the metadata. Can only contain one or more package tags and any number of vendor extension tags.

- *package tag:* Specifies a wrapper for the classes you will define. Can contain one or more class tags and any number of vendor extension tags.

- *class tag:* Defines a class that can be persisted. Can contain any number of field and vendor extension tags.

- *field tag:* Defines a field that can be persisted or ignored. Can contain one collection, map, or array and any number of vendor extensions.

- *collection tag:* Describes the collection. Can contain any number of vendor extension tags.

- *map tag:* Describes a map. Can contain any number of vendor extension tags.

- *array tag:* Describes an array. Can contain any number of vendor extension tags.

- *extension tag:* Used for nonstandard JDO functionality or to convey information to the underlying implementation. Basically it contains the vendor name and a key-value pair.

Listing 10-2 contains a simple example of a metadata file. The file is for an Employee class. Notice that only one attribute is listed; all other attributes are by default persisted if they are not Java transient, static, or final.

Listing 10-2. Employee.jdo

```xml
<?xml version="1.0"?>
<!DOCTYPE jdo SYSTEM "jdo.dtd">
<jdo>
    <package name="com.apress.javapersist.chapter10.bo">
        <class name="Employee">
          <field name="age" persistence-modifier="none"></field>
        </class>
    </package>
</jdo>
```

How You Can Use JDO to Persist Your Objects

For this next section, I will break down a basic JDO application. I will show you the various parts of the application, explaining them one by one. I have broken the application down into separate commands. I tried to create one command for each piece of JDO functionality I will explain.

What I will show you how to create in this section is a simple HR application, building on the work done in earlier chapters. Essentially, you will see how to create a command line tool that will store employees and addresses. It can list stored objects and remove stored objects. It will allow you to associate addresses with employees. Finally, I will show some examples of using the application.

Example Business Objects

The Employee class for this example is a simple Java business object as seen in Listing 10-3. The class has a few attributes, but nothing JDO specific. You need to add a no-argument constructor as I have done here to support the reference implementation's enhancer. Some commercial enhancers add this if it is not present. Keep in mind though that in the final class there will be a public no-args constructor whether you added it or the enhancer did.

Listing 10-3. Employee.java

```java
package com.apress.javapersist.chapter10.bo;

import java.util.*;

public class Employee {
    private long id;
    private String firstName;
    private String lastName;
    private String email;
    private Address address;

    public Employee() {
    }

    public Employee(long id) {
        this.id = id;
    }

    public long getId() {
        return id;
    }

    public String getFirstName() {
        return this.firstName;
    }

    public void setFirstName(String firstName) {
        this.firstName = firstName;
    }

    public String getLastName() {
        return this.lastName;
    }

    public void setLastName(String lastName) {
        this.lastName = lastName;
    }

    public String getEmail() {
        return this.email;
    }
```

```
    public void setEmail(String email) {
        this.email = email;
    }

    public Address getAddressea() {
        return address;
    }

    public void setAddress(Address address) {
        this.address = address;
    }

    public String toString() {
        return "id: " + id + "; "
            + "firstName: " + firstName + "; "
            + "lastName: " + lastName + "; "
            + "email: " + email + "; "
            + "address: [" + address + "]";
    }
}
```

You will also need to provide a metadata file for the employee object. The file in Listing 10-4 is a very simple metadata file. There are no special fields and no implementation specific enhancements. This file will be read by your enhancer and needs to be deployed with your class. Notice that even the application-specific Address attribute is not specified; because it is persistable, it will be taken care of by the implementation.

Listing 10-4. Employee.jdo

```xml
<?xml version="1.0"?>
<!DOCTYPE jdo SYSTEM "jdo.dtd">
<jdo>
    <package name="com.apress.javapersist.chapter10.bo">
        <class name="Employee">
        </class>
    </package>
</jdo>
```

The Address class in Listing 10-5 for your employees is another simple business object. The one interesting feature of this class is the ArrayList of residents. This class actually has a collection-based attribute that you can use for querying.

Listing 10-5. Address.java

```java
package com.apress.javapersist.chapter10.bo;

import java.util.*;

public class Address {
    private long id;
    private String streetLine1;
    private String streetLine2;
    private String city;
    private String state;
    private ArrayList residents = new ArrayList();

    public Address() {}

    public Address(long id) {
        this.id = id;
    }

    public long getId() {
        return id;
    }

    public String getCity() {
        return city;
    }

    public void setCity(String city) {
        this.city = city;
    }

    public String getState() {
        return state;
    }

    public void setState(String state) {
        this.state = state;
    }
```

```java
public String getStreetLine1() {
    return streetLine1;
}

public void setStreetLine1(String streetLine1) {
    this.streetLine1 = streetLine1;
}

public String getStreetLine2() {
    return streetLine2;
}

public void setStreetLine2(String streetLine2) {
    this.streetLine2 = streetLine2;
}

public Collection getResidents() {
    return residents;
}

public void addResident(Employee resident) {
    this.residents.add(resident);
}

public String toString() {
    return  "id: " + id + "; "
        + "line 1: " + streetLine1 + "; "
        + "line 2: " + streetLine2 + "; "
        + "city: " + city + "; "
        + "state: " + state + "; "
        + "residents: " + residents.size();
}
}
```

The metadata file for the Address class in Listing 10-6 is slightly more interesting than the employee metadata file. This file contains a field that is a collection. Notice that you need to specify the type of object that will be in the collection.

Listing 10-6. Address.jdo

```xml
<?xml version="1.0"?>
<!DOCTYPE jdo SYSTEM "jdo.dtd">
<jdo>
    <package name="com.apress.javapersist.chapter10.bo">
        <class name="Address">
            <field name="residents">
                <collection element-type="Employee"/>
            </field>
        </class>
    </package>
</jdo>
```

Performing the JDO Work

In this next section, you will see application code that will work on your business objects. It is in these classes that you will add, list, remove, and modify objects. Figure 10-2 shows how the various commands relate.

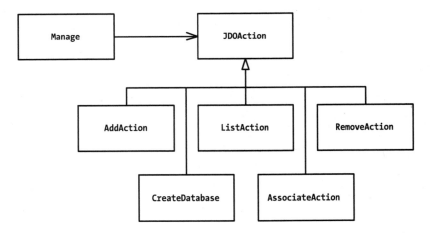

Figure 10-2. Human resources application main classes

All of your JDO commands will need certain functionality that can be shared—for instance, obtaining a reference to a persistence manager, or finding objects to work on. In Listing 10-7 you can see a JDOAction class that contains that functionality. The getPersistenceManager method is used by all subclasses when a persistence manager is needed.

Listing 10-7. JDO Action Is the Superclass of All Your JDO Commands

```java
package com.apress.javapersist.chapter10;

import java.io.IOException;
import java.io.InputStream;
import java.util.Collection;
import java.util.Iterator;
import java.util.Properties;

import javax.jdo.JDOHelper;
import javax.jdo.PersistenceManager;
import javax.jdo.PersistenceManagerFactory;
import javax.jdo.Query;

/**
 * @author rsperko
 *
 * This class is the super class of all our JDO commands. This class provides
 * utility methods for all our JDO work. Specifically this is where we would
 * obtain our connection to our persistence manager.
 */
public abstract class JDOAction {
    private static PersistenceManagerFactory factory = null;

    /**
     * Method getPersistenceManager returns a persistence manager object from
     * the class's static persistence manager factory object.
     */
    protected PersistenceManager getPersistenceManager() {
        if (factory == null) {
            Properties props = loadProperties();

            factory = JDOHelper.getPersistenceManagerFactory(props);
        }
        return factory.getPersistenceManager();
    }

    /**
     * Method loadProperties.
     * @return Properties
     */
    protected Properties loadProperties() {
        Properties props = new Properties();
```

```
        try {
            InputStream in =
                ClassLoader.getSystemResourceAsStream ("jdo.properties");
            props.load (in);
        }
        catch(IOException ioe) {
            ioe.printStackTrace();
        }
        return props;
    }


    /**
     * Method findAll.
     * @param className
     * @param string
     * @return Collection
     */
    protected Iterator findAll(PersistenceManager pm, String className,
        String queryStr) {
        try {
            if("extent".equals(queryStr)) {
                return pm.getExtent(getClass(className), false).iterator();
            }
            else {
                Query query = pm.newQuery(getClass(className), queryStr);
                return ((Collection) query.execute()).iterator();
            }
        } catch (ClassNotFoundException e) {
            e.printStackTrace();
        }
        return null;
    }


    /**
     * Method getClass.
     * @param className
     */
    private static Class getClass(String className)
        throws ClassNotFoundException {
        return Class.forName("com.apress.javapersist.chapter10.bo."
            + className);
    }


    /**
```

```
 * Method all of our commands will override to do their work.
 */
public abstract void execute(String typeName, String[] optional);

/**
 * used by the help message to convey how this action will be used.
 */
public abstract String exampleString();
}
```

Particularly note the getPersistenceManager method. This is the method that all of your subclasses will use to work the JDO implementation. This method loads the properties file that defines what JDO implementation to use and its configuration data.

The other methods in this class are helper methods. To keep the examples simpler, the findAll method that will be shared by the list, associate, and remove commands is in this class. Also, there is a helper method for turning a class base name into an actual class.

To get a better understanding of how the persistence manager is obtained, Figure 10-3 shows a sequence diagram of the relevant objects. Notice that there are two classes involved, the Properties object and the JDOHelper class. The persistence manager factory is an interface obtained from the JDO helper.

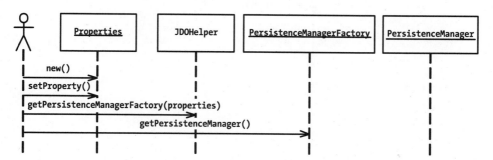

Figure 10-3. Obtaining a persistence manager

Now that you have a superclass where you can obtain your persistence manager, let's look at the class that can add an object to the JDO repository. Listing 10-8 shows the AddAction class, which does most of its work in the execute method. It is here that a transaction is started, an object is persisted, and the transaction is committed.

Listing 10-8. AddAction.java

```java
package com.apress.javapersist.chapter10;

import javax.jdo.PersistenceManager;

import com.apress.javapersist.chapter10.bo.Address;
import com.apress.javapersist.chapter10.bo.Employee;

public class AddAction extends JDOAction {

    /**
     * Add the object
     * @see com.apress.javapersist.chapter10.JDOAction#execute(String, String[])
     */
    public void execute(String typeName, String[] optional) {
        Object obj = buildObject(typeName, optional);
        PersistenceManager pm = getPersistenceManager();

        pm.currentTransaction().begin();
        // Mark the object as persistent
        pm.makePersistent(obj);
        pm.currentTransaction().commit();
        System.out.println("Object stored: " + obj);
        pm.close();
    }

    /**
     * Method buildObject.
     * @param className
     * @param optional
     * @return Object
     */
    private static Object buildObject(String className, String[] optional) {
        Object obj = null;
        if("Employee".equals(className)) {
            Employee emp = new Employee(Long.parseLong(optional[0]));
            emp.setFirstName(optional[1]);
            emp.setLastName(optional[2]);
            emp.setEmail(optional[3]);
            obj = emp;
        }
        else if("Address".equals(className)){
            Address add = new Address(Long.parseLong(optional[0]));
```

```
        add.setStreetLine1(optional[1]);
        add.setStreetLine2(optional[2]);
        add.setCity(optional[3]);
        add.setState(optional[4]);
        obj = add;
    }
    return obj;
}


/**
 * @see com.apress.javapersist.chapter10.JDOAction#exampleString()
 */
public String exampleString() {
    return "    Manage add Employee id FName LName eMail\n"
        + "    Manage add Address id line1 line2 city state";
}
}
```

Figure 10-4 illustrates exactly how an object is persisted. Notice how simple it is to add an object to a JDO data store. All it takes is a call to makePersistent wrapped in a transaction. If the object is enhanced, it is added and ready to be managed by JDO.

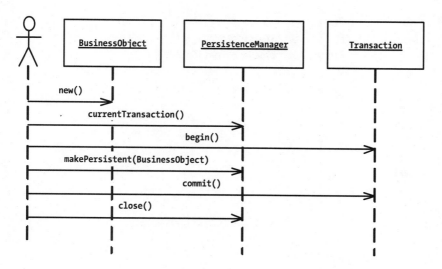

Figure 10-4. Persisting an object

There is an additional helper method in this class for building actual objects that will be added. This method is fairly fragile in that it expects a specific number of arguments in a specific order. It would be a fairly simple exercise to make that code more robust.

Next you want to see the objects you have stored in your repository. The ListAction class in Listing 10-9 is very light because most of your querying functionality is in your superclass to help with other actions. If you look back at the JDOAction class, you see that the findAll method simply calls getExtent or creates a query and executes it. The ListAction then prints out the contents that are returned.

Listing 10-9. ListAction.java

```java
package com.apress.javapersist.chapter10;

import java.util.Iterator;
import javax.jdo.PersistenceManager;

public class ListAction extends JDOAction {
    private Object className;

    /**
     * List the objects that match the query
     * @see com.apress.javapersist.chapter10.JDOAction#execute(String, String[])
     */
    public void execute(String typeName, String[] optional) {
        PersistenceManager pm = getPersistenceManager();
        Iterator iter = findAll(pm, typeName, optional[0]);

        // Run through the objects listing each one
        while( iter.hasNext() ) {
            System.out.println(iter.next());
        }
    }

    /**
     * Show how to use this action
     * @see com.apress.javapersist.chapter10.JDOAction#exampleString()
     */
    public String exampleString() {
        return "    Manage list Employee \"firstName == \\\"LName\\\"\n"
            + "    Manage list Employee extent";
    }
}
```

In Figure 10-5, you can see the how the classes interact to perform the query itself. A Query object is created from the persistence manager. The query is then executed and the resulting objects are available to be worked on.

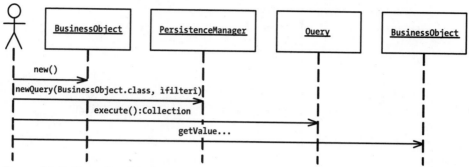

Figure 10-5. Querying for objects

Obviously a management tool should allow removal of employees from the HR application. Listing 10-10 contains the RemoveAction class. This class queries the repository using the findAll method in the JDOAction. It then iterates through the results, removing each from the data store. Removing from the data store is as simple as calling deletePersistent on an object within a transaction.

Listing 10-10. RemoveAction.java

```
package com.apress.javapersist.chapter10;

import java.util.Iterator;
import javax.jdo.PersistenceManager;

/**
 * @author rsperko
 *
 * Remove any objects that match the criteria
 */
public class RemoveAction extends JDOAction {

    /**
     * Remove all instances that match the query
     * @see com.apress.javapersist.chapter10.JDOAction#execute(String, String[])
     */
    public void execute(String typeName, String[] optional) {
        PersistenceManager pm = getPersistenceManager();
        Iterator results = findAll(pm, typeName, optional[0]);
```

```
        pm.currentTransaction().begin();
        // Run through the list of objects deleting each one
        while(results.hasNext())
           pm.deletePersistent(results.next());
        pm.currentTransaction().commit();
    }

    /**
     * Show how to use this action
     * @see com.apress.javapersist.chapter10.JDOAction#exampleString()
     */
    public String exampleString() {
        return "    Manage remove Employee \"lastName == \\\"LName\\\"";
    }
}
```

Finally, I want to illustrate modifying a persistent object. The AssociateAction class, shown in Listing 10-11, will modify both an employee and an address by associating one object with the other. For this to work, the class will query the data store for the objects you want to associate. The execute method will then create a transaction, associate the objects, and commit the transaction.

Listing 10-11. AssociateAction.java

```
package com.apress.javapersist.chapter10;

import javax.jdo.PersistenceManager;

import com.apress.javapersist.chapter10.bo.Address;
import com.apress.javapersist.chapter10.bo.Employee;

/**
 * @author rsperko
 *
 * This class is used to associate one object with another.
 */
public class AssociateAction extends JDOAction {
    /**
     * Associate one object with another
     * @see com.apress.javapersist.chapter10.JDOAction#execute(String, String[])
     */
    public void execute(String typeName, String[] optional) {
        if("Employee".equals(typeName)) {
```

```
        PersistenceManager pm = getPersistenceManager();
        Employee employee = (Employee) findAll(pm, typeName,
            optional[0]).next();
        Address address = (Address) findAll(pm, optional[1],
            optional[2]).next();
        System.out.println("About to associate: " + employee + " with "
            + address);

        pm.currentTransaction().begin();
        // Actually associate the two classes
        employee.setAddress(address);
        address.addResident(employee);
        pm.currentTransaction().commit();
    }
}

/**
 * Show how to use this action
 * @see com.apress.javapersist.chapter10.JDOAction#exampleString()
 */
public String exampleString() {
    return "    Manage assoc Employee \"id==0\" Address \"id==1\"";
}
}
```

The beauty of JDO here is that no work needs to be done other than committing the transaction. If there were an error, the transaction could roll back and everything would return to its original state.

Using the Sun JDO Reference Implementation

There are a couple aspects of the example management application that are specific to Sun's reference implementation. The first is an optional method that creates the database. This same class could be extended to create databases or initialize databases for other implementations.

In this case, I will show you how to create the database file. You can see in Listing 10-12 that this is done by simply adding another property before obtaining the persistence manager factory. The next step is beginning and committing a transaction. That is all there is to it.

Listing 10-12. CreateDatabaseAction.java

```java
package com.apress.javapersist.chapter10;

import java.util.Properties;

import javax.jdo.JDOHelper;
import javax.jdo.PersistenceManager;
import javax.jdo.PersistenceManagerFactory;
import javax.jdo.Transaction;

public class CreateDatabaseAction extends JDOAction {
    /**
     * Method createDatabase will instantiate a new database if needed.
     * @param typeName
     */
    public void execute(String typeName, String[] optional) {
        if("jdori".equals(typeName))
            createJDORIDatabase();
        else
            System.out.println("ERROR: I don't know how to create a "
                + typeName + " database");
    }

    /**
     * Method createDatabase.
     */
    private void createJDORIDatabase() {
        try {
            Properties props = loadProperties();
            props.put("com.sun.jdori.option.ConnectionCreate", "true");
            PersistenceManagerFactory pmf =
                JDOHelper.getPersistenceManagerFactory(props);
            PersistenceManager pm = pmf.getPersistenceManager();
            Transaction tx = pm.currentTransaction();
            tx.begin();
            tx.commit();
            pm.close();
        } catch(Exception e) {
            System.err.println("Exception creating the database");
            System.err.println(e);
            System.exit(-1);
        }
    }
```

```
/**
 * Show how to use this action
 * @see com.apress.javapersist.chapter10.JDOAction#exampleString()
 */
public String exampleString() {
    return "    Manage create jdori";
}
}
```

The last Sun Reference Implementation–specific part is the jdo.properties file that tells the application that it will use that JDO implementation, and this is shown in Listing 10-13. To change JDO implementations, you could simply replace this file and away you go. As I mentioned before, replacing or modifying a property file is a lot nicer than having to recompile the code when making these changes.

Listing 10-13. jdo.properties

```
javax.jdo.PersistenceManagerFactoryClass=com.sun.jdori.fostore.FOStorePMF
javax.jdo.option.ConnectionURL=fostore:jdoriDB
javax.jdo.option.ConnectionUserName=sa
javax.jdo.option.ConnectionPassword=
```

Last but not least is the class that will tie it all together. Listing 10-14 contains the actual Manage class that handles the command line and calls the various JDOAction subclasses. Looking at the constructor, you see your actions created and added to a HashMap. The executeAction runs the actions with arguments.

The usage method first displays a list of all the actions in the HashMap. Next it asks each method to show an example of how it can be used. All of the work gets delegated to the actions themselves.

Listing 10-14. Manage.java

```
package com.apress.javapersist.chapter10;

import java.util.HashMap;
import java.util.Iterator;

/**
 * @author rsperko
 *
 * This class is used to interact with any Java Data Objects implementation.
 * In order to change the JDO implementation that is used, modify the
 * "jdo.properties" file.
```

```
 *
 * Call this class with no arguments to find out how to use it.
 */
public class Manage {
    HashMap actions = new HashMap();

    public Manage() {
        actions.put("create", new CreateDatabaseAction());
        actions.put("list", new ListAction());
        actions.put("add", new AddAction());
        actions.put("remove", new RemoveAction());
        actions.put("assoc", new AssociateAction());
    }

    private void executeAction(String[] args) {
        if(args.length < 2) {
            usage();
            return;
        }
        String actionStr = args[0];
        String typeName = args[1];
        String[] optional = new String[args.length-2];
        System.arraycopy(args, 2, optional, 0, optional.length);

        JDOAction action = (JDOAction) actions.get(actionStr);
        if(action == null) {
            usage();
            return;
        }

        action.execute(typeName, optional);
    }

    public static void main(String[] args) {
        Manage manage = new Manage();
        manage.executeAction(args);
    }


    /**
     * Method usage.
     */
    private void usage() {
        System.out.println("usage:");
```

```
System.out.println("java com.apress.javapersist.chapter10.Manage <act"
    + "ion> <object type> [arg1] [arg2] [argn]");
System.out.println("    actions: " + actions.keySet());
System.out.println();
System.out.println("Examples:");
for(Iterator iter = actions.values().iterator(); iter.hasNext(); ) {
    System.out.println(((JDOAction) iter.next()).exampleString());
}
    }
  }
}
```

Summary

Java Data Objects is a Java API from Sun that is intended to allow write once, store anywhere. Sun went to great lengths to make the standard easy to use and as transparent as possible to developers. Along with the specification, Sun also released a reference implementation to illustrate how the specification should be implemented.

JDO consists of an API and an implementation. The primary classes in the implementation are JDOHelper, PersistenceManagerFactory, PersistenceManager, Query, and Transaction. Most work will be done in JDO with these classes.

In order to make the framework a success, Sun has proposed adding class or source enhancing to give the ability to closely manage persistent classes. Enhancing consists of running a tool against a source file or a compiled class file. The Java code is modified to allow fine-grained control over how the object is used and what happens when values are modified.

Sun has also specified that a class that is enhanced with one enhancer should work with other JDO implementations. This allows some implementations to completely forgo creating their own enhancers and relying on the enhancer provided in the reference implementation.

Querying in JDO is done using JDOQL, which is a combination of classes and strings. It is an object-oriented way to query for objects in a data store. The general way it works is a class is provided to the query, then filters are applied that limit what results come back from the query. JDOQL gives a very rich object-oriented method of querying.

Transactions in JDO are similar to other transactions we have discussed in this book. They do follow the ACID properties. Further transactions are managed through the PersistenceManager class.

CHAPTER 11

Open Source Java Persistence Libraries and Frameworks

THE EVENT ON WHICH THIS fiction is founded has been supposed, by Dr. Darwin, and some of the physiological writers of Germany, as not of impossible occurrence. I shall not be supposed as according the remotest degree of serious faith to such an imagination; yet, in assuming it as the basis of a work of fancy, I have not considered myself as merely weaving a series of supernatural terrors. I am instead going to tell how various pieces and parts from many different people were brought together to create whole entities.

In this chapter I will be discussing several open source Java Persistence libraries and frameworks. The difficulty in writing this chapter is deciding which ones to write about. I am going to try to focus on the projects that seem the most mature and active today. I will talk about Hibernate, ObJectRelationalBridge (OJB), and Castor JDO. Toward the end of the chapter I will list other projects and try to give an idea of what they can do.

I am going to limit the in-depth coverage of libraries to those implementations that are easy to integrate. I hesitate to use products or frameworks where my classes need to extend a single superclass, or implement complex interfaces. You never know what requirements a design or deployment environment will put on your application, so it is not a good idea to commit to these things.

I will use the same codebase when describing all of the frameworks in this chapter. In all cases, I will discuss the same HR application used in Chapter 10. There will be minor variations, but the business objects only vary slightly and the database will not change. Primarily the actions will change to work with the various frameworks.

Just to reiterate how the application works, you have Employee and Address classes. One employee can be associated with one primary address. An address can be associated with multiple employees to accommodate multiple residents in the same household with the same address.

All work is done through a Manager class. The manager can be used to add and remove employees and addresses. The manager can also list all objects that meet a query. Finally, to illustrate modifying objects, it is possible to use the manager to associate an address with an employee.

All of the examples in this chapter will use the same database. The database for this chapter is a MySQL database named chapter11. There are two tables in the database, an Employees table and an Addresses table. Listing 11-1 shows the SQL that will be used to create these tables.

Listing 11-1. Database Creation SQL

```
CREATE TABLE addresses (
  address_id int(11) NOT NULL default '0',
  street_line1 varchar(100) default '',
  street_line2 varchar(100) default '',
  city varchar(100) default '',
  state char(2) default '',
  PRIMARY KEY  (address_id)
) TYPE=MyISAM;

CREATE TABLE employees (
  employee_id int(11) NOT NULL default '0',
  first_name varchar(100) default '',
  last_name varchar(100) default '',
  email varchar(100) default '',
  address_id int(11) default '0' NULL,
  PRIMARY KEY  (employee_id)
) TYPE=MyISAM;
```

You can use such a simple database because you will rely on application-generated unique identifiers and will not implement locking. Otherwise, there could be quite a few more tables that would be used by the various frameworks.

What Is Open Source?

Open source simply means that the source code of the software product is available, the software must be free to give or use without royalties, and the software must allow modification and extension. Beyond these components, there can be other restrictions imposed by licenses, but the software I have listed in this chapter allows you to develop internal applications without needing to release your software. If you plan on extending the software and do not wish to release your changes to the public, you should seek legal council.

While the software's up-front costs are low to none, there can be quite a bit of cost in time spent understanding and learning the software. Some open source software can cost more than their commercial counterparts in this way. If, however, you have people on staff who are technically strong, like to learn, and are attracted to open source software, these products can save your company a lot of money.

There are many different licenses that open source software is released under. For a good definition of open source and a running list of open source licenses, you can check out the Open Source Initiative (OSI) at http://www.opensource.org. Many projects either choose a license from this site or acknowledge when or if OSI recognizes their license.

Hibernate for Persistence

Hibernate is a framework that is intended to be ultra–high performance and very simple to use. The focus of the project is doing one thing and doing it well. The framework can be used either in a stand-alone application or embedded in a J2EE application. Hibernate also provides a partial ODMG 3.0 interface as well as their own persistence API. Hibernate can be obtained from http://hibernate.bluemars.net and is hosted on Source Forge. For this chapter I will discuss Hibernate version 2.

One very nice feature about Hibernate is that without byte code or source code processing, it is still able to provide lazy initialization of values. This is accomplished through collections and the use of proxies generated with CGLIB. These proxies are generated and used at runtime. This can have a great effect on development by keeping the standard Java development cycle of edit-compile-test in contrast to the normal JDO cycle of edit–compile–post process–test.

Another valuable feature of Hibernate is the excellent documentation provided with it. The documentation is not verbose, but is very clear and contains many good examples. The documentation is good enough to the point where most people will be able to get up and running very quickly. This is unfortunately a rarity in open source projects (my own included).

Setting Up Hibernate

Hibernate has the goal of allowing a developer to go from download to using the product in 10 minutes or less. This shows in the fact that all necessary libraries excluding your JDBC drivers are included in the Hibernate download. There is no need to download libraries from all over the Internet before being able to get to work. So the basic process of installing Hibernate means downloading the product from the Hibernate Web site and setting up your classpath.

Once you have installed Hibernate, you need to create a hibernate.properties configuration file for your project. In a stand-alone application, this file will tell Hibernate the JDBC driver, URL, user name, and password necessary to connect to your database. You should also specify the dialect for your database. Optionally, you can specify number of pooled connections, number of cached prepared statements, and connection isolation. It is also possible to specify any number of JDBC driver–specific options. The property file will contain a list of name-value pairs, each separated by equal signs.

In an application server where data sources would be used instead of directly creating connections, you would specify the name of the data source, user name, and password. Optionally, you could specify the JNDI URL, class to be used for InitialContext, and any number of JNDI implementation–specific parameters.

For this example, you will create a hibernate.properties file that uses the MySQL driver and dialect. It will connect to a database named chapter11 running on localhost. Listing 11-2 shows the contents of this configuration file.

Listing 11-2. The hibernate.properties File for Your HR Application

```
hibernate.connection.driver_class=com.mysql.jdbc.Driver
hibernate.connection.url=jdbc:mysql://localhost/chapter11
hibernate.connection.username=root
hibernate.connection.password=password
hibernate.dialect=net.sf.hibernate.dialect.MySQLDialect

## Show executed SQL as Hibernate runs
# hibernate.show_sql=true
```

While this is one way of specifying the configuration data, there are a few others as well. You can programmatically create a java.util.Properties object containing these name value pairs. Hibernate also supports XML files with property tags that would contain the same contents. You can even specify these properties on the command line, adding them into the System properties.

Besides MySQL, Hibernate supports a wide variety of databases. For a complete list, I suggest looking at the documentation on the Hibernate site. Besides listing the supported databases, this site also lists gotchas that you want to be aware of with certain databases or technologies.

For logging, Hibernate uses the Apache commons-logging package. This means that Hibernate will log either through log4j or the JDK 1.4 logging mechanism. If you are using a JDK version less than 1.4, you should create a log4j.properties file to manage your logging output.

Hibernate Mapping Files

As with all object-relational mapping tools, there must be some way to tie a class attribute to a table column. In Hibernate, this is done through one or more XML mapping files. At minimum these files tie a class to a table and an attribute to a column. They can do much more than just that.

Hibernate gives you various ways of specifying these mapping files. One of the simplest is to create a separate XML file for each class that will be persisted. The file should have the same name as the class itself with the extension of ".hbm.xml". If you use this method, the XML files should reside in the same directory as the class files they are associated with. By creating these separate XML files, you can give Hibernate a Java class and it will automatically load the mapping file.

Optionally, multiple classes can be in a single XML file. In this case, the location of the XML file needs to be given to Hibernate so that the mappings can be loaded before Hibernate needs to work with them. Hibernate gives a lot of flexibility; it is possible to indicate multiple XML files even here. You could create one per class; each would then be added individually.

For this example, you will use one XML file called mapping.xml that describes both classes. The name of this file is arbitrary because it can be passed into the Hibernate framework, as you will see later in the Java code that uses Hibernate. This keeps your business object package folder clean. Listing 11-3 shows the XML you will use for Hibernate to manage your Employee and Address classes.

Listing 11-3. Hibernate Mapping File mapping.xml

```xml
<?xml version="1.0" encoding="UTF-8"?>
<!DOCTYPE hibernate-mapping PUBLIC "-//Hibernate/Hibernate Mapping DTD//EN"
          "http://hibernate.sourceforge.net/hibernate-mapping.dtd">

<hibernate-mapping>
    <class name="com.apress.javapersist.chapter11.bo.Employee"
          table="employees">
        <id name="id" column="employee_id" type="long">
            <generator class="assigned"/>
        </id>
        <property name="firstName" column="first_name" type="string"/>
        <property name="lastName" column="last_name" type="string"/>
        <property name="email" type="string"/>
        <many-to-one name="address" column="address_id"></many-to-one>
    </class>
```

```
<class name="com.apress.javapersist.chapter11.bo.Address" table="addresses">
    <id name="id" column="address_id" type="long">
        <generator class="assigned"/>
    </id>
    <property name="streetLine1" column="street_line1" type="string"/>
    <property name="streetLine2" column="street_line2" type="string"/>
    <property name="city" type="string"/>
    <property name="state" type="string"/>
    <set name="residents">
        <key column="address_id"></key>
        <one-to-many class="com.apress.javapersist.chapter11.bo.Employee" />
    </set>
</class>
</hibernate-mapping>
```

For the most part, this file is fairly self-explanatory. A class is associated with a table. An identifier attribute is named and how it is generated is specified. For this example, you use the assigned generator, which means that your application will assign unique identifiers to the objects. Hibernate is more than willing to generate unique identifiers and has several types of IDs it will create including UUID generation (using an IP address rather than MAC address), sequences, or hi/lo values. The code then lists the properties; note that when a property name is the same as the column name, such as email, the column does not need to be specified. Finally, the XML describes relationships.

In this example, the relationships indicate a one-to-many relationship between the Address class and the Employee class. In the employees' listing, you indicate relationship through the many-to-one tag, which contains the employee's address property and the address_id column name. In the address listing, you indicate that there is a "set" property named residents. This means that the Address class must have getters and setters of type java.util.Set. The set ensures that an employee exists in the collection only once.

Hibernate supports several other types of collections including list, map, bag, array, and primitive-array. To use any type of collection with Hibernate, your class must declare a reference of the collection's interface type including java.util.Set, java.util.List, java.util.Map, java.util.SortedMap, and java.util.SortedSet. You must be careful not to try to use methods that are part of implementations of these interfaces because Hibernate will replace the actual implementing class with one of its own for the applicable interface. So even though you know that the set you use in your business object is a java.util.TreeSet you cannot cast the return to that type, as it will be wrapped in a Hibernate java.util.Set implementation.

Besides these simple parts of the listing, Hibernate supports much more including generation of IDs, composite or compound keys, subclasses in the same table, versioning, and timestamping of instances for locking.

Working with Hibernate

Now it is time to look at your HR application, which works with your business objects. As you did in Chapter 10, you will create a Manage class that will in turn utilize one of several actions when it is invoked. Each action will have its own functionality. The functionality you will implement for this exercise is as follows: adding a new object to the data store, listing stored objects, removing any number of objects, and associating one object with another. The full listing of code for this example can be obtained from http://www.apress.com/.

All of your actions will need certain services including obtaining a reference to a Hibernate session. It is from the session that most work will start when using Hibernate. Also, several of your actions, including listing, removing, and associating, will need to query the data store in the same way. For this reason, I am putting these parts in a common BaseAction, as shown in Listing 11-4. One note that I have given before: This code will throw a java.lang.Exception, and this is a very bad practice. I am doing this strictly to simplify the code for this example. I would never do this in real life, and I would never suggest using this code without changing the methods to show the applicable exceptions.

Listing 11-4. BaseAction for Hibernate

```
package com.apress.javapersist.chapter11.hibernate;

import java.util.Iterator;

import net.sf.hibernate.cfg.Configuration;
import net.sf.hibernate.Query;
import net.sf.hibernate.Session;
import net.sf.hibernate.SessionFactory;

public abstract class BaseAction {
    private static SessionFactory factory = null;

    protected Session getSession() throws Exception {
        if (factory == null) {
            // Loads hibernate.properties from the classpath
            Configuration conf = new Configuration();

            // read mapping.xml from the classpath
            conf.addResource("mapping.xml", getClass().getClassLoader());

            factory = conf.buildSessionFactory();
        }
```

```
        return factory.openSession();
    }

    protected Iterator findAll(Session session, String queryStr)
    throws Exception {
        Query query = session.createQuery(queryStr);
        return query.iterate();
    }

    public abstract void execute(String[] args) throws Exception;
    public abstract String exampleString();
}
```

As I said in the earlier section on mapping, you include both of your classes in the same mapping file. The BaseAction class loads that file from the root of a classpath entry. In the downloadable code from Apress, I have placed the mapping file and hibernate.properties in a config directory. That directory must be in the classpath for executing this code.

Note that the BaseAction class has a factory class that is reused across actions. Each action obtains its own session through the getSession method. The find method in this class simply obtains a session, creates a Query object, and returns the java.util.Iterator from it.

Lastly, the base class contains two abstract methods. The first is the execute method. This is the method that each action will override to do its work. To allow for flexibility, I have given it an array of strings as an argument and allowed it to throw an exception. In a real application, I would not suggest either of these because they both indicate a weak design. The abstract method exampleString is used to generate a usage message for the Manager itself. Each action can indicate how it should be used.

The first class you will extend BaseAction with is your AddAction class. The AddAction in Listing 11-5 is used to add new objects to the database. The class is a concrete class that has both the execute and exampleString methods you need.

Listing 11-5. Adding an Object with Hibernate

```
package com.apress.javapersist.chapter11.hibernate;

import net.sf.hibernate.Session;
import net.sf.hibernate.Transaction;

import com.apress.javapersist.chapter11.bo.Address;
import com.apress.javapersist.chapter11.bo.Employee;
```

```java
public class AddAction extends BaseAction {
    public void execute(String[] args) throws Exception {
        Session session = null;
        try {
            Object obj = buildObject(args);
            session = getSession();

            Transaction trans = session.beginTransaction();
            // Mark the object as persistent
            session.save(obj);
            trans.commit();
        }
        finally {
            if(session != null) {
                session.close();
            }
        }
    }

    private static Object buildObject(String[] args) {
        String className = args[0];
        Object obj = null;
        if("Employee".equals(className)) {
            Employee emp = new Employee(new Long(args[1]));
            emp.setFirstName(args[2]);
            emp.setLastName(args[3]);
            emp.setEmail(args[4]);
            obj = emp;
        }
        else if("Address".equals(className)){
            Address add = new Address(new Long(args[1]));
            add.setStreetLine1(args[2]);
            add.setStreetLine2(args[3]);
            add.setCity(args[4]);
            add.setState(args[5]);
            obj = add;
        }
        return obj;
    }

    public String exampleString() {
        return "    Manage add Employee id FName LName eMail\n"
            + "    Manage add Address id line1 line2 city state";
    }
}
```

In the AddAction class's execute method, you see that first an object is created using the buildObject method and the arguments that are passed in. Next a Hibernate session is obtained. A transaction is started, and the object is saved to the session. Finally, the transaction is committed and the session is closed.

Now you want to see the objects you have stored to the database. For this, you will create a list action. The list action will execute a query and print the results to the screen for you. Listing 11-6 shows your ListAction class.

Listing 11-6. Printing Stored Objects with Hibernate

```
package com.apress.javapersist.chapter11.hibernate;

import java.util.Iterator;

import net.sf.hibernate.Session;

public class ListAction extends BaseAction {
    private Object className;

    public void execute(String[] args) throws Exception {
        Session session = null;
        try {
            session = getSession();
            Iterator iter = findAll(session, args[1]);

            // Run through the objects, listing each one
            while( iter.hasNext() ) {
                System.out.println(iter.next());
            }
        }
        finally {
            if(session != null) {
                session.close();
            }
        }
    }

    public String exampleString() {
        return "    Manage list Employee \"from emp in class "
            + "com.apress.javapersist.chapter11.hibernate.bo.Employee "
            + "where emp.id=10\"\n";
    }
}
```

In the ListAction class's execute method, you rely on the BaseAction's findAll method. First you obtain a Session object to use in querying the database. The session and Hibernate query string are passed to the findAll method. The resulting java.util.Iterator is run through to print each object as it is retrieved.

Removing a stored object is performed through the delete method on the Hibernate session. In the RemoveAction class in Listing 11-7, you obtain an iterator of all matching objects, and then remove them from the data store.

Listing 11-7. Removing Stored Objects with Hibernate

```
package com.apress.javapersist.chapter11.hibernate;

import java.util.Iterator;

import net.sf.hibernate.Session;
import net.sf.hibernate.Transaction;

public class RemoveAction extends BaseAction {

    public void execute(String[] args) throws Exception {
        String typeName = args[0];
        Session session = null;
        try {
            session = getSession();
            Iterator results = findAll(session, args[1]);

            Transaction trans = session.beginTransaction();
            // Run through the list of objects, deleting each one
            while(results.hasNext()) {
              session.delete(results.next());
            }
            trans.commit();
        }
        finally {
            if(session != null) {
                session.close();
            }
        }
    }
}
```

```
    public String exampleString() {
        return "    Manage remove Employee \" from emp in class "
            + "com.apress.javapersist.chapter11.hibernate.bo.Employee "
            + "where emp.id=10\"\n";
    }
}
```

The RemoveAction class's execute method calls the BaseAction's findAll with the Hibernate query string. Every object that resolves to that query string shall be returned and deleted through the session. In this method, you wrap your deletions in a transaction to allow for rolling back if there is a problem.

The last action you want to perform with Hibernate is modifying existing objects. We will look at this modification at the same time as we look at managing relationships. In Listing 11-8, you can see your AssociateAction class. This action is used to assign an address to an employee and associate an employee with the address.

Listing 11-8. Associating Objects with Hibernate

```
package com.apress.javapersist.chapter11.hibernate;

import net.sf.hibernate.Session;
import net.sf.hibernate.Transaction;

import com.apress.javapersist.chapter11.bo.Address;
import com.apress.javapersist.chapter11.bo.Employee;

public class AssociateAction extends BaseAction {
    public void execute(String[] args) throws Exception {
        String typeName = args[0];
        if("Employee".equals(typeName)) {
            Session session = null;
            try {
                session = getSession();

                Employee employee = (Employee) findAll(session, args[1]).next();
                Address address = (Address) findAll(session, args[3]).next();
                System.out.println("About to associate: " + employee + " with "
                    + address);
```

```
            Transaction trans = session.beginTransaction();
            // Actually associate the two classes
            employee.setAddress(address);
            address.addResident(employee);
            trans.commit();
        }
        finally {
            if(session != null) {
                session.close();
            }
        }
    }
}

public String exampleString() {
    return "    Manage assoc Employee \"select statement\" "
        + "Address \"select statement\"";
}
}
```

In the AssociateAction class's execute method, you find the first employee and address that match your queries. A transaction is begun. Next, the employee and address are associated with each other. The transaction is committed and the session is closed. This is a basic modification. After this action is run, you can immediately run the ListAction to see that the modification worked.

The last class we will look at in this section is the application object itself. Listing 11-9 shows the Manage object, which is used to run your various actions and display the usage message. This is a very straightforward Java class in which each action is put in a map with a command key. The key is passed in on the command line, and the action is looked up and executed.

Listing 11-9. The Hibernate Manage Application Itself

```
package com.apress.javapersist.chapter11.hibernate;

import java.util.HashMap;
import java.util.Iterator;
```

```
public class Manage {
    HashMap actions = new HashMap();

    public Manage() {
        actions.put("list", new ListAction());
        actions.put("add", new AddAction());
        actions.put("remove", new RemoveAction());
        actions.put("assoc", new AssociateAction());
    }

    private void executeAction(String[] args) throws Exception {
        if(args.length < 2) {
            usage();
            return;
        }
        String actionStr = args[0];
        String[] cmdArgs = new String[args.length-1];
        System.arraycopy(args, 1, cmdArgs, 0, cmdArgs.length);

        BaseAction action = (BaseAction) actions.get(actionStr);
        if(action == null) {
            usage();
            return;
        }

        action.execute(cmdArgs);
    }

    public static void main(String[] args) {
        Manage manage = new Manage();
        try {
            manage.executeAction(args);
        }
        catch(Exception e) {
            e.printStackTrace();
        }
    }

    private void usage() {
        System.out.println("usage:");
        System.out.println("java com.apress.javapersist.chapter10.Manage <act"
            + "ion> [arg1] [arg2] [argn]");
        System.out.println("    actions: " + actions.keySet());
        System.out.println();
```

```
            System.out.println("Examples:");
            for(Iterator iter = actions.values().iterator(); iter.hasNext(); ) {
                System.out.println(((BaseAction) iter.next()).exampleString());
            }
        }
    }
}
```

The Manage class is basic enough that you will use the same class for all of your framework examples. Only the package declaration will change.

Now for the classes you will actually be doing your work with. Your Employee class, shown in Listing 11-10, is a very simple business object. The only points of interest of the class are the fact that you provide a private constructor and private ID setter method. Also, you have a complex value in the address attribute.

Listing 11-10. Employee Business Object for Hibernate

```
package com.apress.javapersist.chapter11.bo;

public class Employee {
    private Long id;
    private String firstName;
    private String lastName;
    private String email;
    private Address address;

    private Employee() {}
    public Employee(Long id) { this.id = id; }

    public Long getId() { return id; }
    private void setId(Long id) { this.id = id; }

    public String getFirstName() { return this.firstName; }
    public void setFirstName(String firstName) { this.firstName = firstName; }

    public String getLastName() { return this.lastName; }
    public void setLastName(String lastName) { this.lastName = lastName; }

    public String getEmail() { return this.email; }
    public void setEmail(String email) { this.email = email; }

    public Address getAddress() { return address; }
    public void setAddress(Address address) { this.address = address; }
```

```
    public String toString() {
        return "id: " + id + "; "
            + "firstName: " + firstName + "; "
            + "lastName: " + lastName + "; "
            + "email: " + email + "; "
            + "address: [" + address + "]";
    }
}
```

The private constructor and accessor are used by Hibernate when instantiating objects. The library does not presume to go directly to the attributes, but instead relies on accessor methods. This gives flexibility in populating transient fields when data is set on the object.

The Address class in Listing 11-11 is a little more interesting in that it has a collection property for residents. Once again, the class has a private no-args constructor and a private ID setter to help the persistence framework.

Listing 11-11. Address Class for Hibernate

```
package com.apress.javapersist.chapter11.bo;

import java.util.*;

public class Address {
    private Long id;
    private String streetLine1;
    private String streetLine2;
    private String city;
    private String state;
    private Set residents = new TreeSet();

    private Address() {}
    public Address(Long id) { this.id = id; }

    public Long getId() { return id; }
    private void setId(Long id) { this.id = id; }

    public String getCity() { return city; }
    public void setCity(String city) { this.city = city; }

    public String getState() { return state; }
    public void setState(String state) { this.state = state; }
```

```
public String getStreetLine1() { return streetLine1; }
public void setStreetLine1(String streetLine1) {
    this.streetLine1 = streetLine1;
}


public String getStreetLine2() { return streetLine2; }
public void setStreetLine2(String streetLine2) {
    this.streetLine2 = streetLine2;
}


private void setResidents(Set residents) { this.residents = residents; }
public Set getResidents() { return residents; }
public void addResident(Employee resident) { this.residents.add(resident); }

public String toString() {
    return  "id: " + id + "; "
        + "line 1: " + streetLine1 + "; "
        + "line 2: " + streetLine2 + "; "
        + "city: " + city + "; "
        + "state: " + state + "; "
        + "residents: " + residents.size() + ";";
}
}
```

Hibernate Query Language

Hibernate has a very complete query language, called HQL, that is object oriented and yet very similar to SQL. It is not, however, OQL. In some ways, this makes the language more powerful. In using this framework, I suggest moving all queries out of code and into resource bundles. While this is always a good idea, it is particularly important when using a nonstandard query language. That way, if anything changes in Hibernate's implementation, you can simply replace the resource bundle.

HQL is very much like SQL in how it is used, and many of the same constructs are available. A basic select statement in HQL consists of SELECT <what> FROM <class> WHERE <criteria>. Where the languages vary is in the what, class, and criteria.

For the most part, when querying with HQL, you will retrieve complete objects. In these cases, there is no need to specify what you want to retrieve; simply adding the class portion of the query will dictate the returned results. If, however, you want to retrieve part of an object, say all first names, that is when you would indicate what is to be retrieved. This further allows for query functions like COUNT, AVG, SUM, and many others.

The FROM part of the query consists of specifying an alias and then indicating which class it relates to. An example would be FROM emp IN CLASS mypackage.Employee. Here you have an alias called emp and a class called mypackage.Employee. In SQL, you would have specified something more like FROM employees emp to indicate the source of the data and an alias.

The WHERE clause of HQL is used to filter results just like SQL. In this case, you filter on attributes of objects that are referenced through your alias. An example could be emp.firstName = 'Jim'. The WHERE clause in HQL can handle many different types of comparators including LIKE, =, >=, <=, <>, !=, is null, and many more including order by and group by constructs.

Other Hibernate Notes

Hibernate supports various other features that we did not discuss in this simple persistence example. Hibernate offers an ODMG API to be programmed to. There are several methods of identifier generation. Lazy loading through dynamic proxies is also available.

ODMG

I mentioned at the beginning of this section that Hibernate supports ODMG. While this is true, it does not support OQL or extents. As with all ODMG implementations, the rest of the API is accessed through a single starting class. For Hibernate, that class is net.sf.hibernate.odmg.Implementation.

Identifier Generation

This example uses application-provided identifiers for your objects. Hibernate provides several strategies for generating keys automatically. Hibernate can work with database-generated auto-increment columns and sequences. Hibernate also provides algorithms for UUID for universally unique identifiers and hi/lo key generation for database unique identifiers.

In order to change the identifier generation, you would simply change the generator tag in the mapping.xml file. For hi/lo, you would use <generator class="hilo.long"/> or <generator class="hilo.hex"/>. For UUID, you would set the class to uuid.string or uuid.hex.

Proxies

Proxies are used by Hibernate to provide for lazy initialization. If you are loading a large number of objects and don't want them fully initialized for memory or performance reasons, you can specify a proxy attribute in the mapping file. When this is specified, all returned values from a query will actually be proxies to the original object. This in-memory replacement of classes is performed using the CGLIB library.

A request to the proxy causes a database access and the actual value is returned. These proxies are subclasses of the original class, which is something that code will need to take into account. If you are using persistent subclasses and try to obtain a subclass in a superclass reference, you will not be able to cast it to its correct class. What that means is that if you request an employee object as a person object, you will never be able to cast that object to an employee object. This can be overcome through use of interfaces where the references are not of the class type, but of the interface type.

ObJectRelationalBridge for Persistence

ObJectRelationalBridge (OJB) is another framework intended for transparent persistence of Java objects. The goal of this project is to provide various persistence APIs built on the same persistence kernel. The way it is built is that the framework has a low-level persistence mechanism based on a `PersistenceBroker` (PB). On top of this, OJB provides ODMG 3.0 and JDO API. This design makes it easy to add different APIs as they become available.

As with Hibernate, OJB works with a wide variety of databases and is very complete in the functionality it provides. Users of OJB can manage relationships, lazy initialization, generated identifiers, and much more. The framework also provides an Object Transaction Management layer to provide transaction functionality to ODMG and JDO.

The OJB project is now part of the Apache DB Project. The project is hosted at `http://db.apache.org/ojb/index.html`. While OJB provides a lot of documentation, development is going very quickly, and some of the documentation is out of date. When working with OJB, the mailing lists and mailing list archives will be the best place to solve problems. For this section, I will discuss version 0.9.9. Like many open source projects, the fact that OJB has not yet reached version 1.0 does not mean you cannot use this product for production work. I would however suggest thorough testing of OJB to ensure that it meets your needs.

Setting Up OJB

OJB is fairly straightforward to install. As with Hibernate, all necessary libraries for building and running with OJB are provided (again, excluding your JDBC driver). At the time of this writing, the binary OJB package contains Jakarta Ant and several other libraries that are used to compile OJB. The OJB site lists what libraries can be excluded for deployment. These same libraries can be excluded from your classpath for these examples.

The next step in setting up OJB is setting up the OJB.properties file. OJB comes with a copy of this file in its documentation. Simply create the file and copy the contents from the documentation into it. Place OJB.properties into a directory that is in your classpath. You should not need to modify OJB.properties for normal work.

OJB.properties contains a reference to the XML file where most of your configuration will start. This file is called repository.xml. A copy of repository.xml is also contained within the documentation. Copy this file into the same directory that you copied OJB.properties to. Keep in mind that OJB uses Xerces XML libraries for reading and processing these files. Xerces does not like working with files that are in directories whose names contain spaces. This isn't a problem with OJB, however, but an issue with Xerces.

For these exercises, you will use a slightly cut-down repository.xml. The file you will use does not include JUnit- or EJB-specific files. Listing 11-12 shows the repository.xml file.

Listing 11-12. repository.xml

```
<?xml version="1.0" encoding="UTF-8"?>

<!-- defining entities for include-files -->
<!DOCTYPE descriptor-repository SYSTEM "repository.dtd" [
<!ENTITY database SYSTEM "repository_database.xml">
<!ENTITY internal SYSTEM "repository_internal.xml">
<!ENTITY user SYSTEM "repository_user.xml">
]>

<descriptor-repository version="0.9.9" isolation-level="read-uncommitted">
    <!-- include all used database connections -->
    &database;

    <!-- include ojb internal mappings here -->
    &internal;
```

```
   <!-- include user defined mappings here -->
   &user;
</descriptor-repository>
```

This file first loads three different files including repository_database.xml, repository_internal.xml, and respository_user.xml. The database file contains information needed for connecting to databases from OJB. The internal file is used by OJB for identifier generation, locking, ODMG functions, and more. The internal file should not be modified, just copied verbatim. The user file we will discuss in the next section, and this is where your classes will be described.

For this book, you will use OJB with MySQL. Before OJB can connect to your database, you need to configure it. With this simple example, you will have one simple database entry in your repository_database.xml file. Listing 11-13 shows this database configuration file.

Listing 11-13. repository_database.xml

```
<jdbc-connection-descriptor
    platform="MySQL"
    jdbc-level="2.0"
    driver="com.mysql.jdbc.Driver"
    protocol="jdbc"
    subprotocol="mysql"
    dbalias="//localhost/chapter11"
    username="root"
    password="password"
    jcd-alias="chapter11"
    default-connection="true"
/>
```

Your database file contains information for your database. As of version 0.9.9, jcd-alias is a required attribute. This attribute is used to connect a PB to a specific database entry. For this example, you set this value to "chapter11". You can think of the jcd-alias as a lookup string for the database.

Building the User Repository

As I mentioned in the last section, all of your classes are defined in a repository_user.xml file for OJB. This file is similar to Hibernate's mapping.xml file in function. This file contains classes and relates them to tables. It also contains fields and relates them to columns. Unlike Hibernate, OJB, when using the repository.xml file listed previously, expects all classes to be defined in the same file.

If you want to create separate mapping files for your classes, you need to add additional ENTITYs and include the files shown in the next listing in the repository.xml file.

Your user file will contain an entry for the Employee and Address classes. Most of your entries will be one-to-one, one attribute to one column. The primary key field is differentiated by the primarykey attribute on the id field. Listing 11-14 shows this user configuration file.

Listing 11-14. OJB repository_user.xml

```xml
<!-- Definitions for com.apress.javapersist.chapter11.ojb.bo.Employee -->
<class-descriptor class="com.apress.javapersist.chapter11.ojb.bo.Employee"
  table="employees">
    <field-descriptor name="id"
        column="employee_id"
        jdbc-type="BIGINT"
        primarykey="true" />
    <field-descriptor name="firstName"
        column="first_name"
        jdbc-type="VARCHAR" />
    <field-descriptor name="lastName"
        column="last_name"
        jdbc-type="VARCHAR" />
    <field-descriptor name="email"
        column="email"
        jdbc-type="VARCHAR" />
    <field-descriptor name="addressId"
        column="address_id"
        jdbc-type="BIGINT" />
    <reference-descriptor name="address"
        class-ref="com.apress.javapersist.chapter11.ojb.bo.Address">
        <foreignkey field-ref="addressId"/>
    </reference-descriptor>
</class-descriptor>
<!-- Definitions for com.apress.javapersist.chapter11.ojb.bo.Address-->
<class-descriptor class="com.apress.javapersist.chapter11.ojb.bo.Address"
  table="addresses">
    <field-descriptor name="id"
        column="address_id"
        jdbc-type="BIGINT"
        primarykey="true" />
    <field-descriptor name="streetLine1"
        column="street_line1"
        jdbc-type="VARCHAR" />
```

```
<field-descriptor name="streetLine2"
    column="street_line2"
    jdbc-type="VARCHAR" />
<field-descriptor name="city"
    column="city"
    jdbc-type="VARCHAR" />
<field-descriptor name="state"
    column="state"
    jdbc-type="VARCHAR"/>
<collection-descriptor name="residents"
    element-class-ref="com.apress.javapersist.chapter11.ojb.bo.Employee">
    <inverse-foreignkey field-ref="addressId" />
</collection-descriptor>
</class-descriptor>
```

Notice that in order to create a one-to-many bidirectional relationship, you create a one-to-one single directional relationship on the employee. On the address you create a one-to-many single directional relationship.

One more factor is necessary for creating the relationships. The class that contains the relationship must have a separate attribute to hold the related key. So the employee object has not only an address field, but also an addressId field. Both fields also need to be listed in the configuration file.

When creating this file, be sure to reference the JDBC-types document that OJB provides. This will tell you exactly what JDBC types to map your Java attributes to. For this example, you have a single Long and several Strings, and this translates to a single BIGINT and several VARCHARs.

Working with OJB

Now let's look at some Java code that leverages OJB. The code you will write is the same application you worked on for Hibernate and JDO. The differences are that you will use a PersistenceBroker and OJB's underlying Query mechanism. This means that there is no query language that can be handed in from the command line, so you will create your own. I will discuss the various OJB query options later when I talk about the Finder class.

There is no need to show the Manager class again because that has remained exactly the same as in the Hibernate example except for the package and import declarations. The Employee and Address classes have some minor changes from versions you have created before in order to support OJB.

The BaseAction class for OJB in Listing 11-15 provides access to a reusable persistence broker to all of the subclasses. In creating the PB, a string is passed in that tells the broker what data source to use. The string "chapter11" is defined in your repository_database.xml file. Once again, the execute and exampleString methods are abstract and need to be implemented by your subclass actions. Unlike Hibernate, in which sessions are created, used, and closed, OJB reuses PersistenceBrokers. In OJB, the concept will include beginTransaction and commitTransaction much like JDO.

Listing 11-15. BaseAction for OJB

```java
package com.apress.javapersist.chapter11.ojb;

import java.util.Iterator;

import org.apache.ojb.broker.PBKey;
import org.apache.ojb.broker.PersistenceBroker;
import org.apache.ojb.broker.PersistenceBrokerFactory;

public abstract class BaseAction {
    private PersistenceBroker broker = null;

    protected PersistenceBroker getPersistenceBroker() throws Exception {
        if (broker == null) {
            // Loads OJB.properties and repository_user.xml from the classpath
            broker
                = PersistenceBrokerFactory.createPersistenceBroker(
                    new PBKey("chapter11"));
        }
        return broker;
    }

    public abstract void execute(String[] args) throws Exception;

    public abstract String exampleString();
}
```

The next class you will look at is the AddAction class in Listing 11-16. This execute method is similar to what we saw in JDO and Hibernate. The method that marks the object as persistent is store. Notice that the broker provides the method to start and commit the transaction. Without the commit, the data would never make it into the database. This class also contains the buildObject method that has been left unchanged from the prior examples.

Listing 11-16. AddAction for OJB

```
package com.apress.javapersist.chapter11.ojb;

import org.apache.ojb.broker.PersistenceBroker;

import com.apress.javapersist.chapter11.ojb.bo.Address;
import com.apress.javapersist.chapter11.ojb.bo.Employee;

public class AddAction extends BaseAction {
    public void execute(String[] args) throws Exception {
        Object obj = buildObject(args);
        PersistenceBroker broker = getPersistenceBroker();

        broker.beginTransaction();
        // Mark the object as persistent
        broker.store(obj);
        broker.commitTransaction();
        System.out.println("Object stored: " + obj);
    }

    private static Object buildObject(String[] args) {
        String className = args[0];
        Object obj = null;
        if("Employee".equals(className)) {
            Employee emp = new Employee(new Long(args[1]));
            emp.setFirstName(args[2]);
            emp.setLastName(args[3]);
            emp.setEmail(args[4]);
            obj = emp;
        }
        else if("Address".equals(className)){
            Address add = new Address(new Long(args[1]));
            add.setStreetLine1(args[2]);
            add.setStreetLine2(args[3]);
            add.setCity(args[4]);
            add.setState(args[5]);
            obj = add;
        }
        return obj;
    }
}
```

```
        public String exampleString() {
            return "    Manage add Employee id FName LName eMail\n"
                + "    Manage add Address id line1 line2 city state";
        }

}
```

Because OJB's `PersistenceBroker` API does not provide an object-oriented query language, you are going to create a `Finder` class that will create its own basic query language. While the PB does not provide a query language, the ODMG API that is part of OJB does provided OQL. There is also a `Query` object that takes SQL. We will not discuss either of these here; for more on ODMG, refer back to Chapter 9.

The language parser I will create for this example is very fragile and simple. Listing 11-17 shows that depending on the number of arguments and the order they are in, the class will create a `Criteria` object. (We discussed this method of querying in Chapter 5 when I showed you how to write your own persistence layer.) The `Criteria` is then handed off to a `Query` object, which is used with the PB to find the matching data.

Listing 11-17. Finder for OJB

```
package com.apress.javapersist.chapter11.ojb;

import java.util.Iterator;

import org.apache.ojb.broker.PersistenceBroker;
import org.apache.ojb.broker.query.Criteria;
import org.apache.ojb.broker.query.Query;
import org.apache.ojb.broker.query.QueryByCriteria;

public class Finder {
    public Iterator find(PersistenceBroker broker, String[] args)
    throws Exception {
        Class clazz = getClass(args[0]);

        Criteria criteria = new Criteria();
        if(args.length == 2) { // class and command
            String cmd = args[1];
            if("all".equals(cmd)) {
                // add no criteria, want to return all
            }
        }
        else if(args.length > 2){
```

```
        String attribute = args[1];
        String comparison = args[2];
        String value = args[3];
        if("equals".equals(comparison)) {
            criteria.addEqualTo(attribute, value);
        }
        else if("notEquals".equals(comparison)) {
            criteria.addNotEqualTo(attribute, value);
        }
    }

    Query query = new QueryByCriteria(clazz,criteria);
    return broker.getIteratorByQuery(query);
}

private static Class getClass(String className)
    throws ClassNotFoundException {
    return Class.forName("com.apress.javapersist.chapter11.ojb.bo."
        + className);
}
}
```

Now that you have created a `Finder` class, you'll add the `ListAction` shown in Listing 11-18. This is a very simple class that iterates through the results the `Finder` class returns and outputs them to `System.out`.

Listing 11-18. ListAction for OJB

```
package com.apress.javapersist.chapter11.ojb;

import java.util.Iterator;

public class ListAction extends BaseAction {
    private Object className;

    public void execute(String[] args) throws Exception {
        Finder finder = new Finder();

        Iterator iter = finder.find(getPersistenceBroker(), args);

        // Run through the objects, listing each one
        while( iter.hasNext() ) {
            System.out.println(iter.next());
        }
    }
```

```
    public String exampleString() {
        return "    Manage list Employee lastName equals LName\n"
           + "    Manage list Employee all";
    }
}
```

Your `RemoveAction` class, shown in Listing 11-19, like your `ListAction` class, finds matching objects and deletes them. One significant difference from `ListAction` is the use of transactions around the call to the delete method of the PB. Only after `commit` is called are the objects actually deleted.

Listing 11-19. RemoveAction for OJB

```
package com.apress.javapersist.chapter11.ojb;

import java.util.Iterator;

public class RemoveAction extends BaseAction {
    public void execute(String[] args) throws Exception {
        Finder finder = new Finder();

        Iterator iter = finder.find(getPersistenceBroker(), args);

        getPersistenceBroker().beginTransaction();
        // Run through the list of objects, deleting each one
        while(iter.hasNext())
          getPersistenceBroker().delete(iter.next());
        getPersistenceBroker().commitTransaction();
    }

    public String exampleString() {
        return "    Manage remove Employee lastName equals LName";
    }
}
```

Your `Finder` class is most used here in the modification of stored objects. `AssociateAction`, shown in Listing 11-20, takes the array of strings and splits it for finding the employee and address objects. Once the objects are found, they are associated with each other. Unlike with JDO and Hibernate, this does not reflect in the database. There needs to be a call to `store` for both objects after that. Next, you commit the transaction and the data is written to the database.

Listing 11-20. AssociateAction for OJB

```java
package com.apress.javapersist.chapter11.ojb;

import java.util.Iterator;

import com.apress.javapersist.chapter11.ojb.bo.Address;
import com.apress.javapersist.chapter11.ojb.bo.Employee;

public class AssociateAction extends BaseAction {
    public void execute(String[] args) throws Exception {
        Finder finder = new Finder();
        if("Employee".equals(args[0])) {
            String[] empArgs = new String[4];
            System.arraycopy(args, 0, empArgs, 0, empArgs.length);
            String[] addArgs = new String[4];
            System.arraycopy(args, 4, addArgs, 0, addArgs.length);

            Iterator iter = finder.find(getPersistenceBroker(), empArgs);
            Employee employee = (Employee) iter.next();

            iter = finder.find(getPersistenceBroker(), addArgs);
            Address address = (Address) iter.next();

            System.out.println("About to associate: " + employee + " with "
                + address);

            // Actually associate the two classes
            employee.setAddress(address);
            address.addResident(employee);

            // Update the database
            getPersistenceBroker().beginTransaction();
            getPersistenceBroker().store(employee);
            getPersistenceBroker().store(address);
            getPersistenceBroker().commitTransaction();
        }
    }

    public String exampleString() {
        return "    Manage assoc Employee id equals 0 Address id equals 1";
    }
}
```

Your business objects need to provide a few things for OJB. The first, as with Hibernate, is they must have no-args constructors. Fortunately, these can be private. One library-specific change is the need to add a new attribute to help with relationships. Notice in Listing 11-21 that the employee object contains not only an address attribute, but also an addressId attribute. From an object-oriented perspective this is redundant. But this is necessary to allow the employee to be associated with the address.

Listing 11-21. Employee for OJB

```
package com.apress.javapersist.chapter11.ojb.bo;

public class Employee {
    private Long id;
    private String firstName;
    private String lastName;
    private String email;
    private Address address;
    private Long addressId;

    private Employee() {}

    public Employee(Long id) { this.id = id; }

    public Long getId() { return id; }
    private void setId(Long id) { this.id = id; }

    public String getFirstName() { return this.firstName; }
    public void setFirstName(String firstName) { this.firstName = firstName; }

    public String getLastName() { return this.lastName; }
    public void setLastName(String lastName) { this.lastName = lastName; }

    public String getEmail() { return this.email; }
    public void setEmail(String email) { this.email = email; }

    public Address getAddress() { return address; }
    public void setAddress(Address address) { this.address = address; }
```

```
    public String toString() {
        return "id: " + id + "; "
            + "firstName: " + firstName + "; "
            + "lastName: " + lastName + "; "
            + "email: " + email + "; "
            + "address: [" + address + "]";
    }
}
```

In Listing 11-22, you can see your address object. The only change in this class from your Hibernate version is that you cannot use a java.util.Set type. Change the residents to a java.util.Collection as shown in this listing.

Listing 11-22. Address for OJB

```
package com.apress.javapersist.chapter11.ojb.bo;

import java.util.*;

public class Address {
    private Long id;
    private String streetLine1;
    private String streetLine2;
    private String city;
    private String state;
    private Collection residents = new ArrayList();

    private Address() {}

    public Address(Long id) { this.id = id; }

    public Long getId() { return id; }
    private void setId(Long id) { this.id = id; }

    public String getCity() { return city; }
    public void setCity(String city) { this.city = city; }

    public String getState() { return state; }
    public void setState(String state) { this.state = state; }
```

```
public String getStreetLine1() { return streetLine1; }
public void setStreetLine1(String streetLine1) {
    this.streetLine1 = streetLine1;
}

public String getStreetLine2() { return streetLine2; }
public void setStreetLine2(String streetLine2) {
    this.streetLine2 = streetLine2;
}

private void setResidents(Set residents) { this.residents = residents; }
public Collection getResidents() { return residents; }
public void addResident(Employee resident) { this.residents.add(resident); }

public String toString() {
    return  "id: " + id + "; "
        + "line 1: " + streetLine1 + "; "
        + "line 2: " + streetLine2 + "; "
        + "city: " + city + "; "
        + "state: " + state + "; "
        + "residents: " + residents.size() + ";";
}
}
```

Other OJB Notes

Now you have seen how to use OJB for basic persistence work. There are a few other important features that I have not talked about yet. As I mentioned earlier, OJB supports several unique identifier algorithms. The library also supports JDO and ODMG APIs.

OJB Proxies

OJB handles the need for lazy initialization through both explicitly created proxies and dynamically created proxies. An *explicitly created proxy* is where the developer creates a class that extends org.apache.ojb.broker.VirtualProxy and delegates method calls to the underlying getRealSubject(). This means that developers need to create proxy objects when they want to lazy load data. While this can seem like more work, put into context this can be a very clear way of handling the situation.

The second way that proxies can be generated with OJB is through *dynamic proxies*. This is similar to Hibernates method of lazy loading; the difference is that OJB relies on the JDK 1.3's `java.lang.reflect.Proxy` class instead of the CGLIB library. In both cases the fact that a class is proxied must be indicated in the repository_user.xml file.

OJB JDO and ODMG APIs

As of this writing, JDO is implemented as a plug-in to Sun's Reference Implementation. There are plans for creating an OJB-specific JDO API; until then users should probably rely on the more mature ODMG API.

OJB's ODMG API is fairly complete and easy to use. The root of the ODMG system is the `org.apache.obj.odmg.OJB` class. From here you can create transactions, databases, and queries. It is also through this interface that you interact with OJB's OQL. The code that you download from `http://www.apress.com` for Chapter 9 uses OJB's ODMG implementation.

Castor JDO

Castor JDO is part of the Castor library, hosted at `http://castor.exolab.org/`. The Castor library is used primarily for conversion of Java objects to XML and SQL. Exolab calls Castor a *data binding framework*. For this chapter, we will focus exclusively on the conversion to SQL. In Chapter 1, I showed how to perform Castor for Java to XML conversion. We will be using version 0.9.4.3 of Castor.

As for the name, Castor JDO does not conform to Sun's JDO specification. JDO does indeed stand for Java Data Objects, but Sun's definition differs from Castor's. Castor has been around longer than the JDO specification has been official. From the Web site the term *Castor* is the scientific name for beaver. Exolab will not say why the project is named after a beaver, but they post lots of speculation.

Castor provides transactions, object caching, lazy loading of data, compound primary keys, and complex relationships—all of the features you want from your persistence libraries.

Setting Up Castor JDO

Installation of Castor is a process of downloading the library from the Castor site. Castor provides several downloadable files, and it is not necessarily clear which is the one you need. Grab the package that contains the JAR files, DTDs, command line tools, and examples. You will also need to obtain a version of Xerces XML library from `http://xml.apache.org/`.

Once you have downloaded and extracted Castor and Xerces, you can set up a classpath containing castor-<version>.jar, jdbc-se2.0.jar (which comes with Castor), xercesImpl.jar, and xml-apis.jar, as well as your JDBC driver.

Configuring Castor JDO

Castor's configuration is very simple and clear. It all starts with a database.xml file. This file specifies the databases to use and references relevant mapping files. Listing 11-23 shows the database.xml file you will use for the example HR application. Notice that the database entry goes to the same database that you use for Hibernate and OJB. The next two entries after the driver load mapping files for address.xml and employee.xml.

Listing 11-23. database.xml

```xml
<?xml version="1.0" encoding="UTF-8"?>
<!DOCTYPE database PUBLIC
    "-//EXOLAB/Castor JDO Configuration DTD Version 1.0//EN"
    "http://castor.exolab.org/jdo-conf.dtd">

<database name="chapter11" engine="mysql">
    <driver class-name="com.mysql.jdbc.Driver"
            url="jdbc:mysql://localhost/chapter11">
      <param name="user" value="root" />
      <param name="password" value="password" />
    </driver>

    <mapping href="address.xml" />

    <mapping href="employee.xml" />
</database>
```

This mapping file is loaded by your JDO class, which you will see in a little bit. The mapping files are loaded separately. The configuration file could optionally contain a reference to a data source instead of the driver. Data sources can also be obtained from JNDI.

Working with Castor JDO

As with the previous examples, you will create object-specific configuration files and then look at how your HR application interacts with Castor to add, query, remove, and modify persistent objects. Lastly, you will look at how your `Address` and `Employee` class have been modified to support Castor JDO. As with OJB, your `Manager` class is unchanged from the Hibernate example.

In Castor JDO, there is only one actual class in the `org.exolab.castor.jdo` package; the rest are interfaces. The one class is the `org.exolab.castor.jdo.JDO` class. This is where all work begins in Castor. From the JDO object you create `Database` instances, which are used to work with the actual database. `Database` objects can be used to handle transactions and create queries.

When working with Castor, all interaction with persisted objects should happen within a transaction. The exception to this is long transactions where Castor makes available a sort of optimistic locking by timestamping objects. I will talk more about long transactions later in this chapter in the section "Long and Short Transactions."

Before you can begin working with the library, you need to tell Castor how to interact with your objects. Like Hibernate and OJB, there are class-specific mappings to tell the framework what fields are persistable and where to store them to. As with the prior two libraries, Castor's configuration files are XML.

For your employee mapping file, you will create an XML file named employee.xml. This file, which should be placed in the same directory as the database.xml file, starts with a description of the class to be persisted and the field to use as an identifier. This is followed by an entry that tells Castor what table to persist these objects to.

Next is a list of fields that will be persisted. In this example, the fields are named based on JavaBean naming conventions. If your accessors are not in the standard get/set format, you can indicate read/write methods in the mapping file.

Finally, in this file is your association to the `Address` class. This is the "one" part of your one-to-many relationship. It is very easy to associate with other classes. By giving Castor the `Address` class, it will look up exactly where to obtain the objects to fulfill this field (see Listing 11-24).

Listing 11-24. employee.xml

```xml
<?xml version="1.0" encoding="UTF-8"?>
<!DOCTYPE mapping PUBLIC "-//EXOLAB/Castor Object Mapping DTD Version 1.0//EN"
                        "http://castor.exolab.org/mapping.dtd">
<mapping>

    <class name="com.apress.javapersist.chapter11.castorjdo.bo.Employee"
        identity="id">

        <map-to table="employees" />

        <field name="id" type="long">
            <sql name="employee_id" type="bigint" />
        </field>

        <field name="firstName" type="string">
            <sql name="first_name" type="char" />
        </field>

        <field name="lastName" type="string">
            <sql name="last_name" type="char" />
        </field>

        <field name="email" type="string">
            <sql name="email" type="char" />
        </field>

        <field name="address"
            type="com.apress.javapersist.chapter11.castorjdo.bo.Address" >
            <sql name="address_id" />
        </field>

    </class>
</mapping>
```

In Listing 11-25, you can see the mapping file for your Address class. Again, the
XML file first indicates which class it is for as well as what field in the class will be
used for identity. Next, the file indicates what table to map to.

Listing 11-25. address.xml

```xml
<?xml version="1.0" encoding="UTF-8"?>
<!DOCTYPE mapping PUBLIC "-//EXOLAB/Castor Object Mapping DTD Version 1.0//EN"
                        "http://castor.exolab.org/mapping.dtd">
<mapping>

    <class name="com.apress.javapersist.chapter11.castorjdo.bo.Address"
           identity="id">

        <map-to table="addresses" />

        <field name="id" type="long">
            <sql name="address_id" type="bigint" />
        </field>

        <field name="streetLine1" type="string">
            <sql name="street_line1" type="char" />
        </field>

        <field name="streetLine2" type="string">
            <sql name="street_line2" type="char" />
        </field>

        <field name="city" type="string">
            <sql name="city" type="char" />
        </field>

        <field name="state" type="string">
            <sql name="state" type="char" />
        </field>

        <field name="residents" collection="set"
            type="com.apress.javapersist.chapter11.castorjdo.bo.Employee">
            <sql many-key="address_id" many-table="employees" />
        </field>
    </class>
</mapping>
```

The final field is the "to-many" part of your relationship to the employee object. Notice that you use the Employees table as the "many" table for this. If you were creating a many-to-many relationship, this would point to a association table.

Now that you have all of your configuration files, it is time to take a look at the application code. As with the prior two examples, we will look first at the BaseAction class to see how to obtain a starting point for the persistence framework. This will be followed with action classes that will handle adding, listing, removing, and associating items.

The BaseAction for Castor JDO can be seen in Listing 11-26. In Castor, your code needs to create a JDO object; this object will be used to provide your subclasses with Database objects. The Database objects are used to do work.

Listing 11-26. BaseAction for Castor JDO

```
package com.apress.javapersist.chapter11.castorjdo;

import org.exolab.castor.jdo.Database;
import org.exolab.castor.jdo.JDO;
import org.exolab.castor.jdo.Query;
import org.exolab.castor.jdo.QueryResults;

public abstract class BaseAction {
    private JDO castorJDO = null;

    protected Database getDatabase() throws Exception {
        if (castorJDO == null) {
            castorJDO = new JDO();
            castorJDO.setDatabaseName( "chapter11" );
            castorJDO.setConfiguration( "config/database.xml" );
            castorJDO.setClassLoader( getClass().getClassLoader() );
        }
        return castorJDO.getDatabase();
    }

    protected QueryResults findAll(Database database, String queryStr)
    throws Exception {
        Query query = database.getOQLQuery(queryStr);
        return query.execute();
    }

    public abstract void execute(String[] args) throws Exception;

    public abstract String exampleString();
}
```

In order to create a JDO object, you need to specify the database name you will extract from the configuration file. You need to specify exactly where it can pick up the configuration file, and you want to associate the JDO object with your ClassLoader. After this is done, you can simply return Database objects.

The findAll method in your BaseAction expects a Database object and Castor OQL. Once these are provided, a simple query is performed. Unlike previous versions of the findAll method, this version returns a QueryResults object instead of an Iterator object. The QueryResults object has many of the same methods that Iterator has, but unfortunately the Iterator method signatures do not allow for exceptions to be thrown. It is for this reason that QueryResults is used.

If you wanted to be consistent because you were switching from another framework to Castor, you could wrap QueryResults in an Iterator implementing class and throw custom DAO-specific RuntimeExceptions. Not the best or cleanest solution, but it is an option.

You must also ensure that the Database object that is passed into the findAll method has already had its transaction begun. Castor JDO does not do anything without a transaction.

The AddAction class for Castor JDO, shown in Listing 11-27, contains your standard buildObject method as well as a Database object to persist the instances created. This class takes arguments in and builds an application-specific object. An instance of Database is obtained upon which a transaction is started.

Listing 11-27. AddAction for Castor JDO

```
package com.apress.javapersist.chapter11.castorjdo;

import org.exolab.castor.jdo.Database;

import com.apress.javapersist.chapter11.castorjdo.bo.Address;
import com.apress.javapersist.chapter11.castorjdo.bo.Employee;

public class AddAction extends BaseAction {
    public void execute(String[] args) throws Exception {
        Object obj = buildObject(args);
        Database database = getDatabase();
        try {
            database.begin();
            // Mark the object as persistent
            database.create(obj);
            database.commit();
            System.out.println("Object stored: " + obj);
        }
```

```
        catch(Exception e) {
            database.rollback();
            throw e;
        }
        finally {
            if(database != null) {
                database.close();
            }
        }
    }
    private static Object buildObject(String[] args) {
        String className = args[0];
        Object obj = null;
        if("Employee".equals(className)) {
            Employee emp = new Employee(new Long(args[1]));
            emp.setFirstName(args[2]);
            emp.setLastName(args[3]);
            emp.setEmail(args[4]);
            obj = emp;
        }
        else if("Address".equals(className)){
            Address add = new Address(new Long(args[1]));
            add.setStreetLine1(args[2]);
            add.setStreetLine2(args[3]);
            add.setCity(args[4]);
            add.setState(args[5]);
            obj = add;
        }
        return obj;
    }

    public String exampleString() {
        return "    Manage add Employee id FName LName eMail\n"
            + "    Manage add Address id line1 line2 city state";
    }
}
```

Once the transaction is started, it is possible to "create" or mark as persistent as many objects as you like. Once all objects have been created in the persistence mechanism, the transaction should be committed. Upon committing the transaction, all data is written to the database.

Now that you have added more data to your database, let's look at querying that data. Castor JDO comes with a very nice OQL. It is OQL that you will pass in from the command line for querying against your data store. As with prior versions, the main work is done in the findAll method. ListAction simply prints the data that is returned.

In Listing 11-28 you can see that there are a couple of differences from prior versions of ListAction. The first is that you begin a transaction before you query Castor. The second change is the use of QueryResults instead of Iterator.

Listing 11-28. ListAction for Castor JDO

```java
package com.apress.javapersist.chapter11.castorjdo;

import java.util.Iterator;

import org.exolab.castor.jdo.Database;
import org.exolab.castor.jdo.Query;
import org.exolab.castor.jdo.QueryResults;

public class ListAction extends BaseAction {
    private Object className;

    public void execute(String[] args) throws Exception {
        Database database = null;
        try {
            database = getDatabase();
            database.begin();
            QueryResults results = findAll(database, args[1]);

            // Run through the objects, listing each one
            while( results.hasMore() ) {
                System.out.println(results.next());
            }
            database.commit();
        }
        catch(Exception e) {
            e.printStackTrace();
            throw e;
        }
        finally {
            if(database != null) {
                database.close();
            }
        }
    }
}
```

```
    public String exampleString() {

        return "    Manage list Employee \"select e from "
            + "com.apress.javapersist.chapter11.castorjdo.bo.Employee e "
            + "where e.id=11\"\n";
    }
}
```

The Castor JDO RemoveAction class, shown in Listing 11-29, performs
similarly to ListAction. The difference is the call to Database.remove instead of to
System.out.println. Again, in this class you begin the transaction, delete the relevant objects, and then commit the transaction.

Listing 11-29 RemovingAction for Castor JDO

```
package com.apress.javapersist.chapter11.castorjdo;

import java.util.Iterator;

import org.exolab.castor.jdo.Database;
import org.exolab.castor.jdo.QueryResults;

public class RemoveAction extends BaseAction {
    public void execute(String[] args) throws Exception {
        Database database = null;
        try {
            database = getDatabase();
            QueryResults results = findAll(database, args[1]);

            database.begin();
            // Run through the list of objects, deleting each one
            while(results.hasMore()) {
                database.remove(results.next());
            }
            database.commit();
        }
        catch(Exception e) {
            database.rollback();
            throw e;
        }
        finally {
            if(database != null) {
                database.close();
            }
```

```
        }
    }

    public String exampleString() {
        return "    Manage remove Employee \"select e from "
            + "com.apress.javapersist.chapter11.castorjdo.bo.Employee e "
            + "where e.id=11\"\n";
    }
}
```

Modifying your business objects can be seen in Listing 11-30, which shows Castor's AssociateAction. This class expects to make two OQL queries. The first result from each query is associated with each other, then the objects are updated through the Database instance.

Listing 11-30. AssociateAction for Castor JDO

```
package com.apress.javapersist.chapter11.castorjdo;

import org.exolab.castor.jdo.Database;

import com.apress.javapersist.chapter11.castorjdo.bo.Address;
import com.apress.javapersist.chapter11.castorjdo.bo.Employee;

public class AssociateAction extends BaseAction {
    public void execute(String[] args) throws Exception {
        String typeName = args[0];
        if("Employee".equals(typeName)) {
            Database database = null;
            try {
                database = getDatabase();

                Employee employee = (Employee) findAll(database,
                    args[1]).next();
                Address address = (Address) findAll(database, args[3]).next();
                System.out.println("About to associate: " + employee + " with "
                    + address);

                database.begin();
                // Actually associate the two classes
                employee.setAddress(address);
                address.addResident(employee);
                database.commit();
            }
```

```
                catch(Exception e) {
                    database.rollback();
                    throw e;
                }
                finally {
                    if(database != null) {
                        database.close();
                    }
                }
            }
        }

    public String exampleString() {
        return "    Manage assoc Employee \"select e from "
            + "com.apress.javapersist.chapter11.castorjdo.bo.Employee e "
            + "where e.id=11\" Address \"select e from "
            + "com.apress.javapersist.chapter11.castorjdo.bo.Address a "
            + "where a.id=121\"";
    }
}
```

The business objects that are used with Castor have a few more restrictions on them than the other frameworks we have discussed, specifically, the need to make all methods used for persistence public as well as provide a public no-args constructor. There is no way for me to feel good about this. Some attributes should only be provided at creation time. However, there is something to be said for not having to write and debug my own SQL, so perhaps it is worth the price. You will need to decide that for yourself.

Listing 11-31 shows your Castor-modified business object. Notice the first constructor is public now. Where OJB and Hibernate required no-arg constructors, they were private before this. Next, notice the setId method. Be careful here. An inexperienced developer could inadvertently change the object in very bad ways with this method. On the upside, you are able to get rid of the addressId field that was necessary for OJB.

Listing 11-31. Employee Class for Castor JDO

```
package com.apress.javapersist.chapter11.castorjdo.bo;

public class Employee {
    private Long id;
    private String firstName;
    private String lastName;
```

```
    private String email;
    private Address address;

    public Employee() {}
    public Employee(Long id) { this.id = id; }

    public Long getId() { return id; }
    public void setId(Long id) { this.id = id; }

    public String getFirstName() { return this.firstName; }
    public void setFirstName(String firstName) { this.firstName = firstName; }

    public String getLastName() { return this.lastName; }
    public void setLastName(String lastName) { this.lastName = lastName; }

    public String getEmail() { return this.email; }
    public void setEmail(String email) { this.email = email; }

    public Address getAddress() { return address; }
    public void setAddress(Address address) { this.address = address; }

    public String toString() {
        return "id: " + id + "; "
            + "firstName: " + firstName + "; "
            + "lastName: " + lastName + "; "
            + "email: " + email + "; "
            + "address: [" + address + "]";
    }
}
```

Your Address class also conforms to the public constraints that Castor imposes (see Listing 11-32). Other than that, this is the same class you have used with the other frameworks. You are able to go back to using a java.util.Set instead of a java.util.Collection in the Castor version.

Listing 11-32. Address Class for Castor JDO

```
package com.apress.javapersist.chapter11.castorjdo.bo;

import java.util.*;

public class Address {
    private Long id;
    private String streetLine1;
```

```
        private String streetLine2;
        private String city;
        private String state;
        private Set residents = new HashSet();

        public Address() {}
        public Address(Long id) { this.id = id; }

        public Long getId() { return id; }
        public void setId(Long id) { this.id = id; }

        public String getCity() { return city; }
        public void setCity(String city) { this.city = city; }

        public String getState() { return state; }
        public void setState(String state) { this.state = state; }

        public String getStreetLine1() { return streetLine1; }
        public void setStreetLine1(String streetLine1) {
            this.streetLine1 = streetLine1;
        }

        public String getStreetLine2() { return streetLine2; }
        public void setStreetLine2(String streetLine2) {
            this.streetLine2 = streetLine2;
        }

        private void setResidents(Set residents) { this.residents = residents; }
        public Set getResidents() { return residents; }
        public void addResidents(Employee resident) {
            this.residents.add(resident);
        }

        public String toString() {
            return  "id: " + id + "; "
                + "line 1: " + streetLine1 + "; "
                + "line 2: " + streetLine2 + "; "
                + "city: " + city + "; "
                + "state: " + state + "; "
                + "residents: " + residents.size() + ";";
        }
    }
```

Other Castor JDO Notes

Castor is a simple-to-use persistence framework that provides many of the things you want for transparent persistence. The framework has a comprehensive OQL. Transactions are supported and lazy loading of data is available.

Castor OQL

Castor actually provides an OQL-to-SQL generator. Internally the framework accepts OQL in, combines it with information provided by the mapping files, and generates SQL. The OQL that is actually recognized is a subset of the ODMG 3.0 specification with a few additions.

In general, a query for your Manager application would look something like `SELECT e FROM com.apress.javapersist.chapter11.castorjdo.bo.Employee e WHERE e.firstName = "FName"`.

Long and Short Transactions

Castor expects objects that are retrieved in one transaction to be modified within the same transaction. This does not lend itself to wrapping the framework in a DAO. The reason is that you want to keep the underlying implementation hidden from the application layer. What would happen is an object is retrieved in one transaction, modified outside the DAO layer. The modified object is then returned to the DAO that intends to persist to the data store.

Castor does have a solution to this: The class needs to implement the `org.exolab.castor.jdo.TimeStampable` interface. This interface adds get and set timestamp methods to the class. On updating the object, the timestamp held for that object is updated. If a second object with the same ID and a different timestamp comes into the update method, an exception will be thrown.

Lazy Loading of Data

Lazy loading is provided by Castor JDO only through collections. There is no concept of proxies in this framework. So only through relationships can you lazy load data. The way Castor works is by replacing the collections with classes that load the requested data in calls to `next` or `get`.

The way this is specified is through an additional attribute on the field tag. Add `lazy="true"` in order to allow for lazy loading. Note, however, that in this version of Castor there is a bug. You cannot use any collection type other than `java.util.Collection` and lazy loading.

Some of the Other Libraries

Besides the libraries discussed previously, there are also libraries that strictly adhere to specifications. For example, several projects are working on pure JDO implementations. To learn how to use these implementations, you can refer to Chapter 10.

The XORM JDO project provides a JDO implementation that uses the GCLIB library, much like Hibernate does, to remove the need for code processing. At runtime, classes are proxied. While this is a nice idea, the requirements of JDO mean that you cannot simply create objects with new. You need instead to use XORM factory methods for generating instances of new objects.

Another promising OR framework is called Cayenne. Cayenne is not transparent because your objects need to extend a root data object name CayenneDataObject. Fortunately, the ObjectStyle group makes this very easy by providing a GUI-based tool for generating the Java code.

Jaxor Framework is an OR mapping library that, like Cayenne, relies on a root object that manages the persistence of all subclasses. Jaxor is reliant on business object hierarchies for things like auditing and shared columns.

These are just a few of the many open source Java persistence libraries that are available. The number is growing, as there is a strong desire today to remove the expense and time that writing a persistence layer takes.

Summary

We probably agree that it is good to not have to maintain code. The best way to avoid maintaining code is to not write it. If used with discretion and some fore-thought, the products in this chapter can save you lots of time and energy. Make sure any product you look at using has a very active developer community; otherwise, you may be the only one upgrading or fixing bugs in the system, in which case any time savings is lost.

In this chapter, we discussed three different open source persistence mechanisms: Hibernate, ObJectRelationalBridge, and Castor JDO. Each of these products provides basic transparent persistence, including persisting any type of business object, complex relationships, and transactions.

CHAPTER 12

Commercial Java Persistence Libraries and Frameworks

MARLEY WAS DEAD: TO BEGIN WITH. There is no doubt whatever about that. And there is no doubt whatever about the question whether it is cheaper to build or to buy. Having explored open source persistence frameworks, we now know that there are options to spending a great deal of our time and energy writing persistence layers. Besides the open source products, there are also the commercial versions. These often seem costly at the beginning of a project, but by the end of almost every project I have been on, a lot more money was spent creating the persistence layer by hand.

While open source persistence frameworks work well in some situations and provide a good introduction to OR frameworks, sometimes you need the features or support provided by a commercial product. For that reason, this chapter will introduce two of the more mature commercial Java OR persistence frameworks, namely TopLink and CocoBase. Now for some history:

In the beginning (object-oriented beginning, at least) there was Simula, after which came Smalltalk. Smalltalk was one of the best-known and loved object-oriented languages used for business software development. Now even waaay back in the days of Smalltalk, there was the need to store objects in relational databases.

In order to fulfill this great need, TopLink was created. TopLink is one of the most mature OR persistence frameworks available. TopLink started life as a persistence framework for Smalltalk. In 1997 TopLink was released for Java. Since then the product has continued going strong. Currently TopLink is owned by and available from Oracle after changing hands a few times in the last couple years.

CocoBase is another very mature Java OR mapping framework. CocoBase was also first made available for Java in 1997 as CocoBase O/R Enterprise. The company behind CocoBase is THOUGHT, Inc.

Both TopLink and CocoBase focus primarily on providing high-performance, transparent persistence to Java applications. Both products also provide Container Managed Persistence or can be used for Bean Managed Persistence when writing Enterprise JavaBeans.

Now that we have covered some history, we can get to work. First we will discuss TopLink. CocoBase will be covered in depth in the second half of this chapter. For both products, you will use the same HR application that was used for JDO in Chapter 10 and for the open source products in Chapter 11. One difference you will note is that I will show you how to use each product's graphical mapping tools rather than writing your own deployment files.

Using TopLink for Java Persistence

As with any product, there are several steps to perform to use TopLink. First I will go through the steps in general, then I will delve more deeply into each step.

The first step is obtaining and installing TopLink. After installing TopLink, you create your database and object model. Then you write your SQL for creating your tables and write your Java objects that you will persist. You use TopLink's mapping workbench to create your deployment file. After you have done all of this, we will look at the application that writes your objects to the database.

Obtaining and Setting Up TopLink

TopLink is currently available from Oracle at `http://www.oracle.com/features/9iAS/index.html?t1as_toplink.html`. You can download an evaluation copy from the Oracle site. Installation on Windows is as simple as running the installation file that is downloaded. Installation for UNIX or Linux is a little more complex, but installation instructions are provided. Once you have downloaded and installed the tool, you need to configure it, which involves a couple of steps.

After you have installed TopLink, you will probably want to test the installation to make sure that everything works. To run the examples, you need to modify the setenv.cmd file that is installed in the TopLink directory. The only necessary modification for this file is adding the correct value for the JAVA_HOME environment variable. This should point to the directory that you have installed Java to (not the bin directory, but the parent of the bin directory, e.g., c:\jdk1.4.x or /opt/jdk1.4.x). You can then run the connection test, which is done through the following command (note that this should be one continuous line):

```
java oracle.toplink.tutorials.gettingstarted.ConnectTest <username> <password>
<database url> <jdbc driver class>
```

TopLink Configuration

Once your installation is tested, you are ready to configure your own environment. The first step in configuring TopLink is to set up your classpath. The classpath for TopLink should include at minimum the files core\lib\toplink.jar, core\lib\xerces.jar, \core\lib\antlr.jar, and your JDBC driver. I suggest adding these JARs to a script or batch file to build you classpath; the code for this chapter can be downloaded from http://www.apress.com and includes just such a file.

These JAR files are the classpath for your environment for building and running the example code from this chapter. As with all previous chapters, I will work from the standpoint that you are compiling and running this code from the command line.

Working with TopLink

TopLink provides a rich and complete workbench tool that you can use for mapping classes to database tables. You can point this tool at an existing database and read the tables or point it at existing Java classes and read them in.

The workbench can be used with any database that has a JDBC 2 or greater driver. Only certain databases are supported out of the box; it is, however, very easy to use a database that is not listed, such as the MySQL JDBC driver.

So before you go any further, you should create your database tables. I have chosen to create two tables in a MySQL database named chapter12. The SQL for creating the tables is shown in Listing 12-1.

Listing 12-1. Create Table SQL for the Addresses and Employees Tables

```
CREATE TABLE addresses (
  address_id int(11) NOT NULL default '0',
  street_line1 varchar(100) default '',
  street_line2 varchar(100) default '',
  city varchar(100) default '',
  state char(2) default '',
  PRIMARY KEY  (address_id)
) TYPE=MyISAM;

CREATE TABLE employees (
  employee_id int(11) NOT NULL default '0',
  first_name varchar(100) default '',
  last_name varchar(100) default '',
  email varchar(100) default '',
  address_id int(11) default '0' NULL,
  PRIMARY KEY  (employee_id)
) TYPE=MyISAM;
```

Now that you have a database, you will need to create your Java classes for the workbench to use. For this example, you will use the same Employee and Address classes that you have seen before. For completeness sake, I have included them here. Listing 12-2 shows the Address class.

Listing 12-2. Address Class for Use with TopLink

```java
package com.apress.javapersist.chapter12.toplink.bo;

import java.util.*;

public class Address {
    private Long id;
    private String streetLine1;
    private String streetLine2;
    private String city;
    private String state;
    private Set residents = new TreeSet();

    private Address() {}

    public Address(Long id) { this.id = id }

    public Long getId() { return id }
    private void setId(Long id) { this.id = id }

    public String getCity() { return city }
    public void setCity(String city) { this.city = city }

    public String getState() { return state }
    public void setState(String state) { this.state = state }

    public String getStreetLine1() { return streetLine1 }
    public void setStreetLine1(String streetLine1) {
        this.streetLine1 = streetLine1
    }

    public String getStreetLine2() { return streetLine2 }
    public void setStreetLine2(String streetLine2) {
        this.streetLine2 = streetLine2
    }
```

```
    private void setResidents(Set residents) { this.residents = residents }
    public Set getResidents() { return residents }
    public void addResident(Employee resident) { this.residents.add(resident) }

    public String toString() {
        return  "id: " + id + "; "
            + "line 1: " + streetLine1 + "; "
            + "line 2: " + streetLine2 + "; "
            + "city: " + city + "; "
            + "state: " + state + "; "
            + "residents: " + residents.size() + ";"
    }
}
```

Listing 12-3 shows the Employee class. As with some of the other frameworks, including Hibernate, you can see that there is a need for a no-argument constructor, but it can be private.

Listing 12-3. Employee Class for Use with TopLink

```
package com.apress.javapersist.chapter12.toplink.bo;

public class Employee {
    private Long id;
    private String firstName;
    private String lastName;
    private String email;
    private Address address;

    private Employee() {}

    public Employee(Long id) { this.id = id }

    public Long getId() { return id }
    private void setId(Long id) { this.id = id }

    public String getFirstName() { return this.firstName }
    public void setFirstName(String firstName) { this.firstName = firstName }

    public String getLastName() { return this.lastName }
    public void setLastName(String lastName) { this.lastName = lastName }

    public String getEmail() { return this.email }
    public void setEmail(String email) { this.email = email }
```

```
    public Address getAddress() { return address }
    public void setAddress(Address address) { this.address = address }

    public String toString() {
        return "id: " + id + "; "
            + "firstName: " + firstName + "; "
            + "lastName: " + lastName + "; "
            + "email: " + email + "; "
            + "address: [" + address + "]"
    }
}
```

The connection between a Java class and a relational table in TopLink is kept in a TopLink descriptor. The descriptor in turn contains the name of the class being persisted, the primary key of the database table, a list of query keys for attributes, mappings between the attributes on the class and the database column, and finally a set of properties that affect the behavior of the mapping. The descriptor is created using the TopLink workbench.

Using the TopLink Mapping Workbench

Once you have installed TopLink on a Windows machine, the workbench should be available from the Start menu. Otherwise, you can find the script to start the workbench in the workbench directory under the TopLink installation directory.

Once the workbench has been started, you will be presented with a Java-based application that should be blank. Your first task is to create a new project. In order to do this, select New Project from the File menu. In the dialog box that appears, set the name to chapter12, choose Other from the available platforms, and then click OK (see Figure 12-1).

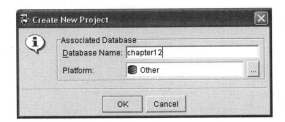

Figure 12-1. Creating a new TopLink workbench project

Upon clicking OK, a Save As dialog box will appear, allowing you to save the workbench project file. Because several subdirectories are created to support the project, I suggest putting the workbench project file into a directory by itself.

The next step in using the workbench is setting the classpath. The classpath you set will tell TopLink how to find your JDBC driver as well as where to find the classes you will be mapping. On the first screen, add these two entries to the classpath in the bottom-right corner of the screen as shown in Figure 12-2.

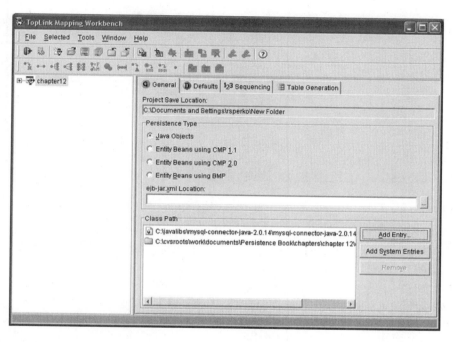

Figure 12-2. Setting the classpath for TopLink

Now you need to tell TopLink where to find your database. This is an important step because the workbench can connect to an existing database and read the available tables and their properties. This helps to remove human error in the process of mapping your objects to tables.

In order to draw your tables into the workbench, you need to set up a database login. The login consists of the applicable JDBC driver class that will be pulled from your classpath. The login will also include the JDBC URL to connect to as well as the applicable user name and password.

To create the database login, you need to first expand the chapter12 project and choose the database portion of the project. This is represented by a blue cylinder. Once the database is selected in the project, the working pane of the workbench will allow you to create database logins (see Figure 12-3).

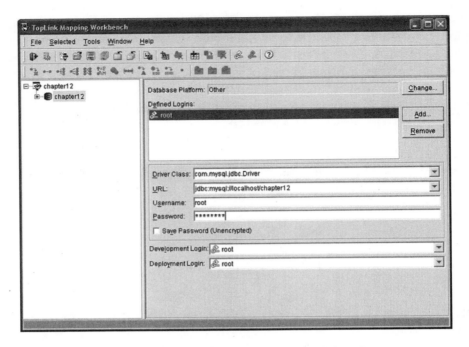

Figure 12-3. Creating a database login in the TopLink workbench

The first step is to click the Add button. This will prompt you for the name you will set for the login information. Set this to the user you will login as. Because I do not cover database security in this book, I will use the inadvisable account of root. I suggest you read the MySQL documentation and set up a nonroot user for your work.

Once you have added a login, fill in the rest of the information on the screen. Set the Driver class to com.mysql.jdbc.Driver. If you have created the database chapter12 on your local machine and have ensured that MySQL is running, set the URL to jdbc:mysql://localhost/chapter12. Then fill in the user name and password as applicable. Your screen should look like Figure 12-3 when you are done.

Now you will add your tables from your database to the project. For this to happen you need to log into the database. This is accomplished by right-clicking the chapter12 database icon and selecting Log in from the menu that appears. This will cause the workbench to log into the database using the selected database login. After the workbench is connected, the database icon will show a green check mark.

To add the tables, right-click the database icon again, this time selecting Add/Update Existing Tables from Database. You will then be prompted with the Import Tables from Database dialog box, which you can see in Figure 12-4. You don't need to change any values on this dialog box, simply click the Get Table Names button. The other fields on this dialog box are for filtering to narrow the tables returned. Since you only have two tables in your database, this is not an issue.

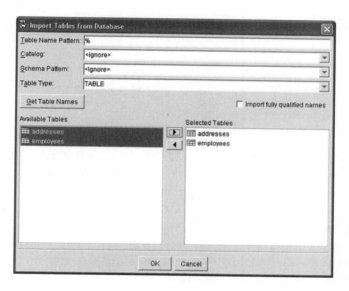

Figure 12-4. Importing tables into the TopLink workbench

When the table names have returned, highlight the Employees and Addresses tables and click the button with a right arrow. This will select the two tables. When you are complete, your workbench should look like Figure 12-4. Click the OK button.

At this point, all of your database configuration for the mapping tool is complete. The next step is to import your Java classes. After that, you will map your classes to the tables. Lastly, you will export your deployment file.

The business object classes you have created are already in the workbench's classpath. You now simply need to add them to the workbench project. For this, right-click the project and choose Add/Refresh classes. From the packages listed, choose the Address and Employee classes, and then click the button with the right arrow. This will mark the two classes as selected, as shown in Figure 12-5. Once this is completed, click the OK button.

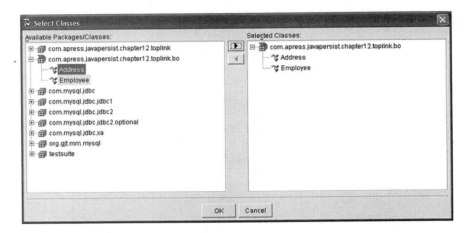

Figure 12-5. Selecting classes to add to workbench project

This next step shows just how nice it is to use a visual workbench rather than write XML by hand. For this step, you will in one fell swoop map most of the properties of your classes to columns in the tables.

Right-click the project root and select Automap. With that menu selection the workbench will recognize that the Address class is related to the Addresses table. The same applies to the Employee class and Employees table. The workbench will recognize and associate almost all of the fields of the classes to the appropriate columns in the database. All of this is done automagically. The workbench uses the names of the attributes and runs through permeations of the name until it either comes up with a match or gives up.

Do not fret if the workbench does not automatically find the field and column match. It is very easy to manually map a field to a column. All you need to do is select the appropriate attribute on the class and click the Direct to Field toolbar button.

There are in this example two fields that did not automatically get mapped. The residents attribute on Address was not deduced by the workbench nor was the address field on the Employee class. These you will map manually. The way these will be associated is through a table reference. A *table reference* informs the workbench of the foreign key relationship between the classes.

To create the table reference, select the address attribute from the Employee class. Make sure that the reference descriptor in the General tab is set to Address. Then choose the Table Reference tab. On the Table Reference tab, click the New button. This will bring up a dialog box that offers to create a new table reference between the Addresses table and the Employees table. All values should be filled in correctly; all you need to do is click OK. When the dialog box is gone, click the Add button. When the association is added to the table, change the employee column from employee_id to address_id. This marks the correct field as the foreign key. Notice that the address attribute loses its warning flag. You have now associated the Employee class to the Address class and completed the mapping for your Employee class.

To associate the Address class to the Employee class, you follow almost the same procedure. The first step in associating the residents attribute with the Employee class is telling the workbench that residents represents a one-to-many relationship. This is accomplished by selecting the residents attribute and clicking the one-to-many toolbar button.

As with the address attribute, you ensure that the reference descriptor is set to the other class, in this case Employee. Then click the Table Reference tab. From the drop-down list, choose the table reference employees_addresses. Upon selection, all warnings should be gone from the screen and the workbench should look like Figure 12-6.

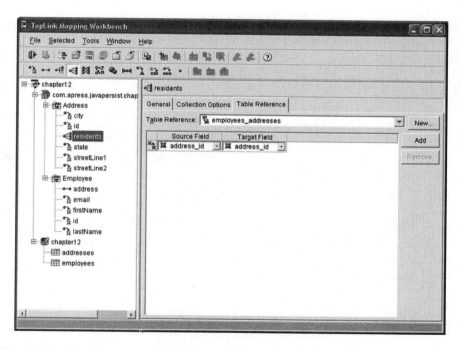

Figure 12-6. The final mapping in the workbench

You have now successfully created your mappings. The mappings contain attribute-to-field mappings as well as a one-to-one and a one-to-many mapping, all of which was done with minimum effort. Next you need to export the deployment XML. This is accomplished by opening the file menu and selecting Generate deployment XML. You will then be prompted with a Save As dialog box.

Export the file as chapter12.xml to a location that you will reference from your Java code in your HR application.

Writing Code for TopLink

Now it is time to look at the code for your HR application. As I said before, this is the same application you used for JDO in Chapter 10 and for the open source frameworks in Chapter 11. I will show you how to create several command objects that will extend one base command object that provides services for the children. The superclass for your commands can be seen in Listing 12-4.

Listing 12-4. TopLink Base Action Provides Services to Children

```java
package com.apress.javapersist.chapter12.toplink;

import oracle.toplink.sessions.DatabaseLogin;
import oracle.toplink.sessions.DatabaseSession;
import oracle.toplink.sessions.Project;
import oracle.toplink.tools.workbench.XMLProjectReader;

public abstract class BaseAction {
    private static Project project = null;

    protected DatabaseSession getSession() throws Exception {
        if (project == null) {
            project = XMLProjectReader.read("config/chapter12.xml");
        }
        DatabaseSession session = project.createDatabaseSession();
        DatabaseLogin login = session.getLogin();
        // user name is provided by configuration
        login.setPassword("password");

        session.login();
        return session;
    }

    public abstract void execute(String[] args) throws Exception;


    public abstract String exampleString();
}
```

The `BaseAction` class includes a few steps necessary to communicate through TopLink. These are all contained within the `getSession` method. This method creates an instance of a TopLink `Project` class if one does not exist. The project is created by reading the deployment XML that was generated from the workbench. Notice that I use a relative path for this file. The file could exist almost anywhere, and provided that I give the correct path, the configuration will be loaded.

Once the project is created, the `DatabaseLogin` is obtained. This is a class that is already a part of the project; you are simply obtaining a reference to it by calling the `getLogin` method. It is possible to set both the user name and password on the database login object, which could be useful if you wanted to track applications or users that were connecting to your database. In this example, I am relying on the user name that was set in the deployment XML and setting the password explicitly. To override the deployment user name, I would simply call the `setUserName` method.

Like OJB, TopLink provides a programmatic query mechanism, which means that you will create a simple language for use in querying. This language will be encapsulated in a `Finder` class. The syntax going into the finder will be class name followed either by the word "all" or an attribute name operator and then a value. You will only support the operators `equals` and `notEquals`. (It is an easy exercise to add additional operators.) A query string could look like this:

```
Employee all
```

or like this:

```
Employee firstName notEquals Wilbur
```

The finder for TopLink is slightly more complex than the one used for OJB. This is because I want to demonstrate two different querying mechanisms. Notice that if the string arguments coming into the find method contains the string "all", the `findAll` method is called. This is the method you want to use if you want all stored instances of the class because it calls `readAllObjects` with no arguments other than the class.

In the second case, notice that the code builds an `Expression` object from the string array in the `buildExpression` method. This method creates an `ExpressionBuilder` object that builds the actual expression that will be used. The expression builder has a nice syntax for programmatically building expressions. All methods on the builder return the correct types to allow daisy chained method calls.

This is one of those situations in which code is fun to write and easy to use, but I would not have designed it this way. It becomes very easy to create long message chains that can be fragile and difficult to understand. In the case of the

ExpressionBuilder, this isn't too much of an issue because the methods are clear and end up reading much like SQL when correctly put together.

Once you have built the expression using the expression builder, you call to the readAllObjects method with arguments of both the class and expression results in a filtered query (see Listing 12-5).

Listing 12-5. Finder Class for Querying TopLink

```java
package com.apress.javapersist.chapter12.toplink;

import java.util.Iterator;
import java.util.Vector;

import oracle.toplink.expressions.Expression;
import oracle.toplink.expressions.ExpressionBuilder;
import oracle.toplink.sessions.DatabaseSession;

public class Finder {
    public Iterator find(DatabaseSession session, String[] args)
        throws Exception {
        Class clazz = getClass(args[0]);

        if(args.length == 2) { // class and command
            String cmd = args[1];
            if("all".equals(cmd)) {
                // add no criteria, want to return all
                return findAll(session, clazz);
            }
        }
        else if(args.length > 2){
            Expression expression = buildExpression(args);
            Vector results = session.readAllObjects(clazz, expression);
            return results.iterator();
        }
        // Do not understand, return null.  Should throw exception.
        return null;
    }

    private Iterator findAll(DatabaseSession session, Class clazz) {
        Vector results = session.readAllObjects(clazz);
        return results.iterator();
    }
```

```
    private Expression buildExpression(String[] args) {
        String attribute = args[1];
        String comparison = args[2];
        String value = args[3];

        ExpressionBuilder builder = new ExpressionBuilder();
        Expression expression = null;
        if("equals".equals(comparison)) {
            expression = builder.get(attribute).equal(value);
        }
        else if("notEquals".equals(comparison)) {
            expression = builder.get(attribute).notEqual(value);
        }

        return expression;
    }

    private static Class getClass(String className)
        throws ClassNotFoundException {
        return Class.forName("com.apress.javapersist.chapter12.toplink.bo."
            + className);
    }
}
}
```

One of the first features you need to implement is storing your objects in the database through TopLink. Writing objects to the database in TopLink consists of starting a transaction, calling the writeObject method on a database session, and then committing the transaction. The execute method in AddAction in Listing 12-6 shows exactly how to store the object.

Listing 12-6. Adding Objects to the Database Using TopLink

```
package com.apress.javapersist.chapter12.toplink;

import oracle.toplink.sessions.DatabaseSession;

import com.apress.javapersist.chapter12.toplink.bo.Address;
import com.apress.javapersist.chapter12.toplink.bo.Employee;

public class AddAction extends BaseAction {
    public void execute(String[] args) throws Exception {
        DatabaseSession session = null;
        Object obj = buildObject(args);
        session = getSession();
```

```
        session.beginTransaction();
        // Mark the object as persistent
        session.writeObject(obj);
        System.out.println("Object stored: " + obj);
        session.commitTransaction();
    }

    private static Object buildObject(String[] args) {
        String className = args[0];
        Object obj = null;
        if("Employee".equals(className)) {
            Employee emp = new Employee(new Long(args[1]));
            emp.setFirstName(args[2]);
            emp.setLastName(args[3]);
            emp.setEmail(args[4]);
            obj = emp;
        }
        else if("Address".equals(className)){
            Address add = new Address(new Long(args[1]));
            add.setStreetLine1(args[2]);
            add.setStreetLine2(args[3]);
            add.setCity(args[4]);
            add.setState(args[5]);
            obj = add;
        }
        return obj;
    }

    public String exampleString() {
        return "    Manage add Employee id FName LName eMail\n"
            + "    Manage add Address id line1 line2 city state";
    }
}
```

The ListAction class simply wraps the finder class just as it did in OJB. The
session is created in the execute method. Then the session and arguments are
passed into the finder. The returned iterator is run through, outputting each object
as it is obtained (see Listing 12-7).

Listing 12-7. Printing Objects Stored in the Database Using TopLink

```java
package com.apress.javapersist.chapter12.toplink;

import java.util.Iterator;

import oracle.toplink.sessions.DatabaseSession;

public class ListAction extends BaseAction {
    private Object className;

    public void execute(String[] args) throws Exception {
        DatabaseSession session = getSession();
        Finder finder = new Finder();

        Iterator iter = finder.find(session, args);

        // Run through the objects, listing each one
        while( iter.hasNext() ) {
            System.out.println(iter.next());
        }
    }

    public String exampleString() {
        return "    Manage list Employee firstName equals LName\n"
            + "    Manage list Employee all";
    }
}
```

The `RemoveAction` method is a great opportunity to see a powerful feature of TopLink, the unit of work. The *unit of work* is an object that allows batching of persistence work. You can create a single unit of work to perform many different persistence-related tasks, then apply them all at once.

While this sounds like transactions, there are actually other benefits to working this way. For one thing, TopLink can optimize exactly how the database calls are made. You will see some other benefits of units of work in the `AssociateAction` class.

In Listing 12-8, you can see that a finder is used to find all matching instances. Immediately after a unit of work is acquired, all objects are deleted through the unit of work. Finally, the unit of work is committed. That call to `commit` is what writes the changes to the database.

Listing 12-8. Removing Stored Objects Using TopLink

```java
package com.apress.javapersist.chapter12.toplink;

import java.util.Iterator;

import oracle.toplink.publicinterface.UnitOfWork;
import oracle.toplink.sessions.DatabaseSession;

public class RemoveAction extends BaseAction {

    public void execute(String[] args) throws Exception {
        String typeName = args[0];
        DatabaseSession session = getSession();
        Finder finder = new Finder();

        Iterator results = finder.find(session, args);

        UnitOfWork unitOfWork = session.acquireUnitOfWork();
        // Run through the list of objects, deleting each one
        while(results.hasNext()) {
          unitOfWork.deleteObject(results.next());
        }
        // apply all deletes to database
        unitOfWork.commit();
    }

    public String exampleString() {
        return "    Manage remove Employee lastName equals LName";
    }
}
```

Now in the AssociateAction class in Listing 12-9, you get to see the unit of work modify objects. The unit of work object is a great feature when it comes to modifying objects because it allows the developer to easily work with copies rather than the original. I have spent much time on various projects making and tracking copies of objects so that either I knew what had changed on the class or I could roll back to the original class state if I needed to without making another database call.

Listing 12-9. Associating and Modifying Existing Objects Using TopLink

```
package com.apress.javapersist.chapter12.toplink;

import java.util.Iterator;

import oracle.toplink.publicinterface.UnitOfWork;
import oracle.toplink.sessions.DatabaseSession;

import com.apress.javapersist.chapter12.toplink.bo.Address;
import com.apress.javapersist.chapter12.toplink.bo.Employee;

public class AssociateAction extends BaseAction {
    public void execute(String[] args) throws Exception {
        DatabaseSession session = getSession();
        if("Employee".equals(args[0])) {
            Employee employee = findEmployee(session, args);
            Address address = findAddress(session, args);

            System.out.println("About to associate: " + employee + " with "
                + address);

            UnitOfWork unitOfWork = session.acquireUnitOfWork();

            // Make copies to work with
            Employee employeeCopy
                = (Employee) unitOfWork.registerObject(employee);
            Address addressCopy = (Address) unitOfWork.registerObject(address);

            // Actually associate the two classes
            employeeCopy.setAddress(addressCopy);
            addressCopy.addResident(employeeCopy);

            // Update the database
            unitOfWork.commit();
        }
    }

    private Employee findEmployee(DatabaseSession session, String[] args)
    throws Exception {
        Finder finder = new Finder();
```

```
            String[] empArgs = new String[4];
            System.arraycopy(args, 0, empArgs, 0, empArgs.length);

            Iterator iter = finder.find(session, empArgs);
            Employee employee = (Employee) iter.next();

            return employee;
        }

        private Address findAddress(DatabaseSession session, String[] args)
        throws Exception {
            Finder finder = new Finder();

            String[] addArgs = new String[4];
            System.arraycopy(args, 4, addArgs, 0, addArgs.length);

            Iterator iter = finder.find(session, addArgs);
            Address address = (Address) iter.next();

            return address;
        }

        public String exampleString() {
            return "    Manage assoc Employee id equals 0 Address id equals 1";
        }
    }
```

The unit of work automatically makes a copy of an object when you register the object with the unit of work. Not only does it make a copy, but the unit of work complains if you try to associate an object that has not been registered with an object that has. This helps to keep you honest.

If you look at the execute method in Listing 12-9, you can see that two objects are obtained from TopLink. You then acquire a unit of work. On registering the objects with the unit of work, you obtain a copy of the object. This is your working copy. Any changes that are made will be made to this version. You then connect the two copied objects together and commit the unit of work.

Another benefit of using the unit of work in this way is that only modified objects will be updated in the commit. You can register various objects, but only modified objects get persisted. This can be a huge performance savings.

Last is the Manage class, which is the starting point of your application. This is shown for completeness in Listing 12-10. It has not changed since prior versions.

Listing 12-10. The HR Application Main Class

```java
package com.apress.javapersist.chapter12.toplink;

import java.util.HashMap;
import java.util.Iterator;

public class Manage {
    HashMap actions = new HashMap();

    public Manage() {
        actions.put("list", new ListAction());
        actions.put("add", new AddAction());
        actions.put("remove", new RemoveAction());
        actions.put("assoc", new AssociateAction());
    }

    private void executeAction(String[] args) throws Exception {
        if(args.length < 2) {
            usage();
            return;
        }
        String actionStr = args[0];
        String[] cmdArgs = new String[args.length-1];
        System.arraycopy(args, 1, cmdArgs, 0, cmdArgs.length);

        BaseAction action = (BaseAction) actions.get(actionStr);
        if(action == null) {
            usage();
            return;
        }

        action.execute(cmdArgs);
    }

    public static void main(String[] args) {
        Manage manage = new Manage();
        try {
            manage.executeAction(args);
        }
        catch(Exception e) {
            e.printStackTrace();
        }
    }
}
```

```
    private void usage() {
        System.out.println("usage:");
        System.out.println("java com.apress.javapersist.chapter10.Manage <act"
            + "ion> [arg1] [arg2] [argn]");
        System.out.println("   actions: " + actions.keySet());
        System.out.println();
        System.out.println("Examples:");
        for(Iterator iter = actions.values().iterator(); iter.hasNext(); ) {
            System.out.println(((BaseAction) iter.next()).exampleString());
        }
    }
}
```

And that is all, folks. The preceding code should give you a basic example of how to use TopLink for storing, retrieving, modifying, and deleting objects. As you can see, TopLink is both easy to use and high performance through caching of changes and batch updates.

Other TopLink Notes

Besides TopLink's standard API, the product provides other ways to use the framework. TopLink provides both a Java Data Objects (JDO) and Container Managed Persistence (CMP) interface to the framework. JDO for TopLink is built on top of the API you have just seen, much like the OJB-provided JDO. Another convenient feature of TopLink JDO is there is no need to process either source or classes. You can use your existing classes.

One feature missing in TopLink JDO is the JDO Query Language. TopLink instead uses its own programmatic query mechanism. Another option for querying is using EJB QL, which TopLink does support. This means that TopLink is not a drop-in replacement for any other JDO implementation.

The reason TopLink provides EJB QL is because it can be used in application servers for CMP. TopLink provides support for BEA WebLogic, IBM WebSphere, and obviously the Oracle9iAS application servers.

Using CocoBase for Java Persistence

As mentioned at the beginning of this chapter, CocoBase is another persistence framework that provides transparent Java persistence. The product itself aims at being very flexible and not restrictive to developers. This, combined with years of evolution, has resulted in a complete yet sometimes confusing persistence product. The confusion comes from just how many ways there are to do the same thing. I will talk a little more about this later.

Obtaining a copy of CocoBase is easy, you simply download an evaluation copy from THOUGHT, Inc. at http://www.thoughtinc.com/cber_info.html. One very nice feature is that THOUGHT provides support for the time of the evaluation period. Besides technical support, you can also use the CocoBase forums on the THOUGHT, Inc. site.

Setting Up CocoBase

Follow the installation instructions that come with CocoBase, or, if you download an evaluation copy, use the instructions that are on the THOUGHT, Inc. Web site. Once you have installed CocoBase, you need to add your JDBC driver to your system's classpath. This will allow the CocoAdmin tool to find it and use your existing database for creating mappings.

The next step you will want to perform is to set up your development environment. This is fairly simple. CocoBase keeps all of its needed files in two places: <CocoBase install dir>\classes and <CocoBase install dir>\demos. You need to have these two directories as well as your own classes directory and JDBC driver in your classpath. After that, you are read to start developing with CocoBase. In version 5 expect a directory restructuring.

Writing Code for CocoBase

For transparent persistence, THOUGHT, Inc. recommends using EJB QL and their CBFacade. EJB QL is provided because Container Managed Persistence is a feature that they offer. The CBFacade is used to wrap much of the complexity of CocoBase and reveal simple clean methods for inserting, updating, deleting, and querying.

When working with CocoBase, you should follow several conventions to simplify your work. Most of these can be overridden, but I would only suggest that if you are mapping legacy code to legacy tables. Otherwise, try to conform as much as possible and enjoy the work that CocoBase will save you.

One of the key conventions in CocoBase is how CocoBase maps columns to class attributes. A *field* is what CocoBase tracks for the database. One part of the field is the field name, which is the column name. Another part that is tracked is the field label. This is the part that will be mapped to an attribute. The convention for the label-to-field tracking is that all labels must begin with a colon (:). The second requirement is that all labels must be all uppercase. To fulfill this requirement, labels follow a convention where underscores separate parts of the name. This means that a class attribute or bean property named "firstName" will have a field label of "FIRST_NAME". In addition, numbers must be prefixed with underscores. This means that "streetAddress1" becomes "STREET_ADDRESS_1".

It is easier working with CocoBase if the objects you are persisting are simple JavaBeans. What that means is there is a no-argument constructor and all persistable attributes are accessed through JavaBean getters and setters. I say "simple JavaBeans" because it is not possible to access indexed properties.

The application I will present for CocoBase is the same one used for all of the transparent persistence frameworks up to this point, a basic HR application. This will consist of an employee and address business object. These objects have a one-to-many relationship in which one address can have multiple residents. Additionally, the application uses the command pattern to execute various parts of the functionality.

Because of this, you will see some simple changes to the employee and address objects in Listing 12-11. Both have no-argument constructors, and I have added a public setter for the id attribute. Because the changes are simple, I will not repeat the classes here.

Listing 12-11. BaseAction for CocoBase, Providing CBFacade to Subclasses

```
package com.apress.javapersist.chapter12.cocobase;

import java.util.Iterator;
import java.util.Properties;
import java.util.Vector;

import thought.CocoBase.CBFacade;


public abstract class BaseAction {

    protected CBFacade getCBFacade() throws Exception {
    public final static String EMPLOYEE_MAP
        = "com.apress.javapersist.chapter12.cocobase.bo.Employee";
    public final static String ADDRESS_MAP
        = "com.apress.javapersist.chapter12.cocobase.bo.Address";
        String url
            = "jdbc:mysql://localhost/chapter12:cocoprop=dynamic.querying=true";

        Properties props = new Properties();
        props.setProperty("cocosource.name", "thought.CocoBase.CocoPowder");
        props.setProperty("cocosource.jdbcdriver", "com.mysql.jdbc.Driver");
        props.setProperty("cocosource.url", url);
        props.setProperty("cocosource.user", "root");
```

```
        props.setProperty("cocosource.password", "password");
        props.setProperty("cocosource.factory",
            "com.apress.javapersist.chapter12.cocobase.BusinessObjectFactory");
        props.setProperty("cocosource.navmodel", "HRAppLinks");

        CBFacade facade = CBFacade.create("thought.CocoBase.CBFacadeLocal");
        facade.connect(props);
        return facade;
    }

    protected Iterator findAll(CBFacade cbFacade, String queryStr, Vector args)
        throws Exception {
        Vector results = cbFacade.executeQLQuery(queryStr, args);
        return results.iterator();
    }

    public abstract void execute(String[] args) throws Exception;

    public abstract String exampleString();
}
```

Creation of a `CBFacade` minimally involves creating a `java.util.Properties` object and populating it with configuration information. The possible properties available are as follows:

- `cocosource.url`: JDBC and CocoBase connection URL, which is required.

- `cocosource.name`: CocoBase driver name, which is required.

- `cocosource.jdbcdriver`: JDBC driver name, which is required.

- `cocosource.user`: User name to log into the database, which is required.

- `cocosource.password`: User password for connecting to the database, which is required.

- `cocosource.navmodel`: Navigation model. This is the name of the model created in CocoAdmin (do not include the .properties extension that the file has). This is optional if you have no relationships.

- `cocosource.autoclose`: Automatically closes JDBC connections this is an optional property which can be set to true or false.

- `cocosource.autotrans`: Automatically create transactions this is an optional property which can be set to true or false.

- `cocosource.autoidentity`: Used for auto-assigning identity to inserted records this is an optional property that can be set to true or false.

- `cocosource.factory`: A class name that the developer creates that helps create and populate business objects. This is optional.

The URL for connecting to `CBFacade` contains two parts. The first is a standard JDBC connect URL. The second part is separated from the first by a colon (:). The second part needs to start with "cocoprop=" and then passes in arguments to CocoBase. At minimum, you should include "dynamic.querying=true" to allow EJB QL to be used.

The `autocommit` argument allows you to indicate whether work will be committed as it is executed or multiple actions will be performed and then the final commit called. This helps optimize the code and allow for transaction support. Another note on this class is that you should add `public static final` attributes to hold onto the map names. This gives you one place that you need to change if the map name changes.

The actual `CBFacade` is created by calling the `create` method with a string argument naming the subclass to create. For this simple example, you create a local facade. It is possible to create a remote version in the same way. THOUGHT, Inc. provides some good documents explaining both facades.

The second method in your `BaseAction` takes an EJB QL query string and a vector of arguments for the query. This is passed into `executeQLQuery`, which returns a vector of results. Similar to the previous examples, a `java.util.Iterator` is returned from this method.

To illustrate some of the flexibility of CocoBase, I have `BaseAction` use a `CocoFactoryInterface` for creating business objects. This is not necessary for the simple objects you are working with, but this does allow for manipulating or modifying data as it comes out of CocoBase. Listing 12-12 shows the `BusinessObjectFactory`.

Listing 12-12. BusinessObjectFactory Allows for Interception or Modification of Data As It Comes Out of CocoBase

```
package com.apress.javapersist.chapter12.cocobase;

import java.util.Properties;

import thought.CocoBase.CocoFactoryInterface;
import thought.CocoBase.CocoProxyM;
```

```
import com.apress.javapersist.chapter12.cocobase.bo.Address;
import com.apress.javapersist.chapter12.cocobase.bo.Employee;

public class BusinessObjectFactory implements CocoFactoryInterface {

    public Object getInstance(Object src,
            Object propertiesIn,
            String objectName) {
        Properties properties = (Properties) propertiesIn;
        try {
            // For each type with custom factory.
            if(BaseAction.EMPLOYEE_MAP.equals(objectName)) {
                Employee employee = new Employee();

                // the following shows how you can manage your own data that
                // comes back from CocoBase
                Long id = (Long) properties.get("ID");
                employee.setId(id);

                CocoProxyM employeeProxy = new CocoProxyM(employee);
                employeeProxy.setPropObjectData(properties);

                return employee;
            }
            else if(BaseAction.ADDRESS_MAP.equals(objectName)) {
                Address address = new Address();

                CocoProxyM addressProxy = new CocoProxyM(address);
                addressProxy.setPropObjectData(properties);

                return address;
            }
        } catch (Exception e) {
            e.printStackTrace();
        }
        return null;
    }
}
```

In the BusinessObjectFactory, if an employee object is requested, you can see that the "ID" value that was passed in is first obtained. Notice that this would be the field label for the attribute as per the CocoBase naming conventions. You could modify or use this value in any way you want before setting it on the newly created

employee. Also notice that all of the heavy lifting in this class is performed by
CocoProxyM; this class populates the business object itself.

Now you need to add some objects to your database. Your AddAction class is
very similar to other versions you have seen. Listing 12-13 shows that you create
your business object and then begin a transaction on the facade. Your code then
inserts the business object and commits the transaction.

Listing 12-13. AddAction for CocoBase

```
package com.apress.javapersist.chapter12.cocobase;

import thought.CocoBase.CBFacade;

import com.apress.javapersist.chapter12.cocobase.bo.Address;
import com.apress.javapersist.chapter12.cocobase.bo.Employee;

public class AddAction extends BaseAction {
    public void execute(String[] args) throws Exception {
        Object obj = buildObject(args);
        CBFacade cbFacade = getCBFacade();

        cbFacade.beginTransaction();
        // Mark the object as persistent
        cbFacade.insert(obj);
        System.out.println("Object stored: " + obj);
        cbFacade.commit();
    }

    private static Object buildObject(String[] args) {
        String className = args[0];
        Object obj = null;
        if("Employee".equals(className)) {
            Employee emp = new Employee();
            emp.setId(new Long(args[1]));
            emp.setFirstName(args[2]);
            emp.setLastName(args[3]);
            emp.setEmail(args[4]);
            obj = emp;
        }
        else if("Address".equals(className)){
            Address add = new Address();
            add.setId(new Long(args[1]));
            add.setStreetLine1(args[2]);
            add.setStreetLine2(args[3]);
            add.setCity(args[4]);
```

```
            add.setState(args[5]);
            obj = add;
        }
        return obj;
    }

    public String exampleString() {
        return "    Manage add Employee id FName LName eMail\n"
            + "    Manage add Address id line1 line2 city state";
    }
}
```

The code for listing your objects is not really any different from the ListingAction class in TopLink. A call is made to BaseAction with EJB QL to find all objects that match the query. The objects are then iterated through, outputting them to standard output (Listing 12-14).

Listing 12-14. ListAction for CocoBase

```
package com.apress.javapersist.chapter12.cocobase;

import java.util.Iterator;
import java.util.Vector;

import thought.CocoBase.CBFacade;

public class ListAction extends BaseAction {
    private Object className;

    public void execute(String[] args) throws Exception {
        CBFacade cbFacade = getCBFacade();

        Iterator iter = findAll(cbFacade, args[1], new Vector());

        // Run through the objects listing each one
        while( iter.hasNext() ) {
            System.out.println(iter.next());
        }
    }

    public String exampleString() {
        return "    Manage list Employee \"select object(e) from Employee e "
            + "where e.firstName='FName'\"";
    }
}
```

Removing objects follows the same convention. As with AddAction, a transaction is started before and committed after. Listing 12-15 shows the CocoBase RemoveAction class. The method called on the facade is delete.

Listing 12-15. RemoveAction for CocoBase

```
package com.apress.javapersist.chapter12.cocobase;

import java.util.Iterator;
import java.util.Vector;

import thought.CocoBase.CBFacade;

public class RemoveAction extends BaseAction {

    public void execute(String[] args) throws Exception {
        CBFacade cbFacade = getCBFacade();

        Iterator results = findAll(cbFacade, args[1], new Vector());

        cbFacade.beginTransaction();

        // Run through the list of objects, deleting each one
        while(results.hasNext()) {
          cbFacade.delete(results.next());
        }
        // apply all deletes to database
        cbFacade.commit();
    }

    public String exampleString() {
        return "    Manage remove Employee \"select object(e) from Employee e "
            + "where e.firstName='FName'\"";
    }
}
```

The last class I will show is the AssociateAction class. Like the classes before this, the associate action is used to show how to modify two business objects and save them, as well as to show how relationships are managed. Listing 12-16 shows the AssociateAction class.

Listing 12-16. AssociateAction for CocoBase

```java
package com.apress.javapersist.chapter12.cocobase;


import java.util.Iterator;
import java.util.Vector;

import thought.CocoBase.CBFacade;

import com.apress.javapersist.chapter12.cocobase.bo.Address;
import com.apress.javapersist.chapter12.cocobase.bo.Employee;

public class AssociateAction extends BaseAction {
    public void execute(String[] args) throws Exception {
        CBFacade cbFacade = getCBFacade();
        if("Employee".equals(args[0])) {
            String employeeQuery = args[1];
            String addressQuery = args[3];

            Employee employee = findEmployee(cbFacade, employeeQuery);
            Address address = findAddress(cbFacade, addressQuery);

            System.out.println("About to associate: " + employee + " with "
                + address);

            cbFacade.beginTransaction();

            // Actually associate the two classes
            employee.setAddress(address);
            address.addResident(employee);

            cbFacade.save(employee, BaseAction.EMPLOYEE_MAP);
            cbFacade.save(address, BaseAction.ADDRESS_MAP);

            // Update the database
            cbFacade.commit();
        }
    }
```

```
    private Employee findEmployee(CBFacade cbFacade, String employeeQuery)
    throws Exception {
        Iterator iter = findAll(cbFacade, employeeQuery, new Vector());
        Employee employee = (Employee) iter.next();

        return employee;
    }

    private Address findAddress(CBFacade cbFacade, String addressQuery)
    throws Exception {
        Iterator iter = findAll(cbFacade, addressQuery, new Vector());
        Address address = (Address) iter.next();

        return address;
    }

    public String exampleString() {
        return "   Manage assoc Employee \"select object(e) from Employee e "
            + "where e.id='101'\" Address \"select object(a) from Address a "
            + "where a.id ='1'\"";
    }
}
```

The Manage class is only different from previous versions in the package names that are imported. This is still the class that is the starting point for your application. I suggest referring back to Listing 12-10 to see the Manage class.

Working with CocoAdmin

The CocoBase CocoAdmin tool is a graphical mapping tool used when working with CocoBase. It is through the CocoAdmin tool that you create all mappings. You also use this tool to create relationships between objects.

How the tool is started depends on what platform it is installed to. For Windows, the tool is added to the Start menu. On UNIX, there is a shell script to start the tool called cocoadmin.sh.

Every time you start the CocoAdmin tool, you are prompted to log on to a database. For this example, you will connect to the same database you used for working with TopLink, namely jdbc:mysql://localhost/chapter12. For this to work, you need to ensure that your MySQL JDBC driver is in your system classpath. Upon starting the server, you are presented with the database login screen shown in Figure 12-7.

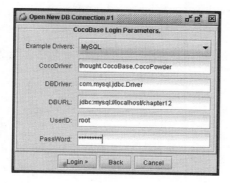

Figure 12-7. CocoAdmin database login

On this screen, choose your database driver, in this case MySQL. Leave the CocoDriver exactly as it is. If you have upgraded to Connector/J, you may need to change the driver class that is shown to com.mysql.jdbc.Driver. Fill in the URL and login information as appropriate.

Upon clicking OK, you will be prompted to install the repository. You should only have to perform this step once. This step creates four tables in your database in which CocoBase stores much of its mapping information. You do not need to do this if you are storing your repository in XML. For this example, you will store the repository in the database. There is no option for MySQL in the repository templates. Microsoft SQL Server is what is suggested by the tool, and this works for MySQL. Figure 12-8 shows the repository creation.

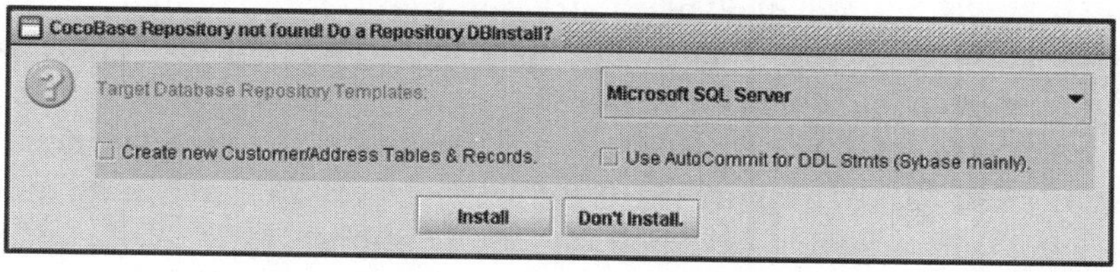

Figure 12-8. Creating the repository in CocoAdmin

This in turn creates the four tables that I mentioned before, which are named cb_fields, cb_clauses, cb_objects, and cb_tables (see Figure 12-9). Where other frameworks store their repository information in external files, CocoBase gives you the option of keeping it with the data. Unfortunately, as I will discuss in more detail soon, not all repository data is stored here by default.

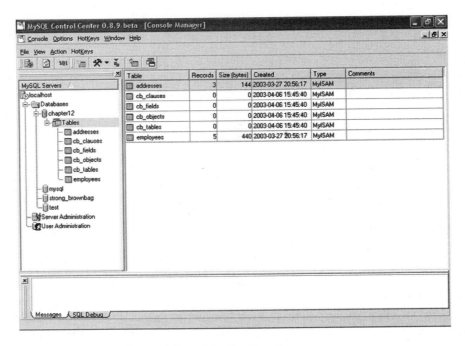

Figure 12-9. Generated repository tables for CocoBase

Next you will be presented with a launcher for various CocoAdmin functions. For this example, you will manually map existing Java classes to your tables. For this reason, simply click the Cancel button. Now you are ready to start mapping.

Your next step is to import your Java classes into the CocoAdmin tool. In order to do this, you select Import Java Class from the File menu. You will be presented with the screen shown in Figure 12-10. It may be necessary to maximize the internal frame in order to see the bottom row of buttons.

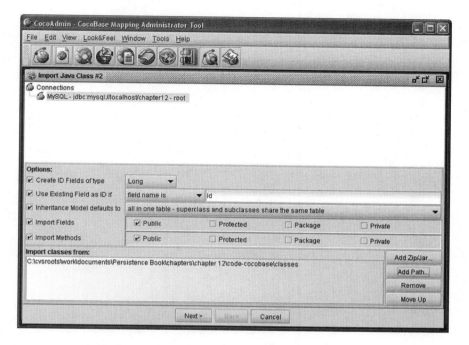

Figure 12-10. Setting up to import Java classes into CocoAdmin

In the Import Java Class screen, first select the connection you want to use from the tree view. Next click the Add Path button. You will be presented with a file dialog box. Navigate to the classes directory where you have compiled your code. When you have selected a connection and added a directory or JAR, the Next button should become enabled as in Figure 12-10.

You will be presented with a warning dialog box listing classes that will be ignored. Provided that Employee and Address are not on the list, it is good that these classes are ignored. Click Continue Import to move to the next step.

On the next screen, you will be presented with a list of all classes that are found with check boxes next to them. Make sure that only Employee and Address are selected. The next screen you will be presented with is a Link Field screen. Simply click Next; you want to explicitly create your links for this example.

Now you are on the final screen for importing your Java classes. This is the screen that will map your classes to tables and attributes to columns. The first step is to map your Employee class. Select the Employee class from the list of objects. You can see that many of the class's attributes already have default values, but they need some massaging to be correct. First change the DB Name for the id attribute to EMPLOYEE_ID as it is in your database. The screen should look like Figure 12-11 when completed.

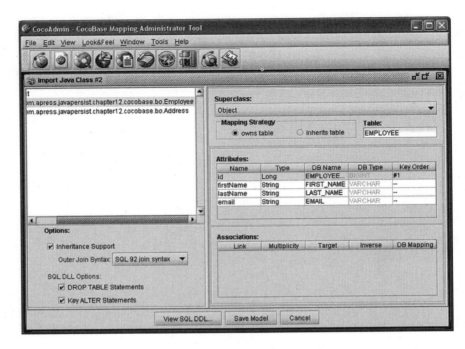

Figure 12-11. Mapping attributes of imported classes in CocoAdmin

Follow the same procedure for the address object. For the address object, change the `id` attribute to ADDRESS_ID. After you have made this change, click Save Model and close the Import Java Class frame. You may be prompted with a warning that the navigation model cannot be saved. Simply click OK.

Your next task is to edit your map. From the File menu, select Edit Map. You will now be presented with the map editor. Your first task in this editor is to correct the Addresses table name. First open the map named com.apress.javapersist.chapter12.cocobase.bo.Address (the Address map). Then open up the "select" mapping child. From here, click the Fields leaf (see Figure 12-12); as you can see, CocoAdmin shows all of the database fields as being part of an ADDRESS table. Your actual table name is ADDRESSES, so you need to make this change. After changing one cell and clicking somewhere else, you will be prompted as to whether to apply to all operations; choose this option.

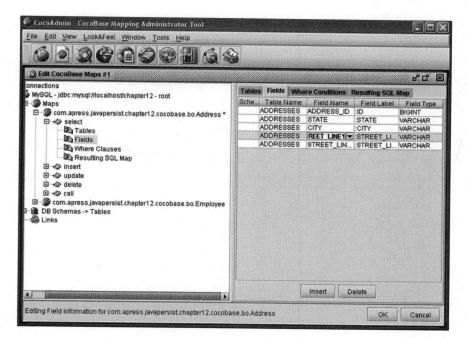

Figure 12-12. Editing the Address map field names to match the database

The next task for the Address map is to correct your street column names. In the "Writing Code for CocoBase" section, I discuss how CocoBase maps bean property names. Since your class contains both streetLine1 and streetLine2, you now have two fields listed by the names STREET_LINE_1 and STREET_LINE_2. Your database, however, is expecting STREET_LINE1 and STREET_LINE2. Click the appropriate cells in the table and make the changes. After you are done, CocoAdmin should look like Figure 12-12. At this point, right-click the map and choose Save Map. This will persist your changes to the database repository.

Now it is time to make some changes to your com.apress.javapersist.chapter12.cocobase.bo.Employee map (Employee map). First select the Employee map, and then open up Fields under the "select" mapping child. Notice that once again your table name is wrong; it should be EMPLOYEES. Make this change and apply it to all operations. Next you need to add another row that will be used to map your one-to-many relationship.

To add another entry to the Employee map, click the Insert button on the editor. A new row will be added to the mapping. In the Table Name column, fill in EMPLOYEES, and for the Field Name column, fill in ADDRESS_ID; this should fill in the corresponding Field Label cell with :ADDRESS_ID. Next, choose a field type of BIGINT. After all of these changes, you will be prompted to apply them to all operations; make sure you do. The Employee mapping should look like

Figure 12-13 at this time. If it does, right-click the Employee map and choose
Save Map.

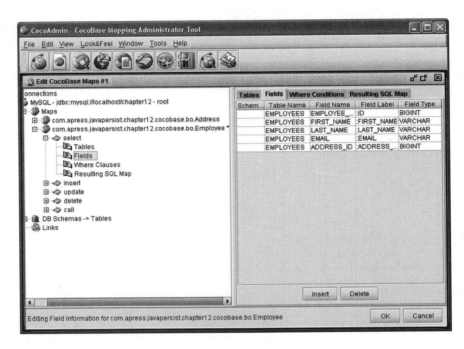

Figure 12-13. Cleaning up the Employee map

Now you need to create your model and link to support your relationship.
Links are connections between maps; a *model* is a group of links. You can have as
many models as you need; for smaller applications, all links can easily reside in
one model. For this application, you will create a model named HRAppLinks.
Right-click the Links node and select New Model. Fill in the name HRAppLinks in
the appropriate text field and click OK.

Your link is created by right-clicking the newly created model, selecting New
Link, and then selecting the newly created link. You are creating a one-to-many
relationship between addresses and employees. To support the connection
between two maps, the link editor has LHS (left-hand side) and RHS (right-hand
side) columns.

For your link, you will select your Address map for the LHS column and the
Employee map for the RHS column. This will automatically fill in the Link Name
and Java Class rows. You want to change the link name in the LHS column to residents to match your get/setResidents method on the Address class. Finally, fill in
both columns' key fields. Key fields refer to field labels, so set the Address (LHS)
role to ID and the Employee (RHS) role to ADDRESS_ID. Check to make sure that

the editor looks like Figure 12-14. If everything is filled in, right-click the model and choose Save Model.

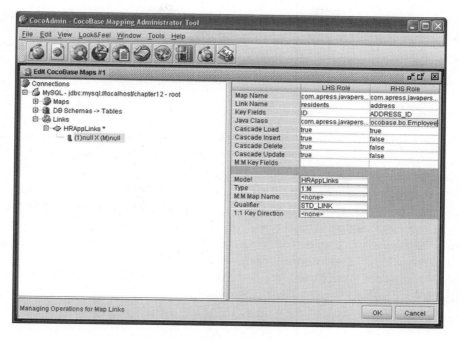

Figure 12-14. Creating the link between the maps

The link that is created is actually stored in a property file named after the model. For this example, you can find the created link in <CocoBase install dir>\demo\resources\HRAppLinks.properties. This file needs to be in your classpath. Since the CocoBase license is kept in the same directory, and both can be found by the Java Virtual Machine as "resources.<file>" off of the classpath, I would leave it there and keep <CocoBase install dir>\demo in the classpath.

You are now read to run the HR management application. If you run into any problems, go back and check the mapping. In my experience with CocoBase 4.5, I have had some trouble with changes being saved by the CocoAdmin tool.

Other CocoBase Notes

What I have shown you in this section is a simple use of CocoBase for transparent persistence. It is very possible to use the framework that underlies the facade to get very fine-grained control over your persistence.

CocoBase also provides object caching, which helps greatly with performance. The cache can often offset most of the performance expense of using the object-relational mapping layer.

If EJB QL does not work for your project, CocoBase also provides `CBQuery`. This is a class that is very similar to SQL, but it is compile-time checked like TopLink's query mechanism. You can use `CBQuery` with the facade as well; I chose to go with THOUGHT's recommendation of EJB QL for this chapter.

Summary

In this chapter, I have shown two popular object-relational persistence layers. TopLink and CocoBase both date back to 1997 and have their roots in object-oriented languages that came before Java.

One great value of these products is their longer lifetime compared to open source alternatives. This means that these products have been tested over and over. You are likely to find more people who have also encountered any problems you experience with these products as well.

The graphical user interfaces of these tools is another distinct advantage. While some open source products are starting to include graphical tools, such as OJB, these products have had them for a while.

Summary

I DO NOT PROPOSE to add anything to what has already been written concerning the loss of the "Lady Vain." Nor will I add much to what has been written in this book. I will however try to summarize the information that we have already discussed.

This book has been about various methods of saving objects to relational databases. This is a hugely important task that almost all significant development efforts need to tackle. Most teams fight their way through the same problem, re-creating the same solution over and over again. My intention with this book is to help you overcome some of the obstacles.

Keep in mind that the purpose of persistence is to save and retrieve objects. It is that simple. If that is not accomplished in a robust manner, then your application and development time is wasted. So use every tool at your disposal to come up with the persistence mechanism that fits your project best.

Be aware of your actual needs. Do not speculate that you need a high-performance object cache if you do not. If a Java serialization will work for you, do that. Try an open source persistence framework if you feel confident that you can support yourself with it. Spend some time evaluating a commercial framework. The savings from this type of evaluation can pay off in a very big way.

All Kinds of Methods of Persisting Objects

Persisting objects means being able to create an object, place it somewhere, and retrieve it at a later time. For Java, there are many different options for this. You can use Java serialization, XML files, object databases, or storage of objects to relational databases.

Java serialization was the first persistence mechanism that Sun provided for the Java language. *Serialization* is a very simple process of converting an object's state and data to a stream of bytes. These bytes can then be stored on a hard disk in a file.

Serialization is quick and free. The facilities are built into the language. There are, however, concerns with this simple mechanism. First and foremost is the inability to use serialization with multiple versions of a Java class. If you store an object and then modify the class, you cannot restore that data to the updated class. There are ways to override this, but then you lose the transparency of serialization.

Another limitation of serialization is querying. There is no facility to find a stored object. It is instead a manual process in which you load all stored objects until you find the one you are looking for. Because of this, applications that store large quantities of objects are likely to perform very poorly.

XML is another way to store objects to a flat file. With XML you have the more manual process of converting your objects to the format, but this can be overcome with third-party libraries. XML is a flexible format that allows the user to overcome some of the limitations that serialization has.

Specifically, it is possible to persist an object to XML, and then read it back into a modified class. This is because you as the developer have complete control over how the object is stored and reconstituted.

Object databases are the last form of persistence that I talked about that does not involve a relational database. An object database is a specialized database that is specifically meant for objects. There is no impedance mismatch with an object database. What gets stored there is exactly what you want retrieved at a later time.

Concerns with object databases are largely due to the smaller user base. This means that it is a lot harder to find people to support these tools. In the past there have also been performance concerns. Most performance concerns have been dealt with through object caching.

Understanding Relational Database Management Systems

A *Relational Database Management System* (RDBMS) is a piece of software that is used to store data. RDBMSs are intended to be very high performance and have a lot of redundancy and fail over. Most companies today store their data in one RDBMS or another.

First let me give a high-level overview. Relational databases store their data in *cells*. Cells are used to store one single piece of data. Related data that is stored in cells is kept in a *row* or *record*. A row is a group of cells. *Columns* describe the data that is in the cell and separate cells within the row. A *table* holds columns and rows. It is the database that holds the tables.

So a relational database is intended to group related data together in a way that is easy to access. To find an employee's first name, I could go to the HR database. In the HR database, I could locate an Employees table. Within the table I could find a specific employee's record. Within that record I could find the column for the first name. At the junction between the row and column, I would find the cell that contains the data that I am interested in.

Views within relational databases are similar to database tables but group together columns that span multiple tables. This can be very useful when working with objects because it is common for data for one object to span multiple tables.

In order to obtain data from a relational database, your software becomes a client to the database server or process. This way there is a separation between managing the data and using the data. Business applications are interested in using data, not managing it.

Transactions are a feature that most serious relational databases support. A transaction is a way of grouping related work together. By grouping the work, you can ensure that either all of the work is completed or none of it is. That way the database does not get into an inconsistent state.

There are several best practices you should follow when working with a relational database. ER diagrams help to design the database and communicate parts of the database. Normalization is the process of breaking up tables to allow for maximum flexibility. The idea is to extract duplicate data into separate tables.

Structured Query Language (SQL) is what is used to communicate with a relational database. So although you are writing Java, you need to write SQL when you have to save, delete, or query the database. All relational databases support SQL of one kind or another.

Using JDBC 1 for Relational Database Work

JDBC is an API that allows consistent and easy communication with a relational database from Java. JDBC was first made available as an add-on to Java 1.0. In Java 1.1 JDBC 1 became a part of the development kit.

Using JDBC, it becomes easy to write Java code that can work with multiple databases. Often only basic changes need to be made to the SQL that is used with JDBC. Those SQL changes are due to inconsistencies between databases.

The JDBC API is actually a group of interfaces that are fulfilled by a JDBC driver. JDBC drivers are provided by any number of companies of any number of databases. This allows the development team to decide on the driver that best fits the project's price/feature/performance needs.

What the JDBC driver actually provides is a concrete implementation for the `java.sql.Connection`, `java.sql.Statement`, `java.sql.PreparedStatement`, and `java.sql.ResultSet` interfaces. The way these work is that you obtain a connection from the driver manager, and the connection obtains a statement or prepared statement that can be used to talk to the database. If data is returned from the database, it comes back in a result set object.

In connecting to the database with the connection, you need to pass in a JDBC URL. The URL for JDBC consists of "jdbc" followed by a protocol, which is followed by a driver-specific string that is used to find the actual database. In this book, we communicate with MySQL, so the URL would look something like this: `jdbc:mysql:<server name>:<port>/<database name>?<options>`.

Once a database connection is made, a statement has various `execute` methods that perform work on the database. There is an `execute` method for modifying the database called `executeUpdate`. There is also an `execute` method for querying the database called `executeQuery`.

When a query is performed, a *result set* is returned. A result set represents the returned data one row at a time. By calling the `next` method on the result set, you move to the next row. On each row you can retrieve the cell's data by calling one of various get methods with either the column name or a column index.

JDBC 1 provides a very simple form of transaction in the fact that you can turn off auto-commit. What that means is that you can set an auto-commit flag on the connection to false. Then many different SQL statements can be sent to the connection. The changes from the SQL will not get written to the database until the commit method is called on the connection.

Besides managing writes, JDBC also allows you to decide what type of reads you want to perform. You can read only data that has been committed. You can specify to read data that has been passed to the database but not committed. A repeatable read gives the confidence that you can read the data multiple times and changes to the database will not affect your results.

When using JDBC, you many want to optimize your code to improve performance of the application. The first place to check when optimizing JDBC is in the SQL itself. Make sure that you are not using expensive queries. Get the help of a database administrator who is well versed in your database to find any database-specific optimizations that you can use.

Prepared statements are often a simple way to improve JDBC performance. A prepared statement is compiled on the server and reused whenever the same query is called. The query in the database is reused with varying arguments.

What Is New in JDBC 2.1 and 3.0

JDBC 2.1 provided new features such as scrollable result sets, batch updates, and handling of advanced data types. Additionally, it included an optional package that contained many server-side features.

A serious issue with JDBC 1 was that you could only move one direction in a result set. The next method was the only way to get to different records in the result set. JDBC 2.1 gives you the ability to move to the next, previous, first, or last record, or go to specific record indexes. All of this is optional; by default, the result set still acts the same as the JDBC 1 version.

Another great feature in result sets that are part of JDBC 2.1 is the ability to modify data in the result set. In this way, you can query the database, then modify it as you work with it. There is no need for the query to make a second call to change the data.

A performance enhancement that JDBC 2.1 provides is the ability to batch updates. You can pass any number of SQL update calls to the connection, and then have them all sent at once to the server. This can be very helpful when adding many instances to the same table, or making many changes to records all at once.

The JDBC 2.0 optional package provides connection pooling, distributed data sources, distributed transactions, and disconnected JavaBeans that hold data. The JDBC 2.0 optional package is meant to contain those parts that a stand-alone application can live without. While connection pooling is always nice, some applications do not need distributed data sources or disconnected data.

A *data source* is an object that is used to create a connection. Unlike the driver manager, the data source can reside anywhere on the network. You do not need to know where. The code that uses it simply knows its name. The name is used to query JNDI and obtain a reference.

The data source allows components that rely on data to be created and distributed without the data they need. The component becomes a client to the data source. This helps separate the functionality and make the application more modular.

The optional package allows you to create *distributed transactions*, which are transactions that span databases. If writing an employee's information involves writing some of the object's information to an HR Oracle database and another part to the same department's DB2 database, a distributed transaction will allow you to ensure that both databases remain in sync. If an error occurs while writing to the DB2 database, the changes to the Oracle database will be rolled back. This gives a much greater level of confidence in the data.

A failing of result sets is where the optional package provides row sets. A *row set* is actually a very flexible interface that allows data to come from any source at all. The row set itself follows the JavaBean conventions, which make it ideal for use with drag-and-drop IDEs. One of the most touted features is the ability to have disconnected data. With a disconnected row set, you can query the database and then pass the found data to a component without leaving a connection open to the database.

JDBC 3 provides more new functionality: savepoints for transactions, parameter metadata for prepared statement arguments, pooling of prepared statements, auto-generated keys, and more. JDBC 3 is meant to better incorporate some of JDBC 2's features and make them part of the basic software development kit.

A *transaction savepoint* is a bookmark in the transaction. At any point that you might want to roll back to, you can create a savepoint. This way transactions do not need to be all or none; they can handle various levels of stable data. This is based on the idea that data has various stages and some are useful. Savepoints can be ignored as well. You can still do a complete rollback.

Auto-generated keys help to prevent multiple calls to the database when inserting new data. Often record keys are based on other data in the database. The normal way this is handled is to lock a table, read the data, create a new key, then write the data and unlock the records. With auto-generated keys, you can simply insert a record and have the database create the key. You can obtain the key from the update statement that was used to write the data.

Parameter metadata allows code to query the possible arguments to a prepared statement. This can include the type, mode, whether nulls are possible, and more. The last new feature for JDBC 3 is *prepared statement pooling*. While connection pooling has been available, now a JDBC driver may keep prepared statement objects around to reuse as needed. This makes this already fast feature even better.

Writing a Persistence Layer

A *persistence layer* is a conceptual layer of code in an application. It is a grouping of related classes whose purpose is to store objects. The advantage of creating such a layer is that you can change where or how you store your objects without disturbing the rest of the application. Even when using a persistence framework, a persistence layer helps to hide the framework, giving you the opportunity to change it at a later time.

Most projects today still write their own object to relational code. This code should reside in the persistence layer. One pattern that Sun has advocated in their Java blueprints is the Data Access Object pattern. This is a class or group of classes that can contain all of the JDBC code that saves the objects.

When inserting objects through a persistence layer, there is sometimes the requirement to create unique identifiers for the objects. While Java does not provide a facility for creating Universally Unique Identifiers in the traditional sense, it does include a cross–virtual machine unique identifier. This allows creation of identifiers that will not conflict with identifiers on any other Java virtual machine in the world.

Inserts, updates, and deletes are all methods available through the persistence layer. By creating these methods and ensuring that there is no connection between the outer method signature and the underlying implementation (like exceptions that are thrown), you can create a robust and flexible persistence layer.

Another feature that a persistence layer must have is a querying mechanism. Without a way to query for data, you might as well use Write Only Memory (WOM). There are many ways to query for data, but most can be broken down into three categories: search methods, query by example, and creating a search language.

A *search method* is a method where what is queried and how it is queried is conveyed by the method name and the arguments that are passed in. For instance, to search for an employee by last name, you might create a method with the following signature:

```
public List findForLastName(String lastName)
```

Search by example is a query type where an object is passed in that represents what you want to find. There are many different variations on query by example, including using actual business objects and creating specific criteria objects.

When querying by example with an actual business object, you simply create an instance of the object that you want to search for. Set the values that you know and pass the object into the persistence layer. The persistence layer will look for any values that are not null and use those as the criteria to search by.

Querying by example with a criteria object is very similar, but instead of creating an instance of a business object, you create a specific criteria object. This

312

makes it easier to convey more subtle requirements such as searching for null matches or asking for greater than or less than values.

A *search language* is best used in situations where the persistence layer is going to be used by many different types of tools and it would be difficult to create type-safe queries. In this situation you need to create a language parser that can read the defined language and make the queries instead.

Persistence-Related Design Patterns

Design patterns are reusable design templates that are conveyed through text. A design pattern describes a problem and then gives a generic solution to the problem. The actual implementation of the solution is up to the developer. Design patterns are also a great form of communication.

Another use of design patterns is to allow a developer who has not seen a problem to find a solution. This is because design patterns are shared knowledge. A developer can read how to solve problems that are outside of their experience in this way.

In this book I showed how to generate SQL using a *Builder pattern*. The idea was to create different Builders to support different SQL statements. An insert statement would come from an `InsertBuilder`, an update statement from an `UpdateBuilder`, and so forth. This allows for consistent usage of objects regardless of what type of SQL they were going to create.

The next pattern that was covered was the *Strategy pattern*. This pattern is used to group related functionality so that it can be changed in and out. For example, different databases have different ways of doing the same thing, such as how dates are formatted. Many databases support different types or formats of dates. The JDBC connection URL also varies based on the database. These two differences can be put together in a Strategy. Then you can create different Strategies for different databases.

The last pattern I showed was an implementation of the *Facade pattern*. In performing a query, you need to interact with a connection, statement, and result set. A Facade query can be created that hides all of this interaction behind a simple interface.

Unit Testing Persistence Layers

Unit testing is a process that is used to reduce the amount of code you need to write and allow for confident modification of a system. In unit testing, the developer creates tests that ensure that each piece of the system is working correctly. These tests are very easily run, making it more likely that the system will be tested as it grows.

Because software that is being developed is in a continual state of flux, unit tests ensure that a change in one area does not break other parts of the system. This allows for a great deal of confidence in refactoring. Unit tests are also a great source of documentation on how a unit or component is meant to be used.

In *test-driven development*, the developer creates a unit test for a unit that does not exist yet. The test is run and fails. Enough code is written to make the test pass, and then the developer moves on. This process ensures that exactly the necessary code is written and no more. It also ensures that the developer stays on track and focuses on how the component is used and whether it works.

JUnit is a unit-testing framework for Java. JUnit is comprised of tests, test cases, and suites. A *test* is a single Java method that exercises another method on another class and ensures that it works correctly.

A *test case* is a class that holds the test methods. The class provides the environment where the test will run. Any resources that are needed by the test should be provided by the test case itself. A *test suite* is an instance of a class that pulls together tests on one or more test cases. A test suite gives a great deal of flexibility in how the tests get run.

When testing persistence layers, the most difficult part is ensuring that the database is in a good state for the tests to run. There are various ways of doing this, including dropping the database between each test, deleting records between tests, or even relying on third-party frameworks like DbUnit. One good way to handle the situation is to delete and reinsert records before each test. That way you are not dependent on previous tests cleaning up after themselves.

Mock Objects is a concept and framework that emphasizes very granular testing of objects. The Mock Objects framework provides classes that allow for out-of-container testing of classes that use JDBC. This is accomplished by providing a mock connection, statement, and result sets.

Enterprise JavaBeans: Container Managed Persistence 2.0/2.1

Enterprise JavaBeans (EJB) are distributed components that follow the EJB specification provided by Sun. While there are three different types of EJBs, entity beans are the type intended to represent data. The EJB 1.1 described a way for entity beans to be automatically persisted by the container they run in. The EJB 2.0 specification improves on Container Managed Persistence (CMP).

For an entity bean to use CMP, it needs to follow some key conventions. The first is that, unlike other entity beans, a CMP bean must be an abstract class. The reason is that the container will extend the abstract class to create a concrete class that will actually be used.

Besides the abstract bean, an EJB also needs remote interfaces that define how to create and interact with the class. Local interfaces define how objects within the container can interact with the bean. Persistent fields can be exposed through one, both, or neither of these interfaces. Attributes that expose relationships to other EJBs can only be described in the local interface.

Persistent fields on CMP entity beans are described through the abstract methods that are defined and the deployment descriptor. The deployment descriptor tells the container which fields are intended to be persistent. How the container stores and retrieves the data depends on the container implementation.

EJB QL is the language that is used to query CMP entity beans. EJB QL is composed of abstract query methods and query strings defined in the deployment descriptor. The methods that need to be created are either `findBy` or `ejbSelect` methods. The query string is a SQL-like language.

Writing to ODMG 3.0

The Object Data Management Group (ODMG) is a committee that created a specification for persisting objects by the same name. The specification they created is not language dependent, though they release language implementation notes. The ODMG is used as an API for many different persistence mechanisms, including some object databases and object-relational frameworks.

The object model for ODMG is based on the Object Management Group's CORBA standard. This is because ODMG can be used with CORBA. Like CORBA, ODMG can in its most ideal implementation be cross-language. The specification defines allowing a stored C++ object to be retrieved in Java or Smalltalk.

The ODMG specification is the first "transparent" persistence that this book addressed. This means that the application does not need to be concerned with how the objects are persisted, the ODMG compliant tool takes care of it. Most of the class and inheritance rules that ODMG requires are already part of Java.

There are several ways to identify objects with ODMG. The first is by object identity. ODMG maintains an application-independent object identifier. How this identifier is generated is not covered by the specification, just that it exists. Another identifier that is allowed is object naming. An object can have an arbitrary name assigned to it. This name can then be used to obtain a reference to the object, which is most useful for root-level objects such as companies or departments.

ODMG also defines a SQL-like language called *Object Query Language*. This language can be used to query for complete or partial objects. While the syntax is clearly defined, there are many implementations that call themselves ODMG compliant that do not provide OQL.

Inserting an object with ODMG is as easy as calling `makePersistent` and passing the object to add to the repository. Deleting an object is as easy as calling `deletePersistent`. Modifying a stored object is as easy as obtaining the object and wrapping the modification in a transaction.

Persistence with Java Data Objects

Java Data Objects (JDO) is Sun's answer to the need for simple, consistent, transparent persistence for Java. JDO is a specification and API released by Sun. There are many vendors that implement the JDO specification in the products they sell.

JDO is loosely based on ODMG. Because many companies have had trouble implementing a complete ODMG product, Sun created a simpler Java-focused solution. There is no intention of persisting a Java object and reconstituting it in C++, for example. The query language has also been simplified.

In order for an object to be persisted with JDO, Sun suggests enhancing the object, either in the form of source code enhancement or byte code enhancement. Either way, the intention is to add code to the accessors of the object that allows for JDO to be notified of changes to the object. Enhancing also gives the ability to lazy load data from the database.

The specification also defines XML files that are used by a JDO implementation to describe classes, fields, collections, maps, and any implementation extensions. The XML files are kept with the classes in a ".jdo" file.

Querying in JDO is performed with the JDOQL, a query language that is based on classes and strings. To query for an instance of an object, you pass the class for the object and a string that contains a comparison of an attribute and the value to match.

Open Source Java Persistence Libraries and Frameworks

Another option for transparent Java persistence is using an open source persistence framework. In this book, I talked about three different open source frameworks: Hibernate, ObJectRelationalBridge (OJB), and Castor JDO.

Hibernate is a framework that is intended to be very high performance and simple to use. The objective of Hibernate is to create a clean and concise persistence framework and not worry about conforming to standards. What they have achieved is an object-relational framework that allows for simple storage of objects, a clean query language, and much more. Hibernate supports complex relationships and lazy loading of data through dynamic proxy objects.

OJB is a framework that is intended to be a platform for supporting various specifications. At this time, the product supports ODMG, JDO, and its own persistence API. OJB is hosted by the Apache Foundation. OJB supports OQL for querying.

The last open source framework discussed was Castor JDO. Castor is intended to convert objects to either XML or SQL. The product is not a JDO implementation, as the name implies, but it is an object-relational persistence framework. The library also supports lazy loading, object caching, compound primary keys, and complex relationships.

Commercial Java Persistence Libraries and Frameworks

This chapter introduced two commercial object-relational products named TopLink and CocoBase. These are two mature frameworks that can vastly simplify a developer's life by taking care of persisting objects. Both products also target J2EE integration by providing Container Managed Persistence.

TopLink is a product that migrated from Smalltalk to Java. The tool handles all of the expected functionality including lazy loading and complex relationships. One great feature that TopLink has is its workbench tool. This is a graphical tool that helps with the mapping of objects to relational databases. This tool will load databases and objects and make it very easy to map the fields to columns. It also makes it easy to create relationships between objects.

CocoBase actually made it onto the Java scene a little before the Java version of TopLink. It also provides a less-intuitive graphical tool called CocoAdmin. While it handles many of the same functions as the TopLink tool, it is a little more awkward to use. CocoBase has an underlying expectation that it works with property objects rather than directly with business objects. This has been remedied in version 4. Now the conversion from property objects to business objects is handled by proxy classes. CocoBase also ships with a very nice facade that makes it very easy to persist and manage persisted objects.

Finally . . .

This is only the beginning. While there is more to learn on all of the topics covered in this book, there are also solutions that were not addressed at all. Be creative, but do not do unnecessary work. Look for products or frameworks that will relieve you of writing code. If none fit, follow best practices as you write your own persistence.

Index